FBI SPECIAL AGENTS ARE REAL PEOPLE

True stories . . . told and written by the present and former Special Agents of the Federal Bureau of Investigation (FBI)

AL ZUPAN

ISBN-10: 0615971733
ISBN-13: 9780615971735

Printed by: CreateSpace
Library of Congress Control Number: 2014921260

Zupan, Al
FBI Special Agents are Real People / by Al Zupan
BISAC: True Crime / General
p.cm.

1. Zupan, Al – 2. United States. Federal Bureau of Investigation. – 3. FBI. Officials and employees – Biography.

Cover design by: Sara Augustine

FIRST EDITION

Printed in the United States of America

Printed on acid-free paper

A BIG THANK YOU !

- A big thank you to God, who makes all things possible.
- Thanks to all of you, both active and retired FBI Special Agents, who have contributed your true personal FBI stories for inclusion in this book.
- Thanks to the thousands of the FBI's Support Employees, whose dedicated work is never heralded and under-appreciated.

"There is no limit to what we can accomplish, as long as we are not concerned with those who will claim credit for our work." (Author unknown)

NOTE BENE !

- The completed rough-draft of the book was sent to the FBIHQ for review and was approved for publication.
- Since all the stories are direct quotes from FBI Special Agents, some of the quotation marks have been eliminated.
- Stories written by the author and fellow FBI Special Agents, both current and retired. Titles of stories by book's author.
- Any profit from the sale of this book will be donated to the Cleveland Chapter of the Society of Former Special Agents of the FBI, for the needs of the Cleveland Chapter.

FBI BY THE NUMBERS (2014)

- **56 Field Offices (also called Divisions), overseen by a Special Agent in Charge (SAC), except for Los Angeles, New York and Washington, D.C., which are headed by an Assistant Director.**

- **380 Resident Agencies (RAs), located in smaller cities in Division's territory. managed by SSRAs).**

- **60+ Legats, overseas FBI offices attached to U.S. Embassies, managed by the Legal Attaches.**

- **35,344 employees, including 13,598 Special Agents.**

DEDICATION

The date, August 9, 1979, will be remembered in the Federal Bureau of Investigation's history as one of the saddest days. Three FBI Special Agents, assigned to two different FBI offices, brutally lost their lives.

Two of the America's finest men, Charles W. Elmore, age 34, and Jared Robert Porter, age 44, were killed by an assailant while in the FBI's Resident Agency office in El Centro, California, out of the San Diego FBI Division.

In an unrelated incident, SA Johnnie L. Oliver, age 35, was shot and killed while pursuing a violent fugitive in the Cleveland, Ohio FBI Division.

Above three Special Agents exemplified the FIDELITY – BRAVERY – INTEGRITY that the FBI men and women represent.

May Johnny, Charles and Jared, as well as thirty three other FBI Special Agents, who died as a direct result of an adversarial action, REST IN PEACE.

To them, their families, and to the families of all the other Special Agents, both active and retired, I dedicate this book.

PROLOGUE

Throughout human history, man has recorded events, whether in written form, by word of mouth, or electronically. The recordings were made to tell a story, to preserve history, to teach and enlighten future generations about life.

All FBI Special Agents have stories to tell. Some stories are sad while others are happy. Some are vivid in our minds while others have long been forgotten. Some have been lost through the years, only to be recounted again, as friends and former co-workers meet and relationships are reestablished.

At various training sessions around the country, at parties, on the X-G's List, over the Internet's various social media, at retirement functions, over a cup of coffee or after a drink or two, all one has to say is..."remember when" and small drops of rain turn into a river of stories that are part of the FBI's unwritten history.

We owe it to the American people, to our families and friends, to tell these stories, so that everyone will know that the FBI Special Agents are real people.

We are men and we are women. We come from diverse backgrounds, races, nationalities and religions and we reflect the society around us. Our backgrounds are as varied as the people that we serve and protect. Some of us attended Ivy League schools and military academies, while others attended small community colleges or Catholic seminaries. Some of us served in the military and survived WW II, Korea, Vietnam and Middle East battlefields, while others protested our military interventions.

We have feelings, we cry and we laugh. We are shot at and we shoot as a last resort. We bleed and we die. We leave for work carrying a gun, a set of credentials and a badge, not knowing if we will return to our loved ones alive and in one piece at the end of the day.

We are saints and we are sinners. The split-second decisions that we have to make at times may haunt us, as attorneys rehash our actions for years after their occurrence. These decisions may make the difference whether we will be "judged by twelve or carried by six". All of us hope and pray that our actions will be just and correct and we will make it home to our loving families.

Many of the stories that are contained in this book will be labeled by some readers as being politically incorrect, provocative, racist and sexist. None of the stories are meant to offend you. Believe me, the stories are real and they deal with life (and death) in the real world that all of us live in today.

There are other stories that cannot be told, in order to protect the sources and assets, businesses, undercover co-opted men and women, double agents outside of the FBI, both in the U.S. and abroad. There are people that have assisted the FBI and their identities will forever be kept a secret. Still other stories would reveal the methods and the means used to achieve some of our successes and losses. These stories will not be in this book, so that the future generations of FBI Special Agents will again resort to the same methods to achieve success.

CONTENTS

THE BEGINNING...

On bare knees, kneeling and slowly moving in a procession on the cold stone floor of a centuries-old Catholic church on Planina Mountain, a mother and her eleven year old son, named Slavko, were making their last pilgrimage.

The two of them came to thank Jesus and His Mother Mary for the favor of leaving the communist country of their birth and begin a new life. A wife was to be reunited with her husband and a child with his father, after eleven long years.

This was the final good bye to the extended family, neighbors and friends they would never see again. As the procession wound around the altar, praying the rosary, the two joined the other faithful in a song dedicated to "Mary from Planina Mountain", bringing tears to all present.

A week later, mother and son left on a train to La Havre, France, and embarked on an ocean liner Queen Elizabeth that was to transport them to "Amerika". The young boy, who was three months old when his father left, to escape a sure death under a communist regime, was to meet his father for the first time.

The boy carried all of his worldly possessions in one child-sized piece of luggage as the two arrived in the USA on Thanksgiving Day, 1956.

On November 30, 1970, the young man, after completing college and his first full time job as a big city cop, and serving as a U.S. Army officer during the Vietnam War, began his training in Washington, D.C. and Quantico, Virginia. Upon completion of his training, he was sworn in as an FBI Special Agent, given a badge # 7906, credentials and a gun.

This book, however, is not my life's story. It is a book of true stories written by hundreds of FBI Special Agents, in their own words, including mine. If you don't like the stories, don't blame me, as I am only a messenger that gathered the stories and outtakes over the last forty four years, and present them in a book form. I welcome your comments via:

- e-mail at alzupan@oh.rr.com
- snail-mail at 2XG LLC, P.O. BOX 40241, BAY VILLAGE, OHIO 44140, U.S.A.

Names of Special Agents, the individuals (subjects) involved in the stories, and the names of the towns and cities, were purposely omitted to protect the innocent and the guilty alike, unless a request was specifically made by the contributing writer of the story to be identified. I am among the guilty.

Yes, FBI Special Agents are real people, who have left various jobs, to pursue a dream and a daily challenge in a career serving fellow human beings. We are special, because we put our lives on the line every day to protect those that we have sworn to serve.

CHAPLAIN'S PRAYER FOR ALL LAW ENFORCEMENT PEOPLE

(Author unknown)

"Tonight, we the citizens of our respective communities, are gathered together in fellowship and happy harmony to pay honor to a dedicated group of men and women, who devote their lives to the rightful promotion of law and order in our land.

Almighty Father, we ask your blessing upon these noble people and we beg you to protect them as they perform their hazardous duties and to shield them from the many dangers which beset them from every side.

Lord! These men and women are people set apart from all the others. Each morning the lawyer goes to his office, the doctor visits his patients, the clerk goes to his store and the laborer to his factory or mill, and each must daily face their own special problems. But dear Lord, these men and women, these guardians of our public and private safety must begin their day by strapping on an armed weapon with the hope and prayer that they may never be called upon to use it, yet knowing full well in the secret of their hearts that before the sun sets they may be called upon to engage in mortal combat with those who live outside the law and in fact, and much too often, are destined to sacrifice their most precious gift, the gift of life, that others might enjoy freedom from fear.

Lord, with sincerity of heart, we beg you to protect these noble men and women from evil obscenities which besmirch their character and deliver them from foul slander that dishonors their profession and their very being.

Finally, dear Lord, we ask you to comfort their wives, husbands and children, in their daily anxieties and to console them in their times of sorrow and help them understand that we know them to be the unsung heroes of our day and that we respect and honor them at all times.

And may all who have made the supreme sacrifice of their lives enjoy perfect happiness and peaceful rest forever. AMEN!"

OUTTAKES

For 47 years, to give some levity to my life, I have collected sometimes useless, but funny and serious stories, about military, the government and law enforcement. The stories interspersed in this book were obtained via faxes, by e-mail, found in desks vacated by my co-workers, or simply placed on my desk by those that knew I collected them.

More recently, since Government's mandated retirement at age 57, these "outtakes" were attachments to e-mails.

I will include some of these stories as "outtakes", in the hope that you will enjoy reading them among the serious stories as written by fellow FBI SAs. If you find some of these to be politically incorrect, I can only say in the English, Polish and German languages…

TUFF SHITSKY UND ES TUT MIR LEID.

ENJOY THE JOURNEY!

OUTTAKE . . .

SIX PHASES OF AN FBI PROJECT
(Author unknown)

1. "Enthusiasm
2. Disillusionment
3. Panic
4. Search for the Guilty
5. Punishment of the Innocent
6. Praise and Honors for the Non Participants"

CHAPTER 1

FIRST OFFICE AGENT

First Office Agent (FOA) is a name lovingly given to an FBI Special Agent straight out of the FBI Academy in Quantico, Virginia, as he/she arrive at their first office of assignment. The name is equivalent of a "90-day wonder" for a U.S. Army Second Lieutenant, straight out of an officer's school, assigned to his/her first unit. FOAs are at the bottom of the pecking order, with wide open eyes, looking at the real world. As they arrive at their first office of assignment, they are bombarded with pearls of wisdom from fellow Special Agents, who have already seen it all and done it all. They are newbies.

In the not too distant past, admonishments were: "Do not drink coffee at your desk in the office, do not make an arrest by yourself, do not drink on the job, do not play with SACs steno pool," but, "do bring donuts to the office on your birthday".

In just a few days, FOAs learn that rules were made to be broken, as common sense prevails. FOAs quickly learn about the "heavies", SAs assigned to criminal squads, as well as the "rubber gun squads," populated by SAs working foreign counter intelligence type cases. This too quickly passes by as the first big case pops up in the office, or for that matter, anywhere in the world where there is FBI involvement. The first big "special", with everyone involved, quickly levels the playing field. There are no "heavies" and no SAs with rubber guns. Everyone has a job to do. Whether you are a CPA or a language trained SA, you are still an FBI Special Agent. You rely on the guy or gal next to you, and they rely on you. Do not screw up. This is not a game. This is for real!

The stories begin . . .

He slept in the class when vouchers were discussed…

" A spanking new SA, straight out of the FBI Academy at Quantico, learned about the government's rule of a '300 mile per day' for travel with a car. This neophyte left Quantico and at the 300 mile marker pulled off the road and went to sleep for the night – in the car since there was no hotel in the vicinity. He did the same thing for the next three nights, sleeping in the car. When he filled out his 'travel voucher', he omitted the names of hotels on the forms that he submitted to the FBIHQ to claim reimbursement. A call from the clerk reviewing the voucher reminded him that receipts from hotels were necessary. He explained the fact that he slept in the car. An SA today would have used a computer and make necessary hotel reservations with the rule in mind."

What happened to the baby?

"SA received orders for his first office. Plan was to travel with his wife and a six month old baby. The day before the planned travel, weather report called for nasty winter blast with travel not recommended the six hundred miles to their destination. What to do with the baby? Leave the baby with grandparents and fly back to pick him up after the storm, or have grandma bring him on the plane. When it came to voucher time, the forms were filled out and no mention was made of the baby. The voucher clerk called and inquired whereabouts of the baby. Grandma brought him a few days later on the plane, and no claim for him was made. That was an incorrect answer. Since baby could not travel alone on the plane, grandma got her ticket paid to bring him." (Common sense prevailed…again)

Laugh at yourself. If you don't, who will…

"Yes, FBI Agents are real people and we come from all walks of life. And of course this means the same stupid things that happen to everyone else occasionally happen to us while we were working cases. I have often talked about this incident as the most embarrassing moment I had in the FBI.

It happened in my first office, and my first case I really got into involved the interstate transportation of stolen property. Now this stolen property was a truckload of farm chemicals. Now this may sound unbelievable, but the total value of loss was $ 250,000.

Several of our suspects in the possession part of the case were farmers in Southeastern Nebraska, and there was no doubt that they were for the most part legitimate businessmen. We pursued the possession part of the charge as we felt there was sufficient evidence they knew they were dealing in stolen property as the purchase price agreed upon was half of the normal retail price. Also, the chemicals were delivered to their farm in unmarked trucks in the middle of the night.

Now as part of the investigation, we served subpoenas at a local bank that held the accounts of a farmer who had considerable land holdings. It was also pretty apparent that he had a considerable amount of loans at that bank, as when we served the subpoenas, the bank president came out and invited us into his office. By his questions, it was obvious he was trying to find out as much information he could from us as he was no doubt worried about the possibility of the farmer defaulting on his loans if he ended up being charged with a crime.

It was a very nice office, with expensive oak paneling and mounted game heads on the wall. I had a terrible cold. So we were all sitting around the big oak desk, the bank president, my partner, and me. I sneezed and of course I blew a huge hunk of snot out of my nose which landed on my pants. So what do you do now? Well, you just casually reach down and pick it off your pants and fling it into the wastebasket. Of course Murphy's Law taking effect you will miss the wastebasket and it will hit the oak paneling. And of course it will make a sound like a big splat. The bank president pretended he did not see it. My partner just shook his head a little and started wondering, 'How did I get stuck with this moron?' And I started wondering if I could get my old job back on the Police Department.

I did mention to my partner after we got outside, 'Hey, at least I did not try and shake bank president's hand on the way out.' And there is my most embarrassing moment in the FBI.

(My mom taught me to always carry two handkerchiefs in my pockets. One to blow my nose and the other to put on a wound to stop the bleeding.)

Best advice I got before leaving Quantico…

"There are three people in the office that you'd better not ever piss off and get mad at you:

1. The SAC's Secretary
2. The Chief Clerk
3. Your Squad Secretary

The titles may have changed over the years, but it's still a good advice today."

Where I be?

"On about the third day in my first office, I took another FOA, who had been in my training class, with me and we went to look for a 26 case fugitive.

Amazingly, we quickly found him, at his last address. Got him into the Bucar, properly cuffed.

Oh, oh . . . neither one of us had the slightest idea where a county or city jail was, to which we could take the prisoner (we hadn't yet had an orientation tour of the city). We were too embarrassed to get on the radio and ask where the jail was.

The prisoner realized our predicament, so he helpfully directed us to the county jail, with which he was quite familiar. So there we were in the 'turn right here . . .' care of our prisoner.

All's well that ends well, I guess."

Who done that?

"Being a 'newbie' in Denver, one of my first leads was to accompany a seasoned agent to conduct an interview. Upon knocking on the door, I was reminded to hold my creds open so the person answering the knock would immediately recognize us as Bu agents. I was nervous but told to follow his lead. When the door opened, the seasoned agent announced his identity, held up his creds, and I dutifully followed suit. I noticed this odd look on the middle-aged gentleman. When he announced to the seasoned SA that his picture was not really a good resemblance, the SA and I looked at his creds and saw a picture of an ape imposed over his picture. Now this seasoned SA had a good sense of humor and an easy laugh but I literally saw steam coming out of his lobster-red face.

When we got back to the office, he took up the issue with the squad's jokester. Did I mention that the victim was a serious work-out specimen? Needless to say, all the lecturing and references in the MIOG regarding professional behavior went down the crapper. All names being withheld for fear of retribution."

A BIG No No!

"A picture of an ape was imposed over a picture of an Afro-American SA, who in turn sued the Bureau."

Make my day…

"In my first office, I was assigned to a "heavy" squad, working fugitives. I was paired with an old-timer who was a fine physical specimen. Despite his age, this former state trooper could walk around a swimming pool on his hands and could definitely physically outmatch most criminals. He carried his FBI issued 38 cal revolver not in a holster, but wrapped in a brown paper bag, secured with rubber bands.

One day, the two of us were searching a house, room by room, guns drawn, for a fugitive. With search almost completed, I asked my partner if he checked the closet next to me in the room. His answer was affirmative. For some unknown reason, I rechecked the closet, with my personally owned and approved back-up weapon, a Colt Highway Patrolman, with a six inch barrel, drawn. The armed fugitive was located there. His small 22 Cal revolver remained frozen in his hands and he gave up. I was not considered a FOA anymore."

OUTTAKE . . .

A BEAR
(Author unknown)

“If you’re a bear, you get to hibernate. You do nothing but sleep for six months. I could deal with that. Before you hibernate, you’re supposed to eat yourself stupid. I could deal with that too.

If you’re a bear, you birth your children (who are the size of walnuts) while you’re sleeping and wake up to partially grown, cute cuddly cubs. I could definitely deal with that.

If you’re a mama bear, everyone knows you mean business. You swat anyone who bothers your cubs. If your cubs get out of line, you swat them too. I could deal with that.

If you’re a bear, your mate expects you to wake up growling. He expects that you will have hairy legs and excess body fat.
Yup.....I wanna be a bear.”

The stories continue . . . .

At your service…

"While completing the FBI Academy and taking classes in Washington, four of us future SAs moved into a room at the old Harrington Hotel, where we shared one room to cut down on expenses. Within five minutes of moving our luggage into the room, and getting situated, we received a telephone call from a young-sounding lady, ostensibly from the 'front desk', asking if we needed any service. The answer was definitely 'negative'. The four of us were convinced that it was probably a test by the 'real' FBI, to check our moral code. As a matter of fact, a small bar located within the same building as Harrington Hotel, was on the list of locations within Washington, D.C. that was off limits to the military because of the number of 'ladies of the evening selling their wares', plying their trade out of the bar."

This is a test…only a test…

"It was my third or fourth day on duty as a FOA in a small southern office. My training agent told me that the ASAC wanted to see me. I straightened my tie, walked down the hall and knocked on the ASAC's door. He told me to come in, close the door and have a seat while he finished some paperwork. Finally, he swiveled his chair to face me and asked how everything was going. While I was telling him how great things were, he reached inside his desk drawer and withdrew a pint bottle of Jack Daniels, held it out to me and said: 'Here, have a snort.'

Time suddenly stopped as I confronted the situation and considered my options, which had to be some kind of a test. I had only two choices, if I took the drink he would think I was a potential problem and if I didn't, he would think I am not a team player and cannot be trusted. I 'wussed' out and said no, thanks, it was too early for me (it was 0900 hrs). A long conversation on life in general ensued. He was a good guy and it was a great office and I absolutely had the time of my life, both official and unofficial, for three years, before I was transferred to my second office. The good times ended forever.

I have often wondered over the years if the Jack Daniels episode was really some kind of test and, if so, did I pass or fail?"

A "gay" fugitive – not...

"I remember my first bureau arrest in my first office. I had a roommate who absolutely loved making arrests. Naturally, he would wake me early and take me with him on his forays. He would go to a fugitive's parents' house and rouse them up. After they professed ignorance of their son's whereabouts, he asked them if they would mind him looking around. The very first place he looked was the closet near the house entrance, where he notices a big pile of blankets, which started to move somewhat, on the floor. My partner, more surprised by this than the fugitive, stepped back and bellowed in his best Bu voice: 'FBI, out of the closet !' And, the fugitive wasn't even gay (not that there is anything wrong with that)."

The naked story

"Four of us FOAs went out to arrest a subject on a Selective Service case. A novelty, since the USA's office avoided Selective Service matters like the plaque. I was along for backup. It was early in the morning when we got to subject's apartment and made entry. It was a one bedroom studio type unit with a bed at the rear of the room with a sheet draped in front like a curtain. We heard some noise from the bed and one Agent pulled the sheet back, exposing subject and girlfriend, both nude. I observed that the girlfriend was a hippy type similar to those we use to see back in the 70's.

She immediately jumped up off the bed and put on a short mid-thigh length robe. We arrested the subject with no problem. The girlfriend promptly ran out of the apartment, down the stairs and across the street, where she was observed in a phone booth. It was a typical cold, drizzly morning and she must have been freezing out there on the street. I don't recall that the ops order covered that scenario."

OUTTAKE . . .

CROCODILE
(Author unknown)

"Never, never, never . . . curse crocodile's mother before crossing the river."

The stories continue . . .

A full field arrestee

"Several of us 'second office Agents' went to arrest a fugitive. We took a FOA with us. We had an excellent description of the fugitive who was also known to be accompanied by his 8 ½ month pregnant wife. We knocked on the door of the fugitive's apartment repeatedly. There was no answer.

We broke down the door and immediately saw the fugitive seated in a chair. The fugitive was naked from his waist down, and his trousers were around his ankles. The fugitive's very pregnant and fully clothed wife had her back to us; she was kneeling in front of her husband giving him oral sex. She turned toward us and dropped what she was doing from her mouth.

We pulled her aside, grabbed the fugitive, and stood him up. We handcuffed the fugitive and pulled his trousers up. However, his 'tool' still protruded from his open fly. The fugitive looked at us and asked that someone tuck it in for him. We all turned toward the FOA, who was wide-eyed and clearly expected the worst assignment ever. Fortunately, the fugitive's wife performed a 'happy ending' for the FOA…instead of for the fugitive."

Help with directions

"Another first arrest out of FBI's Training School. I had arrived in my first office on Sunday afternoon and reported to work Monday morning. I was assigned to a 42 (fugitive deserter) squad and went out that day with a couple of 'old hands' on the squad (first office Agents who had been there for three or four months). Tuesday, there wasn't anyone on the squad available to chaperone a rookie, so I took out a car to drive around the city.

Among my dozens of cases was an old dog that had numerous 45-day (post and coast) checks at the subject's home. I decided I would do my first post Quantico interview, so I knocked on the door. When a young man answered, I identified myself and said I was looking for John Doe. He said he was John Doe., with a correct date of birth. I said he was under arrest. I cuffed him and put him in the car, then I cranked up. After I had driven a few blocks, he asked if we were going to the location where at that time 42's were taken and turned over to the military authorities. I said we were. He said it might be more convenient to turn around and go in the other direction. He then proceeded to give me accurate direction to the place.

When I got back to the office and told what happened, I was reminded that I must not be alone at the time of the arrest, because Bureau rules wouldn't permit it. So I credited the military policeman to whom I turned over the 42 as having helped me with the arrest.

In my entire career, that was the only time someone I arrested had to give me directions as to where I should take him or her."

An oops arrest

"Second or third day on the job in my first office. Told by the supervisor to pick up a map of the city and go out in a car to familiarize myself with the city and its streets. Listened to the Bureau radio, as fellow SAs were chatting on the air, looking for a 42 subject in certain area of the city, giving description of the subject. I looked at the map and realized that they were located just a few blocks away from my location.

I drove through the back alley (no GPS units invented yet) and observed a kid with shaved head and spit shined U.S. Army boots, sitting on the steps of a nearby row house. The looks were a clue to this trained investigator and a former U.S. Army officer, who spent almost two years training recruits in basic training, that this young man must be in the military. When I got out of the car, the young man immediately snapped to attention, probably realizing that I resembled his training officer, short hair, good tan from the hot weather Army post just short six months before.

Asked if he was a deserter from the Army, he responded with an affirmative 'Yes Sir!' Told him he was under arrest, handcuffed him, put him in the Bucar and took him one block away where the other Agents were located, proud that I caught the fugitive they were looking for.

It was not to be. This was not the subject they were looking for, plus, this young man was only AWOL and not yet in the system where he would be of interest to the FBI.

What to do now? 'Unarrest' was not a term in the FBI parlance. A quick meeting with the other Agents, most of whom arrived in their first office just a few weeks ago, determined that the only way out of this problem was to ask the young man if he wished to get a ride to the nearest military recruitment center, which also contained an MP office, where he could turn himself voluntarily in. He agreed. I dropped him off and happily gave my name as the arresting officer, when asked for my ID. I returned to the office and kept my mouth shut.

Next morning, supervisor called me to his office and inquired regarding a notice of arrest that he received from the military, with my name in the space for 'arresting officer'. Needless to say, a proverbial s#2& hit the fan and it smelled bad. My career was on a roll…downhill… fast"!

(U.S. Senator Zell Miller (D-GA) delivered the following statement on the floor of the United States Senate, in May, 2004, on addressing the situation at the Abu Ghraib prison. Has anything changed since then, ten years later?)

"Mr. President, here we go again. Rushing to give aid and comfort to the enemy. Pushing and pulling and shoving and leaping over one another to assign blame and

point the finger at America the Terrible. Lining up in long lines at the microphones to offer apologies to those poor, pitiful Iraqi prisoners.

Of course, I do not condone all the things that went on in that prison, but I for one, Mr. President, refuse to join in this national Act of Contrition over it.

Those who are wringing their hands and shouting so loudly for 'heads to roll' over this seem to have conveniently overlooked the fact that someone's head HAS rolled – that of another innocent American brutally murdered by terrorists.

Why is it? Why is it that there's more indignation over a photo of a prisoner with underwear on his head than over the video of a young American with no head at all? Why is it that some in this country still don't get that we are at war? A war against terrorists who are plotting to kill us every day. Terrorists who will murder Americans at any time, any place, any chance they get.

And yet here we are, America on its knees, in front of our enemy, begging for their forgiveness over the mistreatment of prisoners. Showing the enemy and the world once again how easily America can get sidetracked and how easily America can turn against itself.

Yes, some of our soldiers went too far with their interrogation tactics and clearly were not properly trained to handle such duty. But the way to deal with this is with swift and sure punishment, and immediate and better training. There also needs to be more careful screening of who we put in these kinds of sensitive situations.

And no one wants to hear this, Mr. President, and I'm reluctant to say it. But there should also be some serious questioning of having male and female soldiers serving side by side in these kinds of military missions.

But instead, I worry that the HWA – the Hand-Wringers of America – will add to their membership and continue to bash our country ad nauseam. And in doing so, hand over more innocent Americans to the enemy on a silver platter.

So I stand with Senator Inhofe of Oklahoma, who

stated that he's 'more outraged by the outrage' than by the treatment of those prisoners. More outraged by the outrage. It's a good way of putting it. That's exactly how this Senator from Georgia feels."

The stories continue . . .

Drinking coffee on the job

"My first arrest was a 42 case Army Deserter. Early one morning, another FOA and myself were told to come along on an arrest of this subject whose parents lived at the end of a cul-de-sac. As we approached the house, one senior Agent and the other FOA went to the rear of the house and one senior Agent and I knocked on the front door.

We were met by subject's mother, who advised that the subject had gone out before we arrived but was expected back about noon. She knew about his deserter status and advised he was about ready to turn himself in and face the music.

We all gathered at the front of the house and decided to set up a surveillance to await the subject's return. Well, it so happened that across from the opposite end of the street there was a shopping center, and strategically located in the shopping center was the coffee shop, so the four of us ended up in the shop awaiting the return of the subject to his home. We spent four hours drinking coffee, much to Mr. Hoover's displeasure. During those four hours, most of my thoughts were about the Hoover rule about no coffee while on duty.

About noon, true to his mother's word, the subject pulled up the street, got out of his car and entered the home. We returned to the street, knocked on the door and the subject answered the door., kissed his mom goodbye and said, 'I'm ready'.

Most of my day was spent trying to figure out how much trouble I was going to be in for drinking coffee on the job."

My first arrest the day before I reported for duty

"My first arrest was most unusual. I arrived in my new city on Friday evening and went to the office on Saturday morning just to make sure I could be able to find the office come Monday. Not knowing anything about the office, naturally it was closed, but the clerk on duty came down and opened the door for me to get in. Once I entered and started talking to the clerk, the clerk received a call from a fugitive who wanted to turn himself in. Being just out of the Academy, and the only Agent in the office, I decided that I would make the arrest. The only thing that I knew about the city was the then old train terminal.

I got on the phone with the fugitive and told him to meet me at the water fountains in front of the train terminal. No shit, there was this guy standing out near the water fountains. I placed the fugitive in my car, a 1967 Volkswagen and drove back to the office. Then it hit me. I did not know how to get into the office. Once again, the clerk came down to get me in. Then it hit me again. It's Saturday and what do I do with this guy. The clerk was really great, called the fugitive supervisor who contacted one of the Agents who worked fugitives and he came in, processed the fugitive and took him off my hands.

When I arrived in office on Monday morning for my first day of work, I had accumulated my first stat, arrest of a fugitive, before I even reported for duty. Thanks to the Agent that came in and took the fugitive off my hands…but I had it handled."

The forgotten deserter

"A young SA, in his first office, is ordered to Language School. On about the last day in the field before departing for Monterey, he apprehends a deserter out in the rural area, and brings him to the nearest county jail. Within a day or two, the Agent is gone on his transfer. Unfortunately, he had forgotten to prepare the 'Apprehension Airtel' . He was the only SA on the arrest, so nobody else in the Bureau knew the deserter was in custody, and of course the military didn't know.

Weeks, or it might have been months later, the Sheriff called the field office and inquired about the status of his federal prisoner. I was told that when the SAC learned of this (he was one of the most famous and highly-regarded ones we ever had), he was determined to have the offending SA fired. I guess cooler heads among the old hands talked him out of it.

The offending SA himself eventually became an SAC."

OUTTAKE . . .

(Author unknown – please fill in your own names and positions in the blank space.)

"An airplane was about to crash; there were 5 passengers on board, but only 4 parachutes.

The first passenger said: 'I'm ____________, the best ____ player; My team, ____________________, needs me. I can't afford to die.' So he took the first pack and left the plane.

The second passenger, ____________________, said: 'I am __________________________, the wife of ______________________________ and a potential _________________. I am the smartest ________________ in America's history, so American people don't want me to die.' _______________________ She took the second pack and jumped out of the plane.

The third passenger, _________________, a famous _______________, said: 'I am ___________________, a famous _______________hero and a ___________'. So he grabbed the pack next to him and jumped.

The fourth passenger, a former __________________, said to the fifth passenger, a 10-year-old schoolgirl: 'I have lived a full life and served my country well. I will sacrifice my life and let you have the last parachute.'

The girl said: 'That's OK. There's a parachute left for you. America's smartest person, ___________________, took my schoolbag.' "

The stories continue . . .

Learn from past spill ?

"My first office was deep in the South. When I walked in that first day, I thought I was in a geriatric ward. Never saw so many bald heads and liver spots in one place before. Some offices in those days were considered retirement offices."

On the first day in the office, I was handed to one of the older Agents and told to follow him around and learn the ropes. Later that same day, we went out together to shag a few leads. We got into his car, but before we started out, he said rather solemnly: 'Let me give you some advice.' Oh boy, I thought, here's where the real training begins. 'Never', he said emphatically, 'ever put a cup of coffee on the dashboard of your car.' "

Drinking coffee in the break room

"On the first day in the new office I arrived at the office very early, since I was not sure about that signing in thing. I wondered over to a break room and helped myself to a cup of coffee and took it to my desk. As the senior Agents began filing in, they were looking at me like I had three heads. I must have been asleep at the Academy when that whole drink coffee in the office thing was mentioned. One old timer was kind enough to come over to my desk and advise me that the break room was for the support staff."

Broken picks

"My training Agent was also a FOA, with only a few months experience. The old timers wanted nothing to do with FOAs at that time. Some of the old timers were allegedly sent to this office for various indiscretions. 'Broken picks' I believe was the term used. They later became friendlier when they realized that we weren't going to drop a dime on them for stretching the rules a bit or drinking a beer at lunch."

Interview of a psychic

"A wealthy socialite was missing and a kidnapping case was opened by the FBI. Many callers with information and leads contacted the office. One of these was a female caller, claiming she had information as she was into ESP. As a joke, the SAC, who also oversaw the criminal squad, suggested that I, a FOA, interview the lady … a big lead for a first office Agent. Not to be deterred, I took this as a compliment. I made an appointment with the lady and went out to interview her. The lady stated that she sensed that she knew where the body was…somewhere near a body of water with a word 'horse' included in the title.

Case solved. Body was located at Horse's Creek. The lady became very famous and she assisted police departments on similar cases. Chalk one for the FOA and it was not the only one for me at the same office."

Hi tech tools

"I did my week in office on the squad handling the Watergate investigation. For several days, I frequently saw an older Agent studying documents with a magnifying glass. Hey, this is the real FBI. Finally, said something to my training Agent. He just laughed and said that the guy can't see without the magnifying glass.

Oh well, it was still a great week working on Watergate before the public hardly even knew what it was about."

OUTTAKE . . .

ONE VERSION OF THE ATTACK
(Author unknown)

"Remember the so called wedding party attack in Iraq where the U.S. was accused of killing innocent party guests? Here is the Marine version of it: Assuming this account is way more accurate than what the media has reported, it strongly illustrates either the total incompetence of the media or the agenda driven political bias that compels them to report crap that is not true. Here are some unclassified details I can provide.

Weddings are traditionally held on Thursdays in Iraq to take advantage of Friday as a day of rest – raid took place on Tuesday night.

The only permanent dwelling at the site held large stocks of food, bedding, medical supplies (lots of these . . . was the wedding going to be a cage match of some sort or were the caterers just bad cooks?), ammunition and weapons, as well as an apparent document forging set up. Meat was still frozen solid, not prepared for a wedding feast and there were no stocks of dishes, plates, etc.

Contrary to media reports, no 'Nuptial Tent' was found and a 1KM area around the site was searched – any further away than that would be just too far for the catering staff to walk carrying all those huge platters of food – against union rules.

No evidence of any means of support for the house (like sheep farming which is most common in that area). All evidence pointed to a smuggler way station – fit perfectly the description of several others found in the past.

'Wedding guests' (deceased of course) were almost all men of military age, only a couple of women, no elders at all and only one child (wounded) noted. All dressed as city dwellers, not Bedouins who would hold the wedding at such a location. All of the deceased were sterilized, as in none had any form of ID on them at all. Only ID's found were in a nice neat stack inside the house – and then quite a few less of those than there were people at the site.

Weapons were varied and included RPG's (they really suck when you fire them up in the air for celebration. Yeah, when the rounds come back to earth they make a hell of a bang. There were also military binoculars (when they separate the men and women they have to look at each other with bino's I guess) , and IED making material (party favors?) .

Lots of clothing prepackaged in pants and shirt sets.

There were also no gifts, no decorations, no food set out or left over, and the good bit of money recovered was all in the pockets of the 'guests' (maybe they were just cheap guests). Bottom line assessment: Good hit – no wedding. These were foreign fighters that had just crossed into Iraq and got an early trip to paradise and the martyrdom hall of fame."

The stories continue . . . .

Justice is blind

"My one week with WFO in training school was with an Agent who was legally blind. Real nice guy and still working bad check cases. My main job was getting him on and off buses." (There is definitely a human side to working with the FBI."

Good PR = half the battle

"My first office was in the South. At 5'9" I was the tallest guy in the RA and we called ourselves 'the mighty mights'. Went to the home of a Marine deserter with two terrific Agents. They went upstairs looking for the deserter, while I was listening to the families' lies downstairs. They marched down a shirtless 20 year old stud, who could have probably bounced the three of us all over the house. In transporting him to the PD, he said he thought about fighting, but realized it would be fruitless, given our FBI training.

Thank God for Bureau PR."

One lucky first office Agent

"My first assignment after the training school was in an RA with two other FOAs, each with about 100 assigned cases., mostly deserters and draft dodgers. These cases were mostly one-shot leads to interview the parents and relatives.

So I go alone to the parents' house and nobody answers the door even though I hear noise and conversation in the house. This is about 8 AM. So, I go to the back porch and through the open back door I see about 8 guys drinking beer and playing poker. So, stupid me, I say 'Clem Kadiddlehopper?'and Clem says 'that's me' and comes to the door and I told him that I have to take him back to the Army. He says OK and I take him to the Sheriff's Office so a deputy can claim the $ 50 bounty.

Case closed. I still can't believe how stupid I was."

Lesson not learned

"Being a new Agent with about a month in the field, I was all spiffed with a new suit, a brand new pair of Bostonian shoes, you know, the ones with a thousand eyes. Looking back, I have to admit sans the snap brim hat, I think Hoover would have been proud of my appearance.

We knocked on the apartment door at the location of the subject and his wife answered the door, and as she did so, we heard the fire escape window open and the subject bolting out of the apartment. Being fresh out of the Academy, I was a buffed specimen, who could run the two miles run in a sub 15 minutes. While my partner talked to the wife, I exited the same window as the subject did, and proceeded to climb the fire escape ladder to the roof of the apartment building. Since subject lived on the third floor, he ascended upward toward the sixth floor and the roof.

Man, I was on fire and ready to catch this dope. As I got to the roof, I saw the cross-over to an adjacent building which was connected to two other buildings. But like all city buildings, the heights were different and I had to climb over two separations and jump down about 8 feet to the roof of one of the buildings. As good a shape as I thought I was, the subject was gaining on me.

On one of the roof separations, I slipped and fell on newly tarred surface, ruining my new suit and tearing up my Bostonian shoes. Undeterred, I was now gaining on the subject and as we neared the last roof before an eight foot separation of the two buildings, I watched in horror as the subject leaped to the next roof successfully. By this time, I said to myself, "Are you expletive crazy" and with no rational answer I quit the chase and returned to the apartment where my partner was still talking to the wife.

As he concluded his interview of her, he looked at me and shook his head at my disheveled appearance and the tear in my pants and the tar all over my suit and shoes. As we were walking back to the Bucar, he said to me, 'We do not do this in the FBI, i.e., chase a subject up and down fire escapes and across roofs." He added 'especially for a couple of stolen guns.' I was duly admonished and he said to me to be in the 'O' tomorrow at 5 AM.

I was in the Office at 5 and he said this is how we catch a 'rabbit'. He lit on fire a crumpled up piece of newspaper just outside the neighbor's door and then banged on the door yelling 'FIRE'. Of course, there was a commotion among several neighbors, but the wife opened the door and my partner pushed past her to the bedroom and the subject was still sleeping. My partner took his model 10 revolver and proceeded to screw the barrel in the sleeping subject's ear, waking him up in a very startled state of mind. He was yanked out of bed and handcuffed in his drawers.

Under his bed, on his side, was one of the stolen guns.

The rest is as you would expect. We took him down to the lock up and I learned , or thought I learned, a valuable lesson.

Unfortunately, I had other fugitives in my time in the office, who ran but were caught because I gave chase again and again. Some of us were slow learners, but every time I had to chase down a subject, he went to jail exactly as he was dressed and sometimes that was in his birthday suit.

You just couldn't call this work, it was always pure fun and we laughed at the experience. Even after the real risky ones, what a great job. I want to do it over again, but you just can't, too bad."

Not remembering the rules

"About the third day in my first office, my partner called in sick, so I decided to go out alone to cover a 42 lead. As I pulled up in front of the deserter's wife's house, he came walking down the steps. I was in shock since this guy was a fugitive for over a year. I cuffed him and put him in the back of the Bucar and took him to the office, where another Agent helped me process him.

Later that day, I was called into the SAC's office and was chewed out for making an arrest on my own. I tried to explain that when I was a cop, before joining the FBI, I made many arrests on my own. Wrong thing to say to the boss.

The next day, I again went out alone to cover some leads. I was again called into SAC's office and chewed out for parking the Bucar in SAC's parking spot. Not a good start to my career."

Coffee -YES, Danish - NO!

"As I arrived in my first Office, it was inhabited by a herd of newish Agents like myself and most of the subjects of the horror stories we had been told in training school. After about a month, one of the Agents asked me, as we were waiting for the elevator, if I liked coffee. Of course I said yes. He told me where some Agents stopped and I got my Bucar and drove to the place.

There were about a dozen Agents there and they greeted me cordially. I knew I had made it at that moment. Acceptance! I got a cup of coffee and a blueberry danish and sat down at a table with several of the guys. I took a bite of the danish with relish, but the filling dropped out down my beige jacket onto my beige pants. What a day! I expected to see the SAC all the way to my apartment where I changed my clothes. I wondered how Mr. Hoover managed to show me a good reason not to drink coffee on Bureau time! I had coffee with the fellows many times afterward, but NEVER had another blueberry danish."

Credentials (creds) flying away

"An Agent I went through the Academy with, was transferred to his first Office after graduation. One of his first weeks on the job, he was conducting an investigation which ended on a bridge which spanned several sets of railroad tracks. As the tracks were no longer in use, the area around them had become overgrown with weeds about waist high.

The Agent approached an individual on the bridge and began to identify himself holding his credentials in one hand at arms- length, as we had been taught in the Academy. The individual promptly grabbed the Agent's creds and tossed them over the side of the bridge. (Not exactly how things had gone at Hogan's Alley at Quantico.)

The Agent spent the next two days below that bridge, searching for his creds and never did find them. However, things turned out OK, as several days later he received a call. Someone had found them and turned them in."

OUTTAKE . . .

PHYSICIANS ARE DANGEROUS

(Author unknown and no idea in what year this was written)

- **"The number of physician s in the U.S. is 700.**
- **Accidental deaths caused by physicians are 120,000.**

- **Accidental deaths per physician per year are 0.171..**
- **The number of gun owners in the U.S. is 80,000,000.**
- **The number of accidental gun deaths per year is .0000166.**

Statistically, doctors are approximately 9,000 times more dangerous than gun owners.
Remember, guns don't kill people, doctors do.

Please alert your friends to this alarming threat. We must ban doctors before this gets out of hand.

Out of concern for the public at large, I have withheld the statistics on lawyers for fear the shock would cause people to panic and seek medical attention."

The stories continue . . .

Will the real subject please identify himself?

"First Office Agent story, again. Partner and I were looking for a deserter, who was described as having a tattoo of his first name on his left arm, and the name began with letter "Z". As we were nearing the parent's home, we noticed a young man sitting on the front steps, smoking a cigarette. As we pulled over to the curb, noted a tattoo on the left arm, with the name starting with 'Z'. The young man caught the sight of us and bolted through the front door, slamming the door with a full force.

The two of us cleared the space between the car and the house in about two seconds, as my partner ran to the back of the house and I jumped on the front porch. Tried the door but it was locked. This was a hot pursuit and the adrenalin kicked in, propelling me right through the front door that wisely crashed to the floor. The young man was in conversation with his parents and I was the intruder, as was my partner who entered through the unlocked back door. I announced my identity and the reason for the intrusion, stating that the young man was about to be arrested for being a deserter. Wrong conclusion!

The young man was an identical twin, with both brothers having names starting with 'Z', and tattoos on their left arms. One was Zak and the other one was Zinno. The young man standing in front of us was Zak and Zinno was the one we were looking for. Zinno was not in the house at this time. Parents provided us with baby photos of the twins…identical, as well as a logical explanation. The real subject, Zinno, was arrested a few days later."

(Seems I've had problems with twins before. A friend arranged for a blind date with a female who was a twin that I was not made aware of, but who fronted for her twin sister who needed a date for a HS prom. It was time to terminate a short relationship, since I was never sure who the real date was.)

Arrest stat before training completed

"In about the 12th week of training, we were all hauled to the WFO to be assigned to veteran Agents for the week. I so happened to be assigned to one of the 'heavy' squads. My training Agent asked me if I have my gun and bullets to which I responded that I had my .38 special with 6 rounds in the chamber and a speed loader with an extra six. Trainer said fine and proceeded to tell me that we are going after an UFAP-Armed Robbery subject who was known to carry a .45 auto.

Needless to say, I almost crapped in my drawers right then but tried not to show it. Our first lead was at the home of subject's father. No answer at the door, so we proceeded up the stairs where the trainer pounded on the second floor door. From inside we hear 'Who is it?' and trainer responded with 'PO-LICE' and the door opens. We walk inside and there is this 18-19 year old black female perfectly naked, telling us we had awakened her. We apologized and asked her to put some clothes on. We showed her the picture of the fugitive and she told us she thought he worked at a moving company.

We went out to the moving company, and learned from the manager that the subject will be back by 4 pm and we should be there a little before that time. We came back and the manager asked us to wait in his office and shortly thereafter he brought in the fugitive. We cuffed him and took him to the FBI office where he was processed. One stat claimed and I was not even out of the Academy. What an exciting day.

My first real office was in a Southern state, where I was assigned working 25 and 42 fugitives. I set some sort of a record on bringing in over 100 fugitives in a 18 month period."

Checking SAs IQ

"An FBI instructor in Quantico gave each new Agent the first half of a well-known proverb, asking them to come up with the second half. Their insights may surprise you. Here are the answers from one of the trainees. While reading, keep in mind that these are brand new Agents.

A fugitive in custody....is worth two in the bush.
Don't change horses...until they stop running.
Strike while...bug is close.
It's always darkest before...Daylight Saving Time.
Never underestimate the power of...stenos.
You can lead a horse to water but...you can't stop for a drink on the way home.
Don't bite the hand that...you shoot with.
No news...impossible.
You can't teach an old dog...new math.
If you lie down with dogs, you'll stink in the morning.
Love all, trust...me.
The pen is mightier than the...your 357.
An idle mind is...the best way to relax.
Where there's smoke there's...pollution.
Happy the bride who...gets all the presents.
A penny saved is...not much.
Two's a company, three's...a carpool.
Don't put off till tomorrow what...you should have done today.
Laugh and the whole world laughs with you; cry and... work alone.
There are none so blind as...Stevie Wonder.
Children should be seen and not...arrested.
If at first you don't succeed...spy, spy again.
You get out of something only what you...see in the picture on the box.
When the blind lead the blind...get out of the way.
Better late than...on sick leave."

(Sounds like something I read in Art Linkletter's book Kids Say The Darndest Things.)

Leg of lamb first arrest

"I was assigned to a two man RA and I was a FOA. The SRA tells me he has a lead for a fugitive who is about 15 years old, but is 6'2" and 300 pounds. You can't make this stuff up. He is a fugitive from a civilian gang rape on a military base.

SRA and I leave, accompanied by a county sheriff's deputy., and proceed to subject's grandma's house. As is typical for the FOA, I am sent to cover the rear of the house. The house has been added on and there was no back door or rear windows. Strange house. I go back to the front and grandma has told my partner and the deputy that her grandson is not there and she doesn't know where he is. She gives permission to search the house.

The deputy stays in the front living room with grandma and we proceed to clear each room, finding no one else. My partner pulls down the attic stairs and creeps up to the top, peeking over into the attic with his Kel-Light. He then yells out for the guy to freeze and show his hands. He says that the guy is hiding behind the Christmas tree.

The fugitive is blinded by the light, but tries to move further back behind the tree. Then there is a crashing sound coming from the living room. I run to the living room and there is a giant leg protruding through the sheetrock ceiling between the deputy and grandma. The fugitive's leg was trapped. He wasn't going anywhere.

Turns out that the fugitive was just scared we were going to kill him. It took both deputy and me to push his leg up while my partner covered him with his wheel gun (that's what we carried back then in the late 70's."

Nervous first day in the office

"I reported to my first office in July 1996. I was already perspiring from nervousness about reporting to my first office. There I was, wearing my new 'Hoover Blue' suit, trying not to wilt from the July heat in this SW part of the country. I had driven my own vehicle, a 'pick em up truck', to the office that morning. It was 7 AM. How did I know that I was too early.

I was struggling with my suit jacket and trying to find the right curve to put that paddle holster on my skirt. I was so nervous about reporting in that I left the vehicle keys in the ignition, laid my gun on the front seat, put on my jacket, grabbed my purse from the hood of the truck, locked and closed the door, and…looked in the window and saw my gun...and the ignition keys! What a first day!

I walked to the office and took the elevator up to the reception desk. No one was there. I was too early. I waited in the lobby until someone got off the elevator . It was a female Special Agent. I introduced myself, told her that I was new to the office, and then told her about locking my gun in the truck. She smiled, she laughed, and then took me to see the Administrative Officer, who was another friendly lady. She immediately called the vehicle maintenance mechanic, who came over to the office. I walked him over to my truck, and he quickly did that 'lock-jock' magic to open up the door. I don't think they remember that day, It was probably like any other day for them, but I sure do.

How embarrassing...and I still lock my keys in the car."

GENERAL PATTON'S SPEECH
(Author unknown)

"If General George Patton were alive today and President of the USA, this would be his Fireside Speech:

My fellow Americans:

As you all know, the defeat of Iraq's regime has been completed. Since Congress does not want to spend any more money on this war, our mission in Iraq is completed for now. More missions to follow as we created a vacuum that will be filled with still other sects and fighters, who are preparing to do us harm.

This morning, I gave the order for a complete removal of all American forces from Iraq. This action will be

completed within 30 days. It is now time to begin the reckoning. Before me, I have two lists. One list contains the names of countries which have stood by our side during the conflict. This list is short: The United Kingdom, Spain, Bulgaria, Australia, Norway and Poland are some of the countries listed here. The other list contains the names that are not on the first list. Most of the world's nations are on that list. My press secretary will distribute copies of both lists later this evening.

Let me start by saying that effective immediately, foreign aid to those nations on list 2 ceases immediately and indefinitely. The money saved during the first year alone will pretty much pay for the costs of the Iraqi War. The American people are no longer going to pour money into third world hell-holes and watch those government leaders grow fat on corruption.

Need help with a famine? Wrestling with an epidemic? Call France. In the future, together with Congress, I will work to cut taxes and solve some local problems.

On that note, a word to terrorist organizations. Screw with us and we will hunt you down and eliminate you and all your friends and family from the face of the earth. Thirsting for a gutsy country to terrorize? Try France, or maybe China or Iran.

To Israel and the Palestinian Authority. You, boys. work out a peace deal now. Just note that Camp David is closed. Maybe all of you can go to Russia for negotiations. They have some great palaces there. Big tables, too.

I'm ordering the immediate severing of diplomatic relations with France, Germany, and Russia. Thanks for all your help, comrades. We are retiring from NATO as well. Bon chance, mon amis.

I have instructed the Mayor of New York City to begin towing the many UN diplomatic vehicles located in Manhattan with more than two unpaid tickets to sites where those vehicles will be stripped, shredded and crushed. I don't care about what treaty pertains to this. Pay your tickets tomorrow or watch your precious Benzes, Beamers, and limos be turned over to some of the finest chop shops in the world. I love New York!

A special note to our neighbors. Canada is on list 2. Since we are going to be seeing a lot more of each other, you folks might want to try not pissing us off for a change. Mexico is on list 2. President and his entire corrupt government really need an attitude adjustment. I have a couple of extra tank and infantry divisions sitting around on their ass. Guess where I'm gonna put 'em? Yep, border security. So start doing something with your oil.

Oh, by the way, the United States is abrogating the NAFTA treaty – starting now.

It is time for America to focus on its own welfare and its own citizens. Some will accuse us of isolationism. I answer them by saying 'darn tootin'.

Nearly a century of trying to help folks live a decent life around the world has only earned us the undying enmity of just about everyone on the planet. It is time to cut taxes here because we will not be spending on other people's problems.

To the nations on list 1, a final thought. Thanks guys. We owe you!

To the nations on list 2, a final thought: Drop dead! God bless America.

Thank you and good night."

The stories continue . . .

Toot your horn and he will come

"I will never forget it. My classmate and I were sent to the same office on our first assignment. We were there only a short time when one of the old timers asked if we would be interested in helping with an arrest. We both jumped at the chance and were told to be at the office early the next morning. Now this wasn't just any old timer, while his name escapes me at this time, I can still picture him. Big guy, up in his years, East Tennessee native, was an all American center at the University of Tennessee, a real local hero, known by all.

The two of us carpooled to the office, got into the Bucar, with one of us riding shotgun, the other in the back seat. We drive forever, eventually on dirt roads and through corn fields. The two of us are discussing who is hitting the front door and who is to cover the back of the house.

We get to the lonely house in the country and the old timer pulls right up on the lawn to the front porch, as he is honking the horn. Before we can even jump out of the car, the house door opens and out comes the fugitive, who then gets in the back seat.

That was it! Arrest is over. I think that the old timer chuckled all the way back to the office. But hey, a stat was a stat!"

A shotgun lead for a fugitive that almost had me fired

"I was first office Agent in a new city, assigned to a fugitive squad, with an SAC who served in the capacity of an SAC as well as a Supervisor of the fugitive squad. A UFAP case (Unlawful Flight to Avoid Prosecution) for a double murder out of state, is assigned to me as a case Agent. A lead from another FBI office to check out information from a source that the fugitive was working as a salesman, in an unidentified department store, within 20 miles of the downtown area. No name for the store, no address, only a good description of the subject and a dated photo. Subject described as a white male, no facial hair, a real non-descript individual.

This was a real shot in the dark, needle in the haystack type case, but worthy of being assigned to a first office Agent. No chance in hell of catching the culprit.

Yours truly went for a leisurely ride, alone, to get to know the area 20 miles from downtown. Stopped at the first department store that I found in the suburbs, picked up a large shopping bag and started Christmas shopping on Bureau time and with Bureau's blessing. Walked around in all departments, looking at the salesmen.

One particular salesman made an impression on me as he was talking to a customer. My gut reaction kicked in and my inner feeling was that this was the fugitive, although I was looking at his back and did not see his face yet. I moved in a wide circle in order to get a glimpse of the man from the front. This salesman had a full beard and his name tag did not match the name of my subject, yet my gut reaction persisted that this was my man. If it is possible, half of my brain said yes, half said no. The feeling persisted and any doubt had to be put to rest.

I moved again in a wide circle, to be behind him, as a hungry wild animal stalking its prey. He completed his sale and the customer moved away. There were no other customers or salesmen in the immediate vicinity. This was my chance. Slowly I moved behind his back to be within an arm's reach and softly called out the name that was on my fugitive folder at the office. The man was slowly turning around and before he could finish saying 'You son of a #!:&?', I had him on the ground handcuffed, at the same time telling him that this was FBI and he was under arrest. It was a total surprise to him.

NOW I HAD A PROBLEM! I was a first office Agent, a rookie, a newbie…and the SAC had a rule that the FOAs could not make an arrest on their own. Plus, how do I drive him back to the office, since SAC's rule # 2 was that two FBI Special Agents had to be in a car transporting the arrested person. The official FBI rule was for the arrested person to be placed in the back seat, behind the empty front passenger seat, handcuffed in the back, and the second Agent sitting in the back seat behind the driver. I began to sweat profusely for the first time.

A manager showed up and I quickly described the situation as I was holding the fugitive on the floor by kneeling on him and showing my FBI credentials. Since this was in the days before the cell phones, I asked to use the regular phone to call the office radio room and ask for assistance.

While waiting for a two man FBI unit to show up, the handcuffed fugitive spoke up and told me how lucky I was to find him. Fifteen minutes before, he played a Santa Claus for the store, with hundreds of kids taking turns to sit in his lap. I would never had recognized him in his Santa outfit and his real beard.

This revelation was even a bigger problem for me. IF THE NEWSPAPER PRINTED A HEADLINE STORY ABOUT THE FBI ARRESTING SANTA CLAUS, AND THOUSANDS OF KIDS AND PARENTS WROTE TO MR. HOOVER COMPLAINING AND ASKING WHY THE FBI ARRESTED SANTA, I WOULD BE FIRED FROM THE FBI. My mind raced ahead to a courtroom scene in the movie *Miracle on 34th Street,* with bags of mail from kids addressed to Santa Claus, being brought in and dumped in front of the judge.

The big boss at the office was waiting for me. First he gave me the bad news. A letter of censure was being prepared for the dumb mistake of making an arrest on my own. If the story of Santa's arrest made it to Mr. Hoover's office, I would be quartered and fried and fired for stupidity and the bad publicity that the FBI would receive. (If I were fired then, I would not have enough stories to tell and this book would not have seen the light of day.)

A commendation letter followed instead, and the threat of a letter of censure ended up in the circular file. I was lucky and I admit my stupidity, thanking God for giving me another chance and surviving still other stupid moves during my 32 year career. No wonder I retired on April Fools' Day."

The choppers . . .

"I assisted another Agent in transporting a bank robbery subject, who was a broken down white man, probably in his late 50's. He committed a couple of note jobs. The case Agent arranged for the subject to meet us in a shopping center parking lot.

There to see him off were a couple of his adult children. It was a very low key arrest, something which is a bit of a lost art in today's militarized Bureau.

After driving for an hour or so, case Agent at the wheel skillfully began talking to the subject about the second bank robbery. Well, his technique worked and the subject started feeling sick down in his gut. The driver pulled over and we let the subject get out and he had dry heaves. Nothing came out as he wretched, with the exception of his false teeth, which flew out and hit the turf.

What happened next has stayed with me. The subject simply bent down, picked up the choppers, blew off the bits of leaves, etc. and put them back in his mouth. The drive to the jail continued."

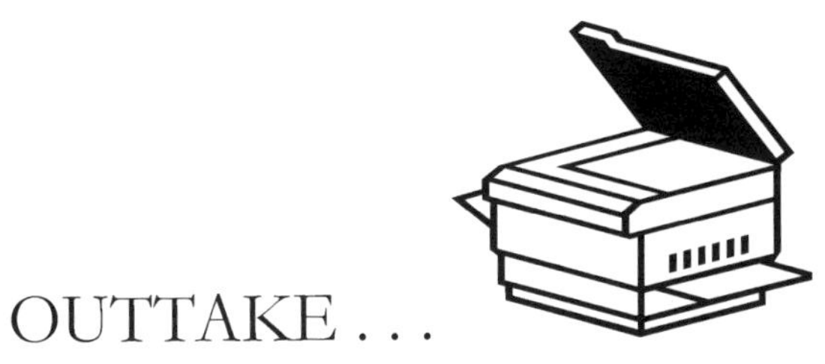

OUTTAKE . . .

ACHTUNG !
(Author unknown)

"Alles Touristen und Non-Technischen Looken Peepers! Das Machine Control ist Nicht fur Gerfingerpoken und Mittengrabben. Oderwise is Easy Schnappen der Springwerk, Blowenfuse, und Poppencorken mit Spitzensparken. Der Machine ist Diggen by Expertzen only. Is Nicht fur Gerverken by Dummkopfen. Das Rubbernecken Sightseenen Keepen das Kottenpicken Hands in das Pockets. So Relaxen und Watchen das Blinkenlights."

The stories continue . . .

A flash on the flesh

"I didn't sleep the night before my first search warrant. The subject was a violent criminal who had successfully robbed a series of banks. The case Agent did not have enough evidence to indict and arrest. The bank video surveillance was pretty good but the subject wore a ball cap to disguise his face. He also wore sunglasses and a shirt with a floral print. The search of residence would hopefully result in the location of clothing depicted on the bank surveillance videos.

I rode to the subject's residence with the case Agent, an old, grizzled and grouchy, cigar-smoking man. A group of other rookie Agents drove in another car. I wondered if those rookies slept the night before. On the ride there, I created every hypothetical scenario in my mind that may result in the use of deadly force. I felt ready for anything this violent criminal may have to offer. While I'm getting focused and putting on my game face, the vet Agent kept talking about his favorite brand of cigar and fly fishing. This really spooked me. I was completely juiced with adrenaline and nerves, but he was acting like the search was just another task in his usual work day.

We parked on the street in front of the subject's house at o'dark thirty. The subject lived in a border line condemned home in a border line condemned neighborhood. The front door was wide open. As soon as I jumped out of the car, I smelled something really bad. Four Special Agents, including myself, approached the front door. The nasty aroma grew stronger with each step towards the front door. Suddenly, twenty to thirty very tiny, harrier terrier-type dogs, resembling long haired rats, started scurrying out of the house. The little rats were quick and darted everywhere, eventually scattering in all directions down the street.

As we entered the house, after knocking and announcing our presence, of course, the aroma began to make my eyes water. It smelled like someone recently spilled a 50 gallon drum of ammonia. Someone tried to turn on lights, but we soon learned that this residence had no electricity. Myself and another Agent were required to clear the family room which was pitch black. As we approached the doorway to the family room, it became obvious that the ammonia smell was emanating from that room. Our eyes were really tearing up. I quickly peeked in to the room in one direction and the other Agent did the same, covering the other side of the room. My heart felt like it stopped. In the pitch black, I thought I saw flesh. I had a flash back to a training scenario at the FBI Academy of the bad guy hunkered down behind a couch in the dark, sighting up his weapon on the arresting Agents entering the room. I told my partner what I saw. His facial reaction mirrored my nerves. We agreed to quick peek one more time, while quickly pointing a flash in the direction of the flesh. I peeked while my partner turned on the flashlight.

There it was – a mass of pale white flesh. I gave a few hard commands and had about a 5 pounds of trigger pull on a 5.5 pound trigger. No response, no movement. The only thing my mind could concoct was that our subject had killed himself. We both turned on our flashlights and stormed the family room.

Much to our surprise and relief, the fleshy mass was on an overweight farm hog. The hog was lying in its own urine – hence the foul ammonia smell.

The subject was not at home. However, he truly lived in a house-size pig sty."

Is it or is it not?

"I was a first office Agent involved in an arrest at a trailer court. Subject's wife claimed that the subject was not there. A male was found in the back bedroom, under the bed, claiming to be subject's twin brother. We had no photo, so we took him to the Office, getting him very upset as a result. He wanted to call an attorney and that got us worried. Perhaps he was telling the truth and was not the subject of our interest. We almost believed in his story.

We took his prints and faxed them to the FBIHQ. A quick answered followed. BINGO! This was our subject and now he admitted that we had the right person. There was no twin brother.

Another case closed in the big city. More to follow on weekly basis."

3rd or 4th husband

"In the summer of 1970, I remember the naked lady we dragged out of the bed she was sharing with her third or fourth husband. He was a Navy sailor who had just returned from Vietnam. It seems she had several husbands in the Navy at the same time, who were all sending her pay allotments to live on. I've always felt bad we ruined that guy's homecoming."

The no reverse Bucar

"After spending the first week or two with my training Agent, I finally went out alone to cover a lead. Needing a Bucar, I headed to the switchboard to pick up a set of car keys. I had been told there were several unassigned old cars that were going to Bucar Valhalla in the very near future and were available for anyone to use. So I grabbed the keys to the only one left., a 1965 Dodge, if my memory serves me correctly. I found it in the basement garage parallel parked near the radio shop. As I got in, the radio tech told me to park it in the same place when I brought it back.

Off I went to do Mr.Hoover's business, looking for an address to cover the lead. I ended up going down a dead end street. When I realized this, I started to make a U-turn. Because the car had a turning radius of two city blocks, I had to stop and put it in reverse to backup and complete the turn. When I did that, nothing happened. The engine roared but the car did not move. I was not going backwards. After several tries, I realized the car had no reverse.

The FBI Agent in me deduced this was the reason the car was parallel parked in the garage and why no one had taken it. I put the transmission back into drive, hopped the curb, drove through a couple of front yards and finally got back on the street, headed in the right direction. I was lucky there were no shrubs, ruts or trees in those yards.

I got back to the office, parallel parked the car in the same spot by the radio shop, and never mentioned the adventure to anyone… until now."

OUTTAKE . . .

AGENT'S DRINKING PROBLEM PAYS DIVIDENTS

(Author unknown)

(Updated prices would really save you a lot of money)

"Since you cannot refrain from drinking, why not start a saloon in your home? Be the only customer and you will not have to buy a license.

Give your wife $ 12.00 to buy a gallon of whiskey. There are 128 snorts in a gallon . . . buy all of your drinks from your wife at 40 cents a snort and in four days, when the gallon is gone, your wife will have $ 39.20 to put in the bank and will have $ 12.00 to start up business again.

If you live 10 years, and continue to buy all your booze from your wife, and then die in your boots from the snakes, your widow will have $ 35,770.00 on deposit, enough to bury you respectfully, bring up your children, buy a house and lot, marry a decent non- FBI man who does not drink and forget she ever knew you."

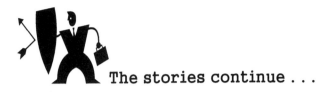

The stories continue . . .

The bucking Bucar

"Five Agents and myself went to arrest a fugitive at his girlfriend's house. As our three Bucars arrived in the area, we saw the fugitive and his girlfriend leave in her car. As we were deciding where to make the stop, he drove into a gas station.

After ordering everyone to close in, my partner and I were the first into the gas station. As I turned the ignition off, my American Motors piece of junk started bucking, making noises, steam coming out of the engine, and would not stop. Embarrassed as we were, we could do nothing except sit there waiting for the Bucar to die a peaceful death.

The noise and commotion, however, caused everyone at the station, including the subject and his girlfriend, to stop what they were doing and watch this spectacle. As it turned out, this diversion caused the other Agents to quietly approach the subjects and effect the arrest.

There are eight million stories in the Naked City, this is one of them."

Bucar accident

"I'm not sure what office this occurred in, but it was real, or at least it has become such an imbedded part of Bucar lore that it seems real to this retired Agent.

The unidentified FBI Agent was in a serious accident in his Bureau steed. The car took most of the damage to the rear bumper area when the skidding Bucar came to rest, rear end first, against a light pole. The resourceful Agent was able to get all cosmetic work done by his contact garage so that no official papers were submitted.

Not so much with the radio equipment, carried in the trunk. The radio unit was destroyed in its mount. He took it into the ET shop with a straight face and told them his radio just quit working.

Whoever the responsible party was will have to tell the rest of the story."

The old switcheroo

"In the mid-60s in a Midwest office, there were several heavies that would sometimes carpool in a Bucar. They would drive their POAs to a particular Rapid Station stop where they would park them before transferring to a Bucar for the ride to the office.

One day, there was a minor fender bender at the station between the fully loaded Bucar and a little old lady in the other car. In the fog and confusion of the moment, one of the Agents was able to substitute his car for the Bucar so that his car appeared to be the one involved in an accident. I think the little old lady was quite confused, but I believe the ruse was successful." (A confidential Bureau source, who has furnished reliable information in the past, but who asked that her identity be fully protected, advised that the guilty party was a Serbian speaking FBI Special Agent, whose contact fixing the car was also of Serbian background, and repaired the car in exchange for one bottle of Slivovitz.)

The pancake Bucar

"In this city, parking on the street is almost impossible. Not for this Agent, apparently. He pulled into a no parking construction zone and, despite our warnings, parked the Bucar. Well, when we returned from lunch to the car an hour later (make that 45 minutes later), the car was flatter than a pancake. A garbage truck had apparently dropped a small dumpster on top of it. Try explaining that one to your ASACS."

The sun in my eyes excuse

"If you live due East of the office and want to use the sun was in my eyes excuse for an auto fixed object collision, you should really remember which direction the sun goes down at night. The second would be if you are involved in an accident and because of the day it is and where you are at once you collect from the other driver because he ran a red light and hit you and you decide to put the car in a shop and get it fixed yourself.

Then because the shop owner is a 137 and you get it fixed at a lower price than the estimate you took to the guy that hit you, what do you do with the difference in the money you collected from his insurance company.

Now remember you have been covering leads and showing up at the BRs in your POA for a week.

Man did I love that job. None of this type of stuff shows up while monitoring second grade recess."

The CYA and the SAs go hand in hand

"As usual, but especially on this one, names / locations will remain anonymous.

Long time ago, in a distant RA that bordered a river separating FBI divisions, an Agent had a Bucar accident. Not a bad one, as he was not responsible but it had to be reported due to damage to the car. Pictures were taken and developed.

One picture of the Bucar showed a dog in back seat looking out the window, at the camera.(It seemed the Agent had to take the dog to vet when the accident occurred.) Somehow, the photo never became part of the 'crime scene' photos."

Tit for tat

"The new supervisor, who always had to have a new car, noticed a scratch on the side of his car. Being a good investigator, he determined that the car parked next to his had done the damage. He pulled the car log, determined who the driver was, and summoned the Agent to his office. He chided the Agent for his poor driving and instructed him to write an accident memo.

The Agent, being one of many years of experience, told the Supervisor what he could do with his memo and denied the incident. The Supervisor, infuriated by this disrespect for his authority, went and got another Supervisor and an ASAC and took them to the garage. He explained the damage to his car and his investigative skills in determining the culprit. He further went and got the spare keys for the offending car and began backing it into its space and talking out the window explaining how the driver scraped his car when his foot slipped from the brake to the gas.

Needless to say, nothing further was said about the incident."

My buddy almost killed me

"I recently reported for duty in a Midwest division from the sunny South. I didn't have a Bucar assigned to me yet, so I was picked up each morning by my good buddy and still a friend today.

My friend was driving a hot, UC Pontiac Firebird and each morning he would come over the hill like a bat-out-of-hell and make a sharp turn into a private road where our townhouse was located. I would wait for him about 7:00 a.m. and he would pick me up.

This particular morning, he was running late and I had walked to the end of the private road to wait for him. At 7:00 a.m. in February it might as well be midnight. Sure enough, after waiting about five more minutes, he came flying over the hill and made the sharp turn onto the private road. There was just one problem. He never saw me standing there.

The front of the Firebird hit me just below the knees. Had he road not been covered with a light snow powder from the night before, he would have literally run me over. As it was, my briefcase flew off to the left, my lunch to the right, and the Firebird hood ornament just missed taking my manhood from me.

As I rolled off the hood onto the fresh snow, he was able to stop the car and jump out with a look of unbelievable horror. At that moment I looked up at him and said, 'So this is the way you greet new Agents to the division?' We both broke up and laughed for at least 3-4 minutes. After I checked to see if anything was broken (There wasn't) and he regained his composure (He thought he had killed somebody) we finally made it into the office. My friend promised to give me strokes on the golf course after nearly taking my life, but of course that never happened. Thank God I don't need strokes when I play him."

Bucar carwash

"Office had a special stop to get the Bucars washed. When we used the services of this particular car wash, we usually ended up getting the car washed and undoubtedly taking back some papers that were found by the cleaning crew. The boss and his crew working there knew every piece of Bureau jargon known to man, as well as classifications, too.

Thank God they were on our side. A lot of butts were saved by the carwash crew. They should have given them a plaque."

Confession – a different approach . . .

"While heading a violent crime squad, I received a call one evening that a badly wanted contract killer was at the Marriott under a known alias. I headed over with three Agents. Night security at the hotel was a PD sergeant. I met him and he said he was available if we needed him. Manager told me subject was drinking about a quart of vodka daily and bringing in hookers every night.

Subject had a partner, also wanted, and was also suspect re killing of a Federal judge. Subject was 6'2" and solid.

His room was empty but we noticed about a 1/3 full bottle of vodka on the bureau. He had left a do not disturb sign on the door.

I set out two of the Agents in the lobby and two of us took a room across from the subject's. The two of us took turns watching through the peephole. About 2 AM we heard a door slam and the do not disturb sign had been removed. Called Agents in the lobby who covered sliding doors of his room. Holding door to our room open with a chair, I called subject's room to tell him that he was surrounded. No answer on the phone, but I didn't think that subject could have passed out so quickly.

We hit the room, looking in the closet, bathroom and under the bed. I looked across the hall and a do not disturb sign was on room next to ours. Looking down the hall and saw subject approaching while leaning heavily on a smaller man. Sergeant and I drew weapons 'FBI – Hands Up'. Subject reached inside jacket. I was waiting for a gun to appear before firing. It was a drunken reflex gesture and his hand came out empty. Slammed both against the wall. Sergeant covered while I cuffed subject who in process toppled over on top of me. Anyway, got subject in room. The other individual was a good Samaritan, a cab driver helping his passenger. He peed in his pants.

I told the sergeant I had been extremely close to wasting subject. He in turn told me that as soon as I would fire he would take out the other guy.

In the room were a number of nude photos of a female. Subject said they were of his wife but she didn't know he had taken them. Had a problem with this, as woman was looking straight at the camera. Also found a pair of woman's panties which appeared too small to have been his wife's. Also found $ 100,000 cash.

Subject was removed to the office. I asked the location of his partner and he said, 'In 20 years I ain't never snitched on nobody.' I told him I had no problem snitching and I was prepared to call his wife and ask her if she knew about the panties we had found. He immediately gave us a number in another city and his partner was arrested the following AM by Bu Agents.

Concerned that the $100,000 would fall into the wrong hands, i.e. defense attorneys, I called the IRS, who by 9 AM appeared and executed a summary judgment for non-payment of taxes and seized the money. Subject is currently on death row."

CHAPTER 2

PEARLS OF WISDOM

"pearl – A smooth, hard, usually white . . . body of varied but usually roundish shape that is an abnormal nacreous growth within the shell of some oysters . . . and forms around a grain of sand . . . and is used as a gem . ."

"wisdom – The quality of being wise . . . following the soundest course of action . . . based on knowledge, experience . . . good judgment; sagacity . . . wise discourse or teaching" (Webster's New World College Dictionary, Fourth Edition)

It follows that pearls of wisdom emanate from the older, wiser, more mature FBI Special Agents, to everyone else in the office . . . sort of a survival manual.

Advice to a new Agent

"The advice I got from an old Agent was: Never miss a chance to eat, go to the bathroom, take a nap, and a few others I won't pass on to protect the guilty."

A secret advice from a hardened old Agent

"The secret of surviving an office inspection is to have one of the best three cases in the office and the inspectors will leave you alone. At the same time, if you have one of these best cases, your supervisor will look good, your ASAC will look like a champ (although he /she may not even be aware of the case that you have) and the SAC will be praised as if he were a God."

The best advice regarding the "Deadly Force Policy"

"The best explanation of the 'Deadly Force Policy' was given to my police training class, by a grizzly old police sergeant in charge of the shooting range, on a big city police department, where I served before joining the FBI. The old man had it right when he stated: **'Better to be judged by twelve than carried by six.'**

He continued: **'When you leave home for your assigned shift, kiss your wife or husband and the kids good bye as you exit the house, promising them that you will see them at the end of the shift, whenever that may be. If anyone will try to do you and those that you have sworn to defend, physical harm, and prevent you from returning to your home safe and sound, and kissing your family at the door, that person has to die, because you want to live. It will be a split second decision, because that is all the time that you will have. The arguments by the attorneys whether you acted correctly, will take months and years, deciding whether your decision was a correct one. Your supervisors and big wigs, the politicians and the newspapers will criticize you, put you through a Maytag Wringer** Washer **and possibly even spit you out. But, you will be alive.'**

At least once a year, in my long law enforcement career with the police department and the FBI, as well as in the military service, I attended mandatory lectures about the use of deadly force policy, as it changed and evolved so that everyone could claim a CYA. It was only the words of that SGT that stayed with me to this day."

The Green Hornet

"From the biggest office out East, comes the story of an unidentified FBI Special Agent who signed in on the radio every morning by saying 'Good morning Central, this is the Green Hornet 10-8'. Central radio played along by saying 'Good morning Green Hornet, you're 10-8 at 0705.'

This went on for years, until one day while the Office was under inspection, the Chief Inspector was walking by the radio room and heard the Green Hornet go 10-8. He stormed into the room, grabbed the microphone demanding: 'This is Chief Inspector O'Brien (an alias), Green Hornet identify yourself!'

After a long pause, while all of the Division listened for the

Green Hornet's true identity, the reply came: 'I'm green, but not that green!"

As the whole Division erupted, one can only imagine the color of the Inspector's face was as red as the Hornet was green."

OUTTAKE . . .

"AN ANALYSIS OF U.S. LAW ENFORCEMENT AGENCIES UPON ENCOUNTERING A PROBLEM SNAKE WITHIN THEIR JURISDICTION"

(author unknown)

FBI:

Searches for, but cannot locate snake. After snake is caught by the local police, FBI forms a Snake Task-Force of 150 Agents, sets up a command center, holds press conference and assumes credit for capture of a snake.

USSS (SECRET SERVICE):

Forms a protective ring of agents around snake and escorts snake to a safe area.

ATF:

Sends SRT team to arrest snake; they expend all of their ammo, then burn the forest down, killing the snake and other local fauna. At a Congressional inquiry, they make a presentation on why additional funding is required to properly train agents how to battle the threat of snakes.

TSA:

Abides by Congressional ruling to prevent 'profiling' of venomous snakes, which requires 'random' snake

inspections. Venomous snake escapes while TSA strip searches non-venomous species.

IRS –CID:

Performs an in-depth investigation of the snake and writes a 100-page summary why the snake should be prosecuted. The investigation is closed and all agents are out of the office by 4:30 p.m.

ICE:

After obtaining permission from the BPA, CBP, FBI, IRS, FINCEN, DEA, FAMS, FEMA, and the Girl Scouts of America, they mail snake a notice to appear on a specified date for a status hearing. Snake never responds and is promptly forgotten.

DEA:

Initiates a Title 3 and an MLAT investigation on the snake's cell phone, after discovering that the above agencies have begun an investigation on the snake. Spends $3M to discover the snake is not Colombian.

U.S. ATTORNEY'S OFFICE:
Declines prosecution out of 'professional courtesy.'

USBP (BORDER PATROL):
Shoots snake."

The Oklahoma City Bombing (OKBOM) lead

"I had only one lead during the case that lasted for months, with probably over one million leads sent out.

A concerned caller notified our office that their daughter's boyfriend resembled the picture of the suspect that was shown on the television, and his demeanor allegedly matched the person of interest.

I made a copy of the picture from the file and proceeded to the caller's home. I met with the parents of the young lady and showed them the picture. They were convinced that their daughter's beau was definitely the man we were after. Their reasoning was as follows:

'One day in the recent past, the young man was so upset with their daughter, that he took a chain saw, and made a convertible car with it, by simply taking most of the car's roof off the large hard-top car that she was driving'.

The recent photo of the boyfriend did not resemble the composite of our subject."

What gets FBI Special Agents in trouble?

"It's the same old story. The three '**Bs**': **B**ooze, **B**roads, and **B**ureau cars."

The ten fatal errors that get you killed

1. "Lack of knowledge; apathy or complacency
2. Taking a bad position
3. Failure to recognize danger signs
4. Poor or no search
5. Failure to handcuff properly
6. Failure to watch the hands
7. Relaxing too soon
8. Making false assumptions
9. Tombstone courage
10. Sleepy or asleep"

Things to remember when making an arrest

- "Have a plan.
- Make it hard to hurt you.
- Issue simple, unambiguous commands.
- Use professional, non-provocative language. You can be firm without being antagonistic. Don't provoke a fight or interference.

- Be assertive, i.e., tell the subject: Who you are / Why you are there / What you expect of them.
- Do not engage in conversation, debate, argument or negotiations with a subject.
- Demand immediate compliance.
- Escalate use of force quickly with any non-compliance. The level of threat you perceive will dictate the forcefulness of initial contact. Subsequent levels of force are dictated by the subject.
- Never relax. Maintain a high threat, worst case mentality.
- Don't get distracted.
- Plan for contingencies, e.g.. passive non-compliance, resistance, outside interference, escape, injuries, etc.
- Always holster your weapon before handcuffing.
- Cuff first and always in the rear, then search high risk areas.
- Once under control, ask the subject questions affecting your safety, e.g.,: Do you have any weapons, drugs, needles?
- Be professional. There may be witnesses or you may need the subject's cooperation at a later time."

Keys to Agent survival

- "Firearms proficiency
- Body armor
- Mental preparation – alertness
- Awareness of threat and surroundings
- Recognition of weapon
- Target discrimination
- Tactics: Approach to subject /
  Position of advantage / Cuffing speed
- Backup assistance
- Will to survive
- Physical conditioning"

My favorite reminders

- "Admit nothing.
- Deny everything.

- Make counter allegations.
- Never cop out."

A two liner to remember:

- "Deny the allegation.
- Defy the alligator."

Incredible statements

- "To do absolutely nothing on your request is also a form of decision.
- Wait for the other shoe to drop.
- Why is it that in today's paperless society, the FBI is buying a larger amount of printing paper as well as TP?"

What an old timer told me and I told a newbie

"There are Old Agents; There are Bold Agents; But there are no Old Bold Agents."

Two of most valuable and memorable pieces of advice

"Be flexible – Provided by a new Agent counselor, an individual completely lacking in flexibility.

Delay will kill you – Provided by a later defrocked ASAC/SAC, who might have retired as an SAC had he been able to delay gratifying his amorous impulses on Butime."

But hey! Better to be a bad example than no example at all."

OUTTAKE . . .

LOVING SPEECH
By Anna Cummins

"Do not save your loving speeches,
for your friends till they are dead.

Do not write them on their tombstones,
Speak them rather now instead."

The stories continue . . .

Advice

"What advice, pithy enough to just take up one or two lines, would I give to new Agents starting out today? Maybe:

- A clear conscience starts with a weasel-worded 302.
- A five-year-old Bucar gathers no 'new' dents.
- 'Gravestone' informants tell no tales to inspectors.
- A clipboard and a worried expression deflect new cases.
- Remember: 'I only have one stomach lining. And they don't transplant those things."

- Two things don't have to pay attention to supervisors – earthquakes and high-stat Agents.
- If you do it right, the only way they'll know you've been banging the book is if you leave DNA evidence.
- A 'blue-flamer' will incinerate everyone on or near the launching pad.
- If the ASAC don't know, it never happened.
- Go ahead and do it: if you're right, they'll understand. (uh huh.)

What about you? What, in two lines or less, would you tell a new Agent, supposing he/she would actually listen?"

What I would tell an FBI Agent in 2014 ?

- "The best thing J. Edgar did was the steno pool. Unfortunately, it has been eliminated.
- Don't drink before noon.
- Return the Bucar full of gas and oil."

More advice…

"The Bureau confuses ambition with ability."

Still more advice…

"They want three bags full. Give them three bags full. Nobody ever looks in the bags anyway."

Advice from a supervisor to the new Agent on a breaking case:

"Just give me the facts, I'll supply the BS."

Advice before the computers took over

"The paperwork that drowns us, keeps us afloat."

Two liners of advice

"If there is the slightest bit of trauma involved, i.e. accident with Bucar or stray firearms shot, etc - - 'I have developed traumatic amnesia and you're only adding to it." (Any psychiatrist will write that on a piece of paper)

"Also proven true: I was in the restroom, looks like me, but? Didn't I see your Bucar with a Christmas tree on the roof?" (counter allegation)

"This is also true and very good advice, given to me once by a great Agent: 'After firing that warning shot (who me?) do not clean your weapon in the office! Hoppes stinks'! "

About haircuts on Bureau time

"Your hair grows on Bureau time so you get it cut on Bureau time.
It didn't all grow on Bureau time. Well, I didn't get it all cut off."

Abe Lincoln's advice . . . to future FBI Agents

"Better to remain silent and be thought a fool, than to speak and remove all doubt."

A more usual, common advice

"If you can't dazzle them with brilliance then baffle them with bulls#%."

FBI Maxims

- "Check your guns – no empty chambers under the hammers.
- Make sure you have a quarter in your pocket to make a call from a pay phone! (Today's Special Agent might not know what a pay phone was.)
- Never holster an empty weapon.
- Different strokes for different folks...different weapons take different magazines."

The rule of three

"Don't respond until they ask for it the third time. If they don't ask for it three times, they don't really want it."

Bureau jargon

"UACB, sutel asap request of mytel dated such and such with cc to SOG." (Actually used term UACB in my e-mail, after waiting over thirty days to get this book approved for publication from the Prepub Unit at FBIHQ. Naturally, their response within 24 hours was that 'the approval letter was sent yesterday'. Today is three days later, and the snail-mail has not arrived. Blame the USPS . . . AGAIN!"

Another jargon worth a chuckle

"Su ur rpt, re my tel. Now kiss my a_ _ and go to h _ _ _."

Pastor's reasoning with God

"My pastor is a quiet type of a guy, living his faith to the fullest. He serves and guides his flock in an inner city Catholic nationality parish, surrounded by the 'hood'. He is a realist, seventy years old, that knows the territory and the multiple homicides and attacks in the area that he serves.

One day, out of the blue, he asked me what I would think if he obtained a CCW permit, noting that he is one of the very few pastors in the inner city that had not been robbed or beaten, whether in the parish house, outside the church building proper, or tending to his flock, consisting of older ladies that still reside in the neighborhood.

His question was somewhat of a shock to me. A man of faith, believing in God's ultimate guidance and protection, thinking of carrying a gun for his own protection. I asked him for his reasoning and his answers were very realistic. Here is what he said: 'I believe that God will protect me, but…there are people out there that would do me harm and I have so much work to do yet in my life and I do not wish some low life, that definitely does not believe in the goodness of God, to end my life on earth this way, by taking my life. I have to live to minister the faithful and attempt to do as much good as possible, in the short time that I have left on earth.'

I gave this Man of God a simple human answer, one that guides my reasoning why I would take someone's life, if my life, the life of my family members or the lives of those that I have promised to protect, was to be ended by a criminal, and it is as follows: I believe in God's protection, but the world is very violent and God is very busy protecting us. So, I am helping God (knowing very well that God does not need my help) in my small way, by carrying a gun at all times, and I am willing to use it. Amen.

Please write your notes on this page, before you

forget, detailing a critical review of the book, and send the notes via an e-mail to me. I love to read constructive criticism and I thank you in advance.

OUTTAKE . . .

Dear Mother and Dad:
(Author unknown)

"Since I left for college I have been remiss in writing and I am sorry for my thoughtlessness in not having written before. I will bring you up to date now, but before you read on, please sit down. You are not to read any further unless you are sitting down, Okay?

Well, then, I am getting along pretty well now. The skull fracture and the concussion I got when I jumped out of the window of my dormitory when it caught on fire shortly after my arrival here is pretty well healed now. I only spent two weeks in the hospital and now I can see almost normally and only get those sick headaches once a day. Fortunately, the fire in the dormitory, and my jump, was witnessed by an attendant at the gas station near the dorm, and he was the one who called the fire department and the ambulance.

He also visited me in the hospital and since I had nowhere to live because of the burnt-out dormitory, he was kind enough to invite me to share his apartment with him. It's really a basement room, but it's kind of cute. He is a very fine boy and we have fallen in love and are planning to get married. We haven't got the exact date, but it will be before my pregnancy begins to show.

Yes, Mother and Dad, I am pregnant. I know how much you are looking forward to being grandparents and I know you will welcome the baby and give it the same love and devotion and tender care you gave me when I was a child.

The reason for the delay in our marriage is that my boyfriend has a minor infection which prevents us from passing our pre-marital blood tests and I carelessly caught it from him.

I know that you will welcome him into our family with open arms. He is kind and, although not well educated, he is ambitious. Although he is of a different race and religion than ours, I know your often-expressed tolerance will not permit you to be bothered by that.

Now that I have brought you up to date, I want to tell you that there was no dormitory fire, I did not have a concussion or skull fracture, I was not in the hospital and I am not pregnant. I am not engaged, I am not infected, and there is no boy-friend in my life.

However, I am getting a D in History and F in Science and I want you to see those marks in their proper perspective.

Your loving daughter, Susie"

CHAPTER 3

THE UNOFFICIAL FBI NUT BOX / COMPLAINT DESK / WALK INS

Definitely not the candied nut variety that one can purchase on the Amazon. These boxes were manufactured by Wayne Novelty Manufacturing Company, and could be ordered in two different sizes, with following nomenclatures: Box, wooden, with lid, antique oak, finger-joints, hinges brass, sliding wooden divider inside, U.S. made, procurement number 7520-285-3143. The one used in my division was size small, with above procurement number, 4 ½"H x 5 ¾"L x 4" W. The larger size was 10" x 7" x 5".

Every FBI division had these boxes. Bigger divisions, such as New York or Washington Field Office, utilized the bigger box, for obvious reasons that I will now explain. These boxes were utilized to keep a paper trail on callers to the FBI switchboard, by writing long hand notes on 3 x 5 cards and placing them in alphabetical order by names of callers. Specifically, they were used to identify persons who bordered on having a mental problem. Because of their usage and the name utilized, FBI divisions were sued and after zillion years of usage, these boxes were eliminated, per order of the FBIHQ.

After all, FBI SAs and support employees that received the phone calls around the clock, did not have appropriate doctoral degrees to establish whether the caller had a problem or not. Nevertheless, boxes served its intended purpose, as you will see from the description of their usage in different divisions.

Full-moon nights came alive

"FBI offices would get hundreds of calls every day and most of the calls were legitimate. Callers were asking for assistance for themselves or volunteer to assist the FBI in their investigation. Unfortunately, a certain percentage of callers, most likely after the regular day hours, offered information that was superfluous and just plain nutty. The info was of no value and absurd. Unless one listened to these callers for a long period of time, one was never sure whether the call was legitimate or not. Many reports were written, reams of paper were used and ended in the trash can. By keeping track of callers with questionable background as to their sanity, a 3 x 5 card would be started, noting person's name and any identifying background and info provided. Any subsequent return call was then checked against the card in the box and the call was appropriately dismissed as being of no value.

The worst nights with dozens of calls would be on a full moon night. I personally believe that after the nut boxes were eliminated, talk show hosts on nightly radio shows took over the clientele, and began a winning combination."

Contact from out of this world

"Some of the callers in my office were telling us stories that were out of this world, in more ways than one. One caller described a recent contact by an extraterrestrial creature via a telephone, followed by nightly hearing noises coming out of the walls or through the windows. These unfortunate souls were asking for help. Some were known to be street people with no fixed address, just wishing to talk to someone that was willing to listen."

Grounding of a bicycle

"One of the regular callers to my office was a street person who utilized a bicycle to get around town for the three meals offered at three different locations. Caller complained hearing voices emanating from the bike's handlebars. What to do? A quite simple solution. 'You have to ground yourself?.' An obvious question from the caller was to get an explanation on how to ground yourself, which apparently was the same answer in all the offices that I have been assigned to. ' Use paper clips attached to your bike and trailing on the ground behind the bike.' Apparently this was a good solution, since I would get a return call weeks later, thanking me for the advice. It worked… and the solution was found right in the box."

What are you talking about?

"I specifically remember prior to one of the first office inspections that I ever went through, that I was told to never, ever refer to the 'nut box' in the reception room when asked about complaint duty procedures. Never saw a nut box, have no idea what you are talking about, don't even know where to find a box like that if Ï needed one… and that was my story and I'm sticking to it."

A dual purpose box

"The nut box made an excellent recipe box and my wife, who use to be a support employee when I first arrived in the new office for me, was overjoyed and asked to get some more, after I told her that the nut boxes had to be eliminated."

Paper clips

"The best grounding system for walkers into our division was a paper clip chain attached to the bottom of the pants or a skirt, depending on the sex of the caller."

"Anything that was aluminum… hats, plates, as well as paper clips, did the job."

Thanks for advice

"All of us can recall those fascinating days on complaint duty when the unbalanced and uninformed would rear their heads during our shift with calls. Always enjoyed the walk-ins during the midnight complaint shift at the office when it wasn't uncommon to send complainants walking away with advice on aluminum hats and paper clip belts for complainants to ground themselves and allow them a peace of mind. And of course, the ones that would call you back and thank you stating that the method worked."

Getting paid to have fun

"My first office had an excellent support employee, a night clerk we called them in those days, who could imitate spoken languages from Eastern Europe to India. He would hand the callers off to pretend doctors and lawyers, who would try to analyze the caller's problems and come up with solutions. It was a blast listening to him. And to think that he even got paid to have fun… clean one, that is."

Foiled glass

"Many a caller who was identified from the nut box was advised to use aluminum foil on glass to prevent radiation from entering his apartment."

OUTTAKE . . .

ESCAPE PROOF

A new FBI building was constructed with completion in 2002. As new office furniture was delivered, each piece of furniture had the following notice attached:

"U.S. Department of Justice
UNICOR
Federal Prison Industries, Inc.

ESCAPE PROOF GUARANTEE

We take great pride in teaching inmates good work

ethics and marketable job skills in order to produce high quality goods and services for our customers. We are committed to your complete and continual satisfaction. If, at any time, an item we have provided does not entirely meet your expectations, we will cheerfully and promptly repair or replace it, entirely at our expense.

Customer inquiries should be directed to:
UNICOR Customer Service Center
Telephone 1-800-827-3168
Website: (None listed)

Questions/Comments
Please call Unicor Forrest City, AR
At (870) 633-3785 or Fax (870) 630-6224"

The stories continue . . .

A diplomatic stalemate

"One complainant, a female of Eastern European heritage, and speaking with a heavy accent, alternated between visits to the FBI office and the offices of a consulate that was in our city. She would report to us new arrivals at the consulate and fellow émigré that were observed at the consulate. Next she would visit that particular consulate again and report on us and how she was received by us. It took a joint meeting, with a few beers, to put an end to her visits on both ends, claiming that each of us was sending her to the others to harass them."

No bags allowed

"Most of the visitors to our complaint room carried numerous paper bags with them. After a while we had to make it a rule that no bags were allowed in the complaint room and folks had to leave bags outside of the building. What followed was the complaints that their valuable bags were stolen."

Calling for help

"In the days of the manual switchboards, we often hooked up two nut jobs so they could talk to each other and solve their problems. That's what happens when mental institutions are eliminated and poor folks have to hit the street. They are calling for help and no one answers them."

FBI rescues a couple

"Did you hear about the couple who solved all their problems at home by calling the FBI number and the two were connected and the problem was solved. Apparently, a face to face communication did not work. Thank you, FBI."

Complaint room supplies

"Our complaint room was well equipped with paper, # 2 pencils, paper clips, rolls of aluminum foil, a red phone to call for help in an emergency, a panic button that could be hit with a foot, large yellow pads, 3x5 cards, barf bag and.........a nut box."

Attorney who changed sides

"The best caller to our complaint line was a former government attorney that fell off the side of the road and sounded like a legit caller, using correct lingo, only to be identified as a person with a mental problem."

Royalty calls

"My favorite call-ins were kings and princesses of foreign extractions, stating that they wished to return back to the country of their birth. Apparently Cuba was not the only country that emptied its mental institutions and shipped their problems to our shores. What a collection of books one could write if all the nut box 3x5 cards were sent to the potential authors."

INS doing FBI a favor and FBI returning it

"INS in our town sent some of their visitors to visit our office so we returned the favor and employees on complaint duty of both agencies had a good laugh."

Talk show hosts in training at the FBI

"Too bad that the night-show hosts were not plying their trade in the days of the nut box. They could have picked up the slack and eliminated some of our visitors.

There is always the 'what if factor'. Wife of an American spy, John Walker, apparently called one of our offices to report that her husband was a spy, but no one believed her as she was apparently very drunk when she called. So you see that it is hard to determine if callers or walk-ins are legit or not."

A dangerous early bird

"One of our visitors to the office complaint room, wishing to speak to an Agent, was an early bird. He was knocking on the side door of the office on the 30th floor before 0630 hours. Somehow he convinced the GSA guards on the first floor, that he had an appointment with the FBI, so they let him up. He rang the door-bell and did not get an immediate response. Kicking at the door followed. The night duty support employee announced on the PA system that someone was trying to break in the door – wishing to speak to an Agent. Three of us that were in the office responded immediately from the lower floor and could hear the commotion and the hard kicking of the metal door. Knowing that other support and SA personnel would soon be arriving to enter through the same door, we knew we had a problem.

What to do? At six feet and a member of the rubber gun squad, and the other two SAs not quite prepared to take on this nut, I volunteered to go out the door and talk to the unruly complainant. I moved closer to the door and told the man that I am an FBI Special Agent and that I wish to come out and talk to him. The individual calmed down a bit and moved away from the door when I asked him to and I was able to communicate with him. He denied having any weapon on him and I asked him to turn around and empty his pockets of everything that was in them. At the same time, I told the other two SAs that I will go outside without a gun and attempt to subdue the unruly visitor. If I failed on the first attempt, I would move back and to the side, giving fellow SAs a clear field of fire, and the two SAs would have to shoot the unwelcome visitor as there was no other choice. We could not take a chance of having the visitor grab the next female support employee to come around the corner and have a hostage situation. The plan worked. I cuffed the fellow, just in time to hand him over to the GSA guards, who were on the way when the problem started. The oldest female support employee also arrived at this time.

The individual was released the same day. Within a week, he was holding police officers from a suburban police department at bay, with a 22 caliber rifle, but surrendered with no shots fired. Another day in the city, part of being an FBI SA."

Death rays handled by Secret Service

"In an office on the East Coast, complaint duty was handled exclusively by young Special Agents, with the exception of an old timer who was on a permanent complaint duty, as he apparently peed some big wig off. We received the regular nut job calls… space ships, death rays and conspiracies to take over the world. We would play a game with these callers. We would listen for about five minutes, then say 'lady (or sir), this death ray thing sounds pretty serious, but the FBI does not handle death rays. The Secret Service does. Do you have their number?'

We would send most of the nut calls to them. They figured it out pretty soon and we would get same callers to call us back."

The walk-in ready to fight

"The closest I ever came to hitting the panic button with a walk-in was in Phoenix. A woman came in to report a crime. I asked her how she knew about the crime, which was sort of logical. She told me the walls in her apartment were talking to her. Just to clarify, I asked if she heard the planning of the crime through the walls. She said no, it was the walls themselves. In trying to get rid of her, I made some comment that made her come unglued, probably tried to refer her to the FCC, for illegal transmission, or something like it. She jumped to her feet, and I thought she was going to come across the desk at me. I figured I could take her, but worried about having to explain it to the rest of the office. Somehow I calmed her down, and got her to see the nice people at the county hospital's mental health wing."

Training did me some good

"Let's see how do I start this one? When I got to the new office, I had three years of vast experience in the FBI on all different criminal squads, plus I was formerly a cop in the Midwest for ten years. So logically, where else would I be assigned to, but to the FCI squad. They needed a Spanish or Chinese speaker. So I recall that when the receptionist decided that a Spanish or Chinese speaker was needed, she called a backup duty SA, which was me. On this particular day, she called regarding something along the lines that there was a nut in the lobby and could I come and talk to him. Of course, go to someone that speaks the language. I forgot the guy's complaint, but do remember him telling me he had just landed his airplane outside on a nearby road. I recall taking him by the elbow and walking him to the elevator and telling him, well you better get back down there and check on your plane. Just as the elevator dinged, signaling its arrival on our floor, he took his hand out of his pocket and was holding an open buck knife. Luckily, I was standing behind him and I believe the training kicked in. I was much younger then and stronger than I am now. I grabbed him by the right wrist from behind and managed to put him in the old bar hammer lock and twist the knife away from him. The receptionist hit the panic button and within seconds I had a ton of help and we were able to handcuff him. So now we have this nut on the floor in handcuffs and what do we do next? The State Penal Code section 51-50 allows for holding a mentally disturbed individual for forty-eight hours if they are a threat to themselves or others.

I remember thinking many more times over the next twenty years we should have used that section of the code in the office more often. Life is an adventure, people."

Be a good listener

"In the infamous John Walker espionage case, his wife made a few calls to the FBI complaint line about her husband's espionage involvement, when she had one too many. The poor lady finally gave up. So I guess the moral is – you gotta listen, at least for a while.

There was an interesting frequent caller at another time. She would start her calls with ' How are you tonight my darling?' I always told her I appreciated her interest."

An important person's lover

"We had a frequent contact in the office who called whenever she got drunk and spoke in an unintelligible mix of five languages. One night our new ASAC, who was an amazing linguist, took her call and sorted out what she was trying to convey. She was the girlfriend of a certain important political leader, who paid her to visit him regularly. The ASAC met with her when she was sober and developed her as a valuable source."

OUTTAKE . . .

"A GUIDE TO GOOD HEALTH

(Author unknown, but possibly an FBI Special Agent with a doctorate degree in BS.)

Q: I've heard that cardiovascular exercise can prolong life. Is it true?

A: Your heart is only good for so many beats, and that's it...don't waste them on exercise. Everything wears out eventually. Speeding up your heart will not make you live longer; that's like saying you can extend the life of your car by driving it faster. Want to live longer? Take a nap.

Q: Will sit-ups help prevent me from getting a little soft around the middle?

A: Definitely not! When you exercise a muscle, it gets bigger.

You should only be doing sit-ups if you want a bigger stomach.

Q: Should I cut down on meat and eat more fruits and vegetables?

A: You must grasp logistical efficiencies.

What does a cow eat? Hay and cord.

And what are these? Vegetables.

So a steak is nothing more than an efficient mechanism of delivering vegetables to your system. Need grain? Eat chicken. Beef is also a good source of field grass (green leafy vegetables).

Q: What are some of the advantages of participating in a regular exercise program?

A: Can't think of a single one, sorry. My philosophy is: No Pain...Good!

Q: Aren't fried foods bad for you?

A: You're not listening. Foods are fried these days in vegetable oil.

In fact, they're permeated in it.

How could getting more vegetables be bad for you?

Q: What's the secret to healthy eating?

A: Thicker gravy.

Q: Is chocolate bad for me?

A: Are you nuts?...Cocoa beans...another vegetable! It's the best feel-good food around (when you pass gas).

Well, I hope this has cleared up any misconceptions you may have had about food and diets.

Now, go have a biscuit...flour comes from wheat, which is a veggie!

And finally; if swimming is good for your figure, explain whales to me!"

The stories continue . . .

A young lady with a confession of a murder

"Just a slow day on a Friday's complaint duty, while assigned to a rubber gun squad, with fifteen minutes to go before the office was to close for the day's business and a three day long holiday weekend in my plan. A young lady called and wanted to meet since she had 'important information regarding a recent case, well publicized in the local newspaper. She wanted to see me today. I believed that she was legit and I made an arrangement to meet her at her parent's home. Thirty minutes later, I met the young lady who handed me a portable cassette tape recorder with a voice recording of a male, describing how he killed another person outside of a strip bar, within five minutes of our office. This was her boyfriend who just a few hours earlier called her and started to tell her the story about the murder. She quickly turned on the cassette recorder and obtained a confession, without his knowledge. She was willing to give me the recording but I had to promise her that she would not have to testify. I was between a rock and a hard place. I made the promise, obtained the tape and met with the homicide unit of the city's police department... which had no other good description of the killer and had to use other means to obtain evidence and bring the subject to justice."

Three interesting complainers in my office

" #1. A captain for an airliner, which was a contract airline for transporting U.S. troops to and from Viet Nam; The captain believed that his entire crew were out to kill him. #2. A motorcyclist who always showed at the office in garb that one might expect to see in a Star Wars movie. This guy showed up at my house one day when I was away and was greeted by my wife, who was also familiar with him, since my wife also worked in the same office. She talked to him through a closed door and was backed up by her sister with a shotgun in hand. Agents later convinced this guy he should never again visit the homes of FBI employees. #3. An old 'Soldier Joe', who claimed to be a WW I vet, who in rumpled military clothes and cane, walked 39 blocks to our office several times each month, shouting invectives along the way. Soldier Joe was never seen again after going berserk in the reception room, shouting and striking his cane on the reception room counter. There was no protective glass above the counter in those days."

Wanted to speak to the real FBI inspector from the TV show

"While serving as the relief night supervisor on a Sunday evening, in a large office, I got a call from a man who adamantly demanded to speak with Inspector Lewis Erskine. After a moment's hesitation, I informed the caller that as it was Sunday night, the Inspector was on television and would be unavailable until the following day. This satisfied the caller. I never found out if the caller called back the next day."

(Efrem Zimbalist, Jr. passed away at his home in the Santa Ynez Valley of California, at age 95, on May 2, 2014. He died of natural causes. Born in 1918, Efrem is a name known to many FBI Agents as Inspector Lewis T. Erskine, from the very successful television show 'The FBI.' The show ran from 1965-1974. For many young Agents of that period, the show was warmly referred to as 'our weekly training film'."

Written by Larry Langberg for June/July 2014 issue of "Grapevine", a publication of the Society of Former Special Agents of the FBI.

Referrals galore

"During a friendly discussion of the nut box/walk-ins with a city policeman, I found out that the police officers routinely always referred their callers to the FBI."

FBI does not pick up dead dogs, BFI does

" An old copy of the FBI's magazine, The Investigator, noted that the switchboard operator in one of the offices received calls from local citizens, wanting to know if the FBI 'picked up dead dogs'."

Complaint room supplies

"Every FBI division had a complaint room where walk-ins were interviewed. Even though there was no SOP regarding what supplies had to be on hand in the room, every division I served in had the same supplies, as follows: panic button, handcuffs, gun, large box of paper clips, reams of paper to write on, 3 x 5 cards or larger, depending on the box itself, TP, aluminum foil, pens and # 2 pencils."

Nut-boxes for sale on E-bay

"Unbelievable! Saw the wooden nut boxes for sale on e-Bay for $ 19.95 plus postage. Just wonder if those buying them were retired Special Agents of the FBI, to bring back memories, or collectors of antiques who had no idea that the FBI called them nut boxes. Or were sellers possibly fellow Special Agents who collected the boxes when they were eliminated by the offices and thrown away.

At least the seller was politically correct by not calling them nut boxes. What are you talking about? I never saw anything marked 'NUT BOX' around the FBI offices where I worked."

CHAPTER 4

DICTIONARY OF BU-SPEAK, BU JARGON, ABBREVIATIONS, DEFINITIONS, ACRONYMS, BUREAU SLANG, COMMENTS WRITTEN ON REPORTS

Every agency and office, whether in the federal government or in private business, can probably be accused of using identical jargon, abbreviations and comments . . . . some most probably invented and utilized by the "empty suits" in positions of authority. Why should the FBI be any different?

In the FBI, you can merely add "Bu" in front of any word and you have a new word to use in your communications.

- **Special Agent**.... The lowest rank on the totem pole of FBI professional cadre, an SA, an Agent, an FBI Special Agent, a hump.

- **What is the status of**..........I've been asked, now you've been asked and you better come up with an answer.

- **Staff Duty**.............That which comes to all except the most evasive.

- **Duty Roster**...A mass of red and blue marks which always come up indicating you.

- **It's a good experience**... I've never done it either so better you than me.

- **What about this?....** I need some type of an answer in case I'm asked the same question.

- **To ASAC**...being sent to an Assistant Special Agent in Charge of an FBI Field Office; "The buck passer"; a good person to know to keep you out of trouble with the SAC.

- **To SSA**... SSA is a Supervisory Special Agent, Buck passed again, Last stop at a squad level.

- **I'll be back later**... In case somebody with a need to know asks, I'm expected back at any time, but you know I won't be back until the following day.

- **I'm going to get a haircut**... Can you think of a better excused absence for the rest of the day?

- **I am developing sources**... I am somewhere where I should not be.

- **It's good training**.... When you don't know what else to call it.

- **Sorry about that**.... You'd do the same to me if you had the chance.

- **File it**.... Unless you know what to do with it.

- **Character guidance**....The hour you try and set the chaplain straight.

- **Concur generally**....Have not read the document and don't want to be bound by anything I might say.

- **In conference**....Don't know where he/she is.

- **Kindly expedite**....For God's sake, try to find the papers!

- **Passed to higher authority**....Pigeon-holed in a more sumptuous office.

- **In abeyance**....A state of grace for a disgraceful state.

- **Giving him the picture**....A long, confusing and inaccurate statement to a newcomer.

- **Appropriate action**....Do you know what to do with this?

- **Under consideration**....Never heard of it and do not want to hear it now.

- **Under active consideration**....We'll have a shot at finding it in our files.

- **Has received careful consideration**....A period of inactivity covering the time lag.

- **Have you any remarks?....**Give me some idea of what it's all about.

- **Project is in the air**....Am completely ignorant of the subject.

- **You will remember**....You have forgotten, or never knew because I don't know.

- **Transmitted to you**...Hold the beef awhile. I'm tired of it.

- **It is requested**....Please take a look and write another endorsement.
- **It is recommended**.... We don't think it will work, but stick your neck out and try.
- **Historical record**....A hysterical record of incomplete, obsolete and useless information.
- **For necessary action**....We don't know what they want; We don't know what to do with it; you do it.
- **For compliance**....Sure it is silly but you have to do it anyway.
- **Immediate action**....We've stalled it long enough; now you do something.
- **Returned without action**....Just try to put the blame on us; How should we know if you can hardly tell.
- **For signature**....I thought it up; you take the rap for it.
- **You were called by**....I couldn't answer the question so I dropped your name to account for my lack of knowledge.
- **Reply no later than**....I need your answer to make one of my own.
- **FOUO document**....A confusing designation affixed by confused people.
- **For Official Use Only**.... CYA if it works or does not work.
- **Palace Guard**.... Older SAs who were personal friends of the SAC and counted on to produce and keep the heat off the SAC.

- **TUD time**.... Time under the desk; the ass kissers who were close to the SAC or ASAC or Supervisor or all of them together and spend many hours in their offices.

- **TUG Time**.... Ass kissers who were pulling Supervisors attention away from others.

- **Lead**.... An assignment to be carried out by you, given to you in a written form, from another office or from your supervisor.

- **Flims**y.... A lead on a thin copy of paper, mostly used in applicant cases where hundreds of leads in one case were handled by many SAs.

- **Eye....**A lead car in a surveillance with view of the subject

- **105**....A foreign Intelligence case designation.

- **91**....Bank robbery case designation.

- **134**.... Counterintelligence source designation.

- **137**.... Criminal source designation.

- **42**....AWOL case designation.

- **170**.... Ghetto informant designation.

- **UCA**.... SA working undercover.

- **RIP**...Recruitment in place.

- **Asset**....A source, provider of info.

- **Letter of Censure**.... A bad boy/girl report card.

OUTTAKE . . .

THINGS YOU'D LIKE TO SAY AT WORK, BUT CAN'T
(Author unknown)

- I can see your point, but I still think you're full of S@#$.
- I don't know what your problem is, but I'll bet it's hard to pronounce.
- How about never? Is never good for you?
- I see you've set aside this special time to humiliate yourself in public.
- I'm really easy to get along with once you people learn to worship me.
- I'll try being nicer if you'll try being smarter.
- I'm out of my mind, but feel free to leave a message.
- I don't work here. I'm a consultant.
- It sounds like English, but I can't understand a word you're saying.
- I like you. You remind me of when I was young and stupid.
- You are validating my inherent mistrust of strangers.
- I have plenty of talent and vision. I just don't give a d@#%.
- I'm already visualizing the duct tape over your mouth.
- I will always cherish the initial misconceptions I had about you.
- Thank you. We're all refreshed and challenged by your unique point of view.

- **The fact that no one understands you doesn't mean you're an artist.**
- **Any connection between your reality and mine is purely coincidental.**
- **What am I? Flypaper for freaks?**
- **I'm not being rude. You're just insignificant.**
- **It's a thankless job, but I've got a lot of karma to burn off.**
- **Yes, I'm an agent of Satan, but my duties are largely ceremonial.**
- **Do I look like a people person?**
- **This isn't an office. It's hell with fluorescent lighting.**
- **I started out with nothing and still have most of it left.**
- **Sarcasm is just one more service we offer.**
- **If I throw a stick, will you leave?**
- **Errors have been made. Others will be blamed.**
- **Whatever kind of look you were going for, you missed.**
- **I'm trying to imagine you with a personality.**
- **A cubicle is just a padded cell without a door.**
- **Can I trade this job for what's behind door # 1?**
- **Too many freaks, not enough circuses.**
- **Nice perfume. Must you marinate in it?**
- **Chaos, panic, and disorder – my work here is done.**
- **How do I set a laser printer to stun?**
- **I thought I wanted a career, turns out I just wanted paychecks.**

The stories continue . . .

- **BAA**.... Black Agents Association (Yes, it exists!)
- **FAA**...Female Agents Association
- **WAA**.... White Agents Association (No such organization, since it would be prejudicial – YOU figure!)
- **Perp**.... The bad guy that SAs are after.
- **Dead Drop**.... A location where classified documents were stashed and payments made by spies/intelligence officers.
- **RA**.... Resident Agency, an FBI office in another city, outside the main office.
- **SSRA**...Senior Resident Agent in charge of an RA.
- **Heavies**.... The older, mature SAs that have been around the block a few times.
- **Alibi**... A CYA excuse on the firing range why the round did not go off or why the weapon was not fired.
- **Atta Boy**.... An award recognizing a good deed.
- **Misur**.... Microphone surveillance
- **Tesur**.... Telephone surveillance
- **Elsur**... Electronic surveillance
- **RUC**.... Return upon completion.

- **DOA**.... Dead on arrival
- **BUAP**....FBI applicant
- **Old Dog**.... An old case that has been worked before or not worked on properly.
- **GOA**.... Gone on arrival.
- **Sub-fug**....Sub File for a fugitive.
- **FOA**...First office agent, similar to a 90 day wonder in the military.
- **Nitel**...A teletype sent after normal day duty hours.
- **Teletype**-A machine transmitted communication.
- **Rebel Rouser Index form**.... A fill-in form for exactly what it says, describing someone that may be a trouble-maker. Form was eliminated after Mr. Hoover's death.
- **FD-302**.... A bread and butter form to report on something, anything, to denote who, what, where, when, how.
- **Blue slip**....A voucher for getting paid for approved expenses.
- **OA**....An operational asset.
- **IA....** An informative asset.
- **Roto**r.... A metal circular filing system for different cases worked on the squads.

- **Rotor girl**.... In the past, usually a female clerk managing and keeping the squad rotor and the cases up to date.
- **Bucket**.... A stationary place for a surveillance, usually an individual room or apartment. Also known as a **Lookout** or an **LO.**
- **Bumper lock** ....A tight surveillance, right on person's a$&.
- **Lip lock** ....Same as above.
- **A Possible**....All K5 (kill-zone) on the target
- **OP**.... Office of preference, a dream sheet that every SA filled out, hoping to get to his city of preference.
- **Case Agent**.... An SA assigned a case.
- **Group I and Group II**....Undercover operations
- **T-4** ....Body transmitter
- **SPC** ....Security Patrol Clerk
- **Unsub**.... Unknown Subject
- **Humint**.... Human intelligence
- **FBIHQ**.... FBI Headquarters, Seat of all knowledge, A place where empty suits decided fates of cases worked by the humps.
- **New York Split**.... Number of SAs enjoying good dinner and multiple drinks while some SAs ordered steaks and vintage drinks and others had a hamburger and "just a glass of water, please" and the one check comes and the total is divided equally and %$&*@ follows.

- **Bucar**.... An FBI issued car for use of SAs. Also Bu car.
- **CONUS**.... Continental U.S.
- **O & A**.... Open and Assign (As assigning a case to an SA).
- **FOL**.... A password for Friend of Louie Freeh when he was the FBI Director.
- **TS**....Top Secret or Tuff Shitsky in Polish.
- **FNU LNU**....First name unknown, Last Name unknown.
- **Locals**.... Local police department personnel in the area that you worked.
- **Indices Card**.... 3 x 5 cards used to record info prior to computerized indices.
- **Legat**.... SAs assigned overseas working out of U.S. diplomatic establishments.
- **OC**.... Organized crime
- **FLAP**... Foreign language availability program.
- **Balloon**.... Taking an unexcused absence in PM from work after you signed in to work your assigned tour of duty. A big NO NO!
- **A Rabbi**.... An SA in a high supervisory position that was a close friend of yours and could help you if you got in trouble or help you in advancement or an OP transfer. You did not have to be of Jewish religion as Catholics, Mormons as well as Amish have used a rabbi.

- **A handle**... A form of a balloon taken in AM.
- **Red-balled**.... Stopped by the red traffic light while conducting surveillance.
- **K5**.... Kill zone on the shooting targets.
- **VOT**.... Voluntary overtime
- **A Green Hornet**.... A communication from the FBIHQ, on green paper telling you that you screwed up on a Bureau rule or regulation. The paper was to be filed in the case file but it was many times filed in the "circular file" by the "heavies".
- **Circular file**... The trash can
- **Mahogany Row**.... Offices of the heavies at the HQ level.
- **Blue Flamer**.... An SA who was trying to become an empty suit.
- **Ponies**.... An actual report or a write-up to be used by others as a sample, so as not to reinvent a proverbial wheel.
- **RUC**.... Return upon completion. A report can be either P for pending, C for closed or RUC.
- **SPC**....Security Patrol Clerk
- **Unsub**.... Unknown subject
- **UACB**.... Unless Advised to the Contrary by the Bureau; A method used by field offices to force someone at the HQ to tell them not to do something;
- **Retread**.... A person that had to be recycled to prove his worth.

- **KMA**.... Kiss my behind (as used by SAs that were ready to retire.

- **Post and Coast**... Term used to show in the case file that you did some work on the case within a certain time frame so that the SSA knew you were making progress.

- **In-Service....** Training done outside your office space for the purpose of updating your knowledge and expanding your group of friends.

- **In conference**.... Don't know where he/she is.

- **Kindly expedite**.... For God's sake, try to find the papers.

- **In abeyance**.... A state of grace for a disgraceful state of affairs.

- **Give him/her the big picture**.... A long, confusing and inaccurate statement given to a newcomer.

- **Appropriate action**.... Do you know what to do with this?

- **Under consideration**.... Never heard of it but we are working on it.

- **Have you any remarks**.... Give me some idea what this is all about.

- **Project is in the air**....I am completely ignorant of the subject matter.

- **You will remember**.... You have forgotten or never knew because I don't know.

- **It is recommended**.... We don't think it will work, but stick out your neck and try.

- **For compliance**.... Sure it is silly but you "gotta" do it anyway.
- **For your signature**.... I thought it up; you take the rap for it.
- **You were called by**.... I couldn't answer the question so I dropped your name to account for my lack of knowledge.
- **Short-timers calendar**....With 90 days to go before retirement, some Agents snapped together 90 paper clips and hung them from the ceiling, removing one each day until only one was left...and it was time to ride into the sunset.

CHAPTER 5
A GALLIMAUFRY OF STORIES

The reader has to remember that many stories in this book were part of a different era, stretching from the 1960's to the early 2000. Undeniably, the reality was that one did not have to be politically correct in those early days. Some of the stories reflect those times and are un-excusable. Authors protected to avoid being besmirched.

We are closed today

"In early 2002, there was an intensive fugitive hunt for a stockbroker who had masterminded and operated a multi-million dollar Ponzi scheme.

The subject had been on the run for about four weeks, and had traveled throughout the country. We were always 24 hours behind him, and amazed by the speed and distance he was able to travel.

On a Saturday afternoon, in a rare break from the case, the Special Agent in charge of the investigation was taking his daughter and four friends to their church basketball game. The Agent received a call that the long sought-after subject was at the Federal Building where the FBI office was located, trying to give himself up.

As it turned out, the subject walked into the Federal Building which, being Saturday, was relatively quiet. The subject, who was the focus of intense local and national media attention, identified himself to the security guard on duty, and stated his desire to surrender to authorities. The security guard told him the building was closed, and to come back Monday."

"A lupus in mouton mufti"

"A great legacy left behind by the late Joe Stipkala. Joe was convinced that nobody at the FBIHQ was really reading the communications they were receiving from the field. To prove it, he used the phrase, 'a lupus in mouton mufti' in a communication. Lupus is Latin for wolf, mouton is French for sheep, and mufti is Hindi for clothes.

As suspected, no one from FBIHQ ever called him to question it."

"A word for the day"

"A long quiet day of report writing in the squad bullpen area, with ten plus Agents doing the same. One particular squad member, to break the quiet trance, asked if anyone knew the definition of a certain word. None did. An idea was hatched.

We came up with 'A word for the day', one word that none of us knew the meaning of, but could easily be found in a dictionary. Everyone on the squad would use that word in their communication to the FBIHQ that day. The idea was to rattle the great minds at the FBIHQ, and force the reader to look up the word in the dictionary. We took turns looking up a word and posting it on a 3x5 card and pinning the card on the bulletin board, to everyone's amusement.

The program lasted a few weeks, until two different communications landed in the same FBIHQ office, on two different desks of Bureau Supervisors who were in a quandary about a particular word's meaning. The plot was discovered and a telephone call was received. 'Just a coincidence I guess', was the reply.

The program was laid to rest. It was fun and educational for us, street humps, as well as for the empty suits, as long as it lasted."

The $20 chase

"An FBI Agent and a county sheriff's deputy were cruising an area where they had information a fugitive they were looking for was hanging out. As they were rounding a corner, they spotted him at the same time he spotted them. They exited the car and the chase was on. Unlike most chases, this one was long and drawn out, and lasted many blocks. At times, the chase came to a complete standstill, with the fugitive, as well as my partner and I, bent over, hands on knees, trying to catch their breath, looking at each other. Then as soon as someone would catch their breath, they'd start out again and everyone began the chase again.

After two or three times of stopping and trying to catch his breath and deciding we were not gaining distance on the fugitive, my partner and I found some guy on the street during one of the stops, who was watching the chase, and offered him $20 to go tackle the guy. The guy accepted the offer and the chase was over. My partner paid him his well- earned $ 20."

OUTTAKE . . .

JOHN GOTTI'S TAX TIPS

(Author unknown)

"You can deduct the entire piano even if you bought it just for wire.

Guys who escape from the trunk of car may be considered tax losses.

No matter how much he relies on you, a funeral director does not count as a dependent.

You must actually kill someone in your home for it to qualify as a 'place of business'.

Three simple words for the auditor: 'How's your family?'
When reporting income, be plausible. No pizzeria in the world takes in 3 million dollars a day."

Stories continue . . .

The ugly . . .

" (small 'a' on purpose because this man does not deserve to be called an FBI Special Agent.) Earl Edwin Pitts became an 'agent' for the Russian KGB and its successor agency, the SVRR.

From 1987 to 1992, Pitts was involved in espionage activities and then became dormant. From August, 1995 to December, 1996, Pitts was ensnared in a 'false flag' (sting) operation run by the FBI. He provided classified information to what he believed to be the SVRR, but was actually the FBI 'handlers'. His KGB 'handler' defected to the U.S. and named Pitts as a Russian 'mole'.

Pitts was sentenced to 27 years in jail on June 27, 1997. May he rot in hell."

Double ugly . . .

" 'agent' (same type of scumbag as above with a different name) Robert Philip Hanssen, aka 'Undertaker', sold out the FBI's family jewels as a spy for the Russians. He made a deal with the devil and the prosecutors to avoid the death penalty. He was sentenced to a life in jail, without parole, in exchange for giving the U.S. Government a full account of the information given to the Russians. A number of good people died as a result of his spying. May he rot in hell, because one of my "friends" had to die because of him."

A steno typo error

"The vagaries of the Gregg Shorthand System sometimes resulted in a 'look-alike' word creeping into dictated material. An Agent, whose team had arrested a mid-level mobster at 5 AM in bed with his paramour, had dictated to an office secretary the FD-302 on the arrest, and he got the finished report back that afternoon.

One sentence read: 'Subject was arrested in bed with his power mower'."

Don't fool your wife

"One clever Agent hit upon a simple plan to save money, without the knowledge of his wife.

Each time he got a raise, he would announce it proudly at home, quoting a figure half the actual amount of the increase. He then banked the difference.

This went on for many years, until, at a Christmas party, his wife was comparing salary rates with the wife of another Agent who had the same time of service. When she discovered what her husband was actually making, she confronted him and he had to 'fess up'.

Next month, she booked a three week trip for them both, touring all the capitals of Europe, while their house was being redecorated.

The total cost was slightly more than the Agent had saved over those years with his 'fool the missus' scheme."

No key

"During a large scale Sunday roundup of several gamblers whose warrants were issued in secrecy, about 24 Agents, in teams of two each, were rounding up the subjects, cuffing them, and escorting them back to the office, to be photographed, fingerprinted and interviewed.

My partner and I returned with our assigned gambler in cuffs, but when we got to the office, we discovered that neither one of us had a handcuff key. We checked the vault but all the keys had been charged out and we couldn't find anyone in the office that had one.

I recalled that one of the most experienced Agents in the office had told me once that he could open a pair of cuffs with just the insert of a government ballpoint pen. Fortunately, he was in the office to bail us out. While he prepared the pen's metal insert (consisting of tearing the end slightly and peeling it back just enough to simulate the key) I went back to the subject and told him with a straight face: 'Mr. Hoover requires all Agents to pick a set of handcuffs once every two months, just so we'll be aware of how it can be done and insure that no subject does it in our custody. This particular Agent is due for his training this month, so he will take your cuffs off.'

The Agent appeared on cue, jiggled his pen insert in the cuffs and

opened them in a trice."
(This technique does not work if the cuffs have been double locked.)

Cuffed pants

"Early 1970s, followed a deserter home in a 95 degree day in a Southern state. As he pulled into his driveway, I blocked his vehicle in. I put him up against the car, hands on the roof, and went for my cuffs, half in the middle of my back, the other half tucked in my pants.

As I went to grab them, the loop in the pants opened and promptly locked around my belt. Where in hell is the key, find that, and try unlocking my pants with a key I can't see to put it in a slot I can't see, all while the subject is asking what the hell is going on. As time passed, and there was way too much of it, traffic backed up and stopped for the show. The subject wanted to turn around to see what the hell I was doing that attracted so much attention.

Keeping him busy with no free hands took some incredible threats which made no sense, even to me, and dripping sweat was not helping undo the cuffs.

After eternity, and it was all of that and more, I freed my pants and cuffed the guy. Fortunately, he never knew how stupid the scene had been."

Rear sight

"I was working on the Violent Crimes Fugitive Task Force in an East Coast city. We were making some early morning arrests in December and it was about 35 degrees outside that morning. One of the Task Force members, now a SSA, was sitting in his car doing paperwork or talking on the radio, I'm not sure which, while the rest of us went to the door.

We were entering the front door of the subject's house when this Agent notices a window on the side of the house being opened. Out of the window jumped a male individual. The SA, being the astute investigator he was, figured this must be the guy we were after, so he left the car and began a foot pursuit. During the pursuit he noticed that the guy he was chasing wasn't wearing a stitch of clothing. Our man followed the guy over the fence and finally caught up with him on a second fence.

He grabbed the guy (I'm not sure where he grabbed him) and pulled him to the ground and cuffed him.

The guy is now laying on the ground, buck naked in 35 degree weather at 5:00 AM, and looks up at the Agent and says, 'Is there a problem, officer?'

Once the Agent got him back to the cars, no one of course wanted to transport him in their car. The guy had to stand out in the cold until we could get some clothes. The poor guy was so cold waiting for his clothes that he bent over onto the hood of one of the cars to warm himself from the engine heat. Not a pretty sight."

Some-days never come . . .

"SA Johnny Oliver was one of three FBI Special Agents that was shot and killed on August 9, 1979. If Johnny were alive today, he would remember the discussion he had with yours truly, a week before he was killed.

Johnny asked for a ride home and I obliged. He rode in my newly purchased pickup truck and exclaimed that 'Someday I want to have a pickup truck just like this one.' I reminded Johnny that some-days never come. For him, some-day was a mere one week later. For the rest of us, it is an unknown date with destiny.

As Johnny's dead body was carried on a stretcher out of an inner city housing project, citizens derisively cheered and clapped, according to a local newspaper report, because a law enforcement officer, another 'pig', doing his job, was killed."

OUTTAKE . . .

NOTICE
(Author unknown)

"The objective of all dedicated company employees should be to thoroughly analyze all situations, anticipate all problems prior to their occurrences, have answers for all these problems, and move swiftly to solve these problems when called upon . . .

However . . .

When you are up to your ass in alligators, it is difficult to

remind yourself that your initial objective was to drain the swamp."

The stories continue . . .

Quotes from Jackie Presser
(From JP's co-worker)

"Jackie Presser was one of the nation's most controversial union chiefs when he died in 1988. He was well known to the Cleveland's FBI, because of his alleged Mafia connection and his alleged informant status for the FBI.

Here are some of Jackie's favorite quotes:

- 'Faults are thick when love is thin.
- Hypocrisy is the Vaseline of political intercourse.
- Who never climbed, never fell.
- When you're desperate and it's close . . .
- If man could have half his wishes, he would double his troubles.
- When the lights are dim, he turns up the heat.
- Lying is taking responsibility for reality.
- Life is what happens when you are busy making plans.
- I am willing to run the gauntlet as long as I am driving the car.
- All the red lights tell me to go.
- The guys with pointy shoes and finger nails so polished they hurt…
- They were so vicious that you didn't know they had cut off your arms until you felt your hands hit the floor.
- When you face a situation not covered by written or verbal instruction, you should use your discrepancy.' "

Signs observed in the FBI offices…

- **"MAKE IT AGENT PROOF"**

Due to Special Agents of the FBI often doing stupid things and coming up with careless mistakes because they were not using common sense at times.

- **"I AM THE BOSS HERE –AND ONLY HERE – ACCORDING TO MY WIFE"**

The owner of this sign knew perfectly well who the real boss was at home.

- **"I AM THE BOSS IN THIS HOUSE – but I have my wife's permission to say so"**

A sign hanging above a workshop table of an Amish man who enjoyed hearing stories about life in the FBI. Even a strictly religious Amish man, with dominant male upbringing, was cognizant of the real boss in the house, with LARGE letters in the first part of the sign and SMALL letters in the end.

- **"FIRST I GOT A NIGERIAN LETTER, THEN I GOT ONE FROM OBAMA"**

Seen in a small two man RA in the Mid-West. Nigerian letters on the internet are an obvious scam. How about Obama's?

- **"IF A CLUTTERED DESK IS A SIGN OF A CLUTTERED MIND, WHAT DOES AN EMPTY DESK SIGNIFY?"**

Observed in a South East FBI office on a wall behind an Agent's desk.

- **"EINSTEIN WAS A CLUTTERER"**

Which one of the above two signs is correct? YOU decide !

- **"ALL WHO ENTER THIS OFFICE PUT A SMILE ON**

MY FACE. SOME WHEN THEY ARRIVE, OTHERS WHEN THEY LEAVE"

Only in NY would an SAC dare to have above sign in his office.

- **"IF IT AIN'T BROKE, DON'T FIX IT"**

Couple of my bosses in the Bureau would charge in and change things for the sake of changing them, even though they were working pretty damn well to begin with.

- **"THERE IS NO LIMIT TO WHAT WE CAN ACCOMPLISH AS LONG AS WE ARE NOT CONCERNED WITH THOSE WHO WILL CLAIM CREDIT FOR OUR WORK"**

True meaning to above sign could be found in any office setting, not necessarily only in the FBI.

- **"HOME OF THE UNCOLAS"** . . . with a picture of a ramshackle old house

This sign was hanging all over the office, specifically in areas occupied by support employees. It was hung to portray the disparity in pay raises between the Agent personnel and the support employees, after Special Agents received a very nice COLA boost in pay in the 1980's. Fortunately, support employees were eventually given a COLA of their own and the signs disappeared.

- **"A LACK OF PLANNING ON YOUR PART IS NOT AN EMERGENCY ON MY PART"**

Secretaries in my East Coast office had these signs in their cubicles, to let the Agents know how they felt about our emergencies that had to be handled NOW !

- **"SPECIAL AGENT ___________________"**

Most of the Agents had above nameplate with their name on their desks. One of the Special Agents merely had a nameplate that stated:

"ORDINARY AGENT _______________"

- **"I'M NOT BOSSY, I JUST HAVE BETTER IDEAS"**

Sign that I had on my desk. I also had a sign that stated: "WORRYING MUST HELP . . . 95% OF THE THINGS I WORRY ABOUT NEVER HAPPENED".

- **"I AM NOT ALLOWED TO DRIVE THE TRAIN OR EVEN RING THE BELL BUT LET THIS DAMN THING JUMP THE TRACK AND SEE WHO CATCHES HELL"**

I may not have this exactly right, since it was a long time ago, but I recall above sign behind SAC's secretary's desk. She was the real power in the office.

- **"MR. HOOVER IS BACK AND HE IS PISSED"**

One of my favorite signs that I had on my desk.

- **"OUR DAY BEGINS WHEN YOUR DAY ENDS"**

Sign hanging in a Detroit, Michigan Police Department Homicide Bureau.

- **"FIGHT CRIME – SHOOT BACK"** and **"MY KID WAS INMATE OF THE MONTH AT FLORIDA STATE PRISON"**

Two of the bumper stickers that I had on my desk and still have.

- **"IF YOU NEED IT AND DON'T HAVE IT, YOU MAY NEVER NEED IT AGAIN"**

  A sign with a picture of a S&W Chief Special revolver in the early 1970s on the wall of the NIS office in the Washington Navy Yard.

- **"FRIENDS ALWAYS WELCOME . . . RELATIVES BY**

APPOINTMENT ONLY"

Sign I have at the entry to our home. Not that any of them pay any attention to above sign. In our kitchen, where everyone gathers, of course, a sign says:

- **"THE BEST THINGS IN LIFE AREN'T THINGS".**

- **"IF MOMMA AIN'T HAPPY, AIN'T NOBODY HAPPY". My wife's favorite.**

- **"IN GOD WE TRUST . . . OTHERS MUST SIGN"**

Marine Corps Supply NCOs had above sign over the doors into the supply room.

- **"HOW CAN YOU KNOW WHERE YOU'RE GOING IF YOU DON'T KNOW WHERE YOU'VE BEEN"**

My favorite sign for new Agents dealing with the sacrifice/history of our Agents.

- **"WE TRAINED HARD, BUT IT SEEMED THAT EVERY TIME WE WERE BEGINNING TO FORM UP INTO TEAMS, WE WOULD BE REORGANIZED. I WAS TO LEARN LATER IN LIFE THAT WE TEND TO MEET ANY NEW SITUATION BY REORGANIZING; AND A WONDERFUL METHOD IT CAN BE FOR CREATING THE ILLUSION OF PROGRESS WHILE PRODUCING CONFUSION, INEFFICIENCY, AND DEMORALIZATION."**

Above sign was on the wall by an Agent's desk in my division.

- **"WHEN I WANT YOUR OPINION, I WILL GIVE IT TO YOU."**

Three of us gave above sign to an Executive Assistant Director who had a great sense of humor. He was so damn smart, that when we thought 'A' was the answer to a problem, he was already on 'D'.

- **"IGNORANCE CAN BE CORRECTED, BUT STUPID IS**

FOREVER."

While summoned to a meeting with a high muckety-muck at FBIHQ, and asked what I thought of the proposed solution to a given problem, I could only laugh and point to his sign.

- **"I KNOW YOU BELIEVE YOU UNDERSTAND WHAT YOU THINK I SAID, BUT I AM NOT SURE YOU REALIZE THAT WHAT YOU HEARD IS NOT WHAT I MEANT."**

A good sign to see after a speech by the supervisor.

- **"IF YOU DON'T HAVE TIME TO DO IT RIGHT THE FIRST TIME, WHEN WILL YOU HAVE TIME TO DO IT OVER AGAIN?"**

Not sure which office I saw this sign in, but thought it was great then and have plagiarized it many times since.

OUTTAKE . . .

NOTICE
(Author unknown)

DUE TO THE CURRENT ECONOMIC SITUATION, THE LIGHT AT THE END OF THE TUNNEL WILL BE TURNED OFF...

The stories continue . . .

- **"DO NOT DRINK ON THE JOB, DON'T PLAY WITH MY STENO POOL."**

A sign in my first SAC's office. About a month later, the word came out that the SAC totaled a new Bureau car while drunk, and replaced it with an identical new car. Unfortunately, shortly after this happened, an annual office inspection took place and while checking Bucar VIN numbers, Inspectors found out that one car did not belong in the car inventory.
The SAC "retired" and obtained a job with another federal agency, with offices in the same building as the FBI.

- **"THE EQUIPMENT YOU NEED WAS GIVEN TO THE AGENT WHO JUST LEFT – SHE HAS THE MOST IMPORTANT CASE IN THE BUREAU."**

A favorite sign of mine, on the door to the Equipment Room.

- **"I'D RATHER BE DOWN HERE, WISHING I WAS UP THERE . . . THAN UP THERE, WISHING I WAS DOWN HERE."**

The aircraft mechanic that worked on the Bureau airplanes had above sign on his shop wall.

- **"THIS AIN'T BURGER KING. YOU CAN'T HAVE IT YOUR WAY."**

Sign in the jail cell in one Alabama's Sheriff's jail.

- **"NOBODY IS COMPLETELY WORTHLESS, THEY CAN ALWAYS BE A BAD EXAMPLE."**

My Unit Chief had above sign in his office at the FBI Academy.

- **"EVEN MOTHERS LIE"**

When I was at WFO, I had a friend cross-stitch a sign with flowers and above truism.

- **"INFORMANTS ARE NOTORIOUS LIARS, SELF SERVING, AND TOTALLY WITHOUT HONOR, BUT THE INFORMATION THEY PROVIDE IS FASCINATING."**

Above sign hung in my squad area.

- **"YOU CAME INTO THIS ROOM WITH GOOD LOOKS AND VALUABLE INFORMATION. YOU WILL LEAVE WITH ONLY ONE OF THEM."**

  A sign in the interview room of a local police department detective office.

- **"HALF TRUTH IS BETTER THAN HALF LIE"**

A sign I saw somewhere during my Bureau career and noted it's presence on a 3 x 5 card, since it made an impression on me.

WHAT DO THE LETTERS FBI STAND FOR?

The correct answer is Fidelity, Bravery, Integrity. Unfortunately FBI initials have appeared on t-shirts, sweat shirts and other pieces of clothing, that have nothing to do with the real FBI.

Unauthorized use of the FBI seal, name and initials are subject to prosecution under Federal Criminal Law, including Section 701, 709 and 712 of Title 18 of the U.S. Code. What follows are some of the examples of different meanings given to the letters FBI as well as stories re the initials.

- FEMALE BODY INSPECTOR
- FOREIGN BORN IRISH
- FULL BLOODED IRISH
- FULL BLOODED ITALIAN
- FAMOUS BUT INCOMPETENT
- FROM BIG ISLAND

- FULL BLOODED INDIAN

DUMPSTER JUMPING

"When conducting legitimate dumpster jumping for the FBI, for the purpose of collecting evidence of a crime, I always wore a shirt with initials BFI on the front as well as on the back. What does BFI mean? BFI stands for a legitimate business, Browning – Ferris Industries, which sold out to Allied Waste, which was acquired by Republic Services. BFI was the 2nd largest nonhazardous waste management provider in the U.S.

BFI ad stated: "Homeowners and businesses in 39 states in the U.S. and Puerto Rico pledge allegiance to Republic Services and the trash collection for which it stands."

When I was assigned to WFO, my family often traveled to Gettysburg, Pa and eventually purchased some weekend property from a low key local real estate agent. His wife inquired as to my profession and my answer was a simple BFI, the trash company. No questions on her part followed.

Years later, as I was being transferred, I finally told her the truth. I worked for the FBI, but was a bad speller, plus, FBI was picking up human trash. She was upset but laughed anyway."

FAT BOYS

"A routine interview of a female whose name was used by an applicant as a character reference. When showing my FBI credentials, the female noted that her husband "also belonged to the FBI". When asked where he is presently serving, the female stated that he is not, but has a shirt to prove that he is with the FBI. Since I never heard of him I asked additional questions. She stated that on his shirt it states that he belongs to the **FAT BOYS INSTITUTE**. So much for respect for the real FBI."

FBI NICKNAMES

"Popeye"

As a young man entering the FBI, I resembled a Hollywood actor, Gene Hackman, aka Popeye Doyle, in the movie French Connection. I wore a hat, described as a pork pie type hat, just like Hackman, and started to be called Popeye by the squad mates. Numerous times I was asked by females if I was Hackman, since they wanted his autograph. I even used his

"Poughkeepsie" line from the bar bust in the movie. The nickname stayed with me throughout my career.

"Mortician"

Nickname given to the agent hanssen (caps reserved for the good guys) that went bad and volunteered to become a spy for the Russians. He always wore dark clothing, was tall and somber, and somehow resembled a mortician. His nickname was a truism, as many good people died because of him.

"The Kraut"

The German speaker on the squad, otherwise a true Irishman.

"Salt"

An SA whose real last name was a brand of salt.

"Jug-head"

A Yugoslav speaker (actually there is no such thing as a Yugoslav language, since one speaks either Slovenian, Croatian, Serbian, Macedonian or Shiptar languages. Instead of Y for Yugoslavia, the true spelling uses J as the first letter in the spelling of Jugoslavia. The SA was actually an Italian by birth.

"Father"

An SA who was a Catholic priest before he became an SA.

"T-Rex"

A fairly tall Special Agent with short arms.

"Mister"

(Emphasis on "I", pronounced as "ee") An Agent born in an Eastern European country who never lost his accent. (I agree with you, GH.)

"Shorty"

The shortest Agent on the squad, a Navy veteran, who was very familiar with an asset, who was very tall and built like a giant and whose nick-name was also "Shorty."

"Don Juan"

This particular Agent got his nickname in between his two marriages. There was a story of his love for a gal who had an equivalent of the 1942

Buick bumpers . . . you need some imagination to figure this out. To help you identify this fine fellow, here is another hint: At age 65 he could still fit into his Bureau issued FBI gym shorts. . . and he still owns them.

BUREAU CAR (BUCAR) STORIES

"The chain reaction"

"I was a supervisor of a large criminal squad, and in order that I would not be bored, SAC decreed that I would also be responsible for all Bucar matters.

One morning, past coffee time, my small cubicle was invaded by 10 or 12 Agents, who alluded to the fact they 'might have a slight problem.'

Inquiries determined this group of Agents held a mini strategy meeting in a restaurant, which was well known to them for its apple fritters and coffee. This meeting site was located at the bottom of a hill and they safely (almost) parked their Bucars parallel to the curb, all facing down-hill. Picture this: Bucar 1 through 6 were parked on the lower stretch of the hill, and Bucar 7 was parked behind a civilian vehicle, at the top of the hill.

When the civilian vehicle left the area, Bucar 7, parked by 'I thought I set the hand brake,' started on its way down the hill, initiating a chain reaction involving all of the Bucars, and knocking #1 into the street.

What to do? Anyone hurt? No. Any third party injured or damaged? No. Solution = 'Get out of here, you're giving me a headache. I couldn't explain it if I tried, we'll work it out.' And we did."

"A stolen or snowed-in Bucar?"

"An SA checked out a Bucar and drove to his destination, where he parked the vehicle during a snow storm. The SA went into the building and presented the case to the U.S. Attorney. About an hour later, SA came out, unlocked a car, covered with snow, believed to be his Bucar. He drove the car to the Bureau garage and parked. It was on a weekend.

On Monday, another SA checked out the keys to a car. However, he could not locate the car in the garage. A big investigation was conducted to locate the stolen Government property . . . one Bucar. It was located still parked in the original parking spot, still covered with snow. The car in the contract garage was then checked and found to be reported to the Police Department (PD) as being stolen. The same keys worked in both ignitions.

The PD recovered the stolen car. They claimed the recovery value of the car for stat purposes, I suppose, as well as recovery value of the Bucar."

"Driving a stolen Bucar ?"

(Same office as previous story, but different SA involved, and different SA writing the story, neither of them knows of the two different stories until they will read this book.)

"I took the keys for an available Bucar from the Key board and headed for the garage. Found the make and color of the car, started the car and drove off on a lead to be covered that morning outside the headquarters city, in an RA territory.

About an hour into the trip, picked up an FBI radio message regarding a stolen Bucar, with a description and license plate. Jogged the info down on a piece of paper and continued driving, Every 10 minutes, same wanted message for a stolen Bucar, and a note for everyone to be on the lookout. Funny, description fit the vehicle that I was driving. Pulled over to the side of the road and checked the license plate. I was driving a stolen Bucar, according to the FBI radio.

I contacted the radio and advised them that the wanted Bucar is in my possession. Was advised in turn to return to the office immediately.

Yep! The same key fit two different Bucars in our car pool, same make and model and same color.

No recovery claimed for stat purposes."

"Companies A, B, C"

"Office rule regarding Bucar accidents was the same all over the country. If you were involved in an accident, you had to get three separate estimates for car repair from three separate businesses approved by the FBI. These estimates were then given to the SA that was tasked to interview witnesses and write a report. The SA tasked to do so was the one who had the last accident before you did, and so on, with you doing the interviewing and writing the report on the next accident.

So off I went to one of the repair shops on the list, asking for an estimate. The friendly manager reached into top drawer on the right side of his desk and pulled out an estimate sheet with 'company A' on the letterhead. He pulled another sheet from drawer # 2 for 'Company B' and a third one from drawer # 3 for 'Company C'. The estimates differed by $ 20 each, more or less. Same shop space, same owner, three different businesses. I had my three estimates, assured by the manager that this was an acceptable practice in all shops."

"Sex causes rear-ending . . ."

"While driving I heard a fellow SA from the RA on his Bureau radio requesting assistance, stating that he had been in an accident at a stop light. I responded since I was only about five minutes away.

Upon arriving, I observed his car on the side of the road with a Jeep CJ parked just behind him. As I approached, the SA advised me that he got rear ended at the stop light by the Jeep with two occupants. The driver was a young athletic looking male and the passenger was a very cute young lady.

The male driver walked up to me and said that he needed to talk to me in private. I figured he was going to tell me that he was cut off by the other driver and he was not at fault, or something similar. He was a college football player on scholarship to one of the preppy schools. He said that he got excited and ran into the Bucar. He apologized profusely. I asked him what the excitement was all about.

After making sure that his girlfriend was far enough away so that she could not monitor the conversation, he said that while they were at the stop light, he and his girlfriend decided to have sex - - like immediately. He was behind the Bucar at that moment so he wanted to back up to cross over the road and take the frontage road where they could pull off in a more remote area. He hit the accelerator as he looked to the rear, but was so excited that he forgot to shift into reverse. The result was a rear end collision with the Bucar.

I wrote up the FD-302 and the accident case was assigned to another Agent. The two of us still occasionally laugh about that accident case when we do our weekly golf outings."

"A marked FBI car"

"In this Midwest division we used snow tires that went on every fall and came off every spring. They were stored at the contract garage and had the car number and FBI written in white chalk, on the side wall which was black.

Of course, on a nice spring day, trying to be inconspicuous, on

surveillance, a school child knocked on the car's window and said, 'you're the FBI'. I asked him why he thought that. He said: 'It's written on your tires.'
To the car wash and advise everyone else."

"Tire chains"

"I went out in a Bucar with an experienced Agent who was saddled with this rookie.

It began to snow, and being from Florida, I hadn't driven in snow since I was a student at Michigan. I asked the experienced Agent what were the ramifications of an accident in a bucar when it was possibly caused by snowy conditions on the street. He replied that standard Bureau policy was for Bu cars to have chains on when it snowed.

He said that we would get out of the car, wipe the blood off our eyes, take the chains from the trunk, put them on the car and then check to see if there were any injured in the other car.

Always good to receive the real skinny from the voice of experience."

"Bucar is not Agent-proofed"

"One of the Agents rolled the Bucar over, going around the curve. As this two-man RA was in a remote area of the state, the only Agent available to conduct the accident investigation was his fellow Agent in the RA..

During the course of the investigation, the investigating Agent asked his buddy how fast he was going around the curve when he rolled over. The driver stated that he was driving within the speed limit and was going just 45 mph. The investigating Agent said 'all right, that's what I will report, but just between you and I, how fast were you really going?" The driver insisted that he did not exceed 45 mph on the curve and a big argument ensued.

Finally, the investigative Agent said, 'I'll show you that you won't roll the car going 45 mph.

You guessed it! He got in the Bureau car and hit the curve at 45 mph and rolled his Bureau car over."

"Do not park in this space"

"I thought I would mention one incident which happened to me back in 1955.

I was working the 4 to midnight shift and had parked my POA on the Mall, until after 6 P.M., as usual. After everybody had left the FBI parking area for the evening, I slipped out of the building to bring my car into the basement parking area. I found a real nice space near the elevator and left the car there until midnight.

The fun began the next day when I arrived at work. An inspector summoned me to his office and informed me that I had parked in 'Miss ___________'s space the night before. When she returned to work late in JEH's office, her space was taken. She went home and took a cab back to the building. There were about 200 empty spaces nearby the night before, but she preferred not to park in another's space. They checked my license tag number through DMV and had caught the culprit.

You can be certain I never parked in that space again. For those of you who didn't know Miss ___________, you're too young ."

"Do idling miles on a car count?"

"While working out of an RA in one of the Southern states in the early 60's, I was told that I would receive a low mileage car that was being transferred out of the seat of government. When I received this car with only 12,000 miles showing, I could not have been more pleased even if it was a salmon colored Hudson. In spite of the low mileage, the car was in repair shop every other week over a period of several years.

On one occasion, I parked the car near a large wooded area and assisted the Sheriff's office in trying to locate a fugitive. We caught the individual late in the evening and since we were nearer the road where I had parked the Bucar, I invited the Sheriff and some other officers to walk to my car to take the fugitive to jail. We walked over two miles to where the car should have been, to find it gone. We had to then walk another mile or so with the fugitive to a farm house to call for transportation. I then learned that my friendly wrecker driver happened to see the salmon Hudson on the side of the road, and thinking it had again broken down, he loaded it up and took it to the repair shop.

I later learned that while the Hudson only had 12,000 miles when I received it, the car had over 150,000 idling miles as it had been used as a stationary surveillance car at its original office."

"AC in Bucars during Hoover era"

"I never heard of anyone doing this in HQ city, but several RAs were known to have installed the under dash air conditioners in their cars. When the Inspectors came, the AC was removed for a few days and after they had gone, it was re-installed and recharged for another year. When they got a new car, they tried hard to get the same make/model, but if not, purchasing a different compressor mounting bracket usually took care of everything." (In Hoover era, when cars were delivered with the AC, these were removed . . . since G-men could tough it out and save money for the taxpayers, by cars getting better mileage. In St. Louis, in early 70s, none of the cars had AC, and during the summer months, most of the interviews were conducted by 0900 hours, since Agents did not wish to be thoroughly drenched due to humidity. After all, we had to wear suits whatever we were doing.)"

"The possessed and evil Bucar"

"While assigned to an East Coast city during the 1980s, a squad-mate of mine on the OC squad was driving into the office one morning and he stopped in a bank parking lot to use an ATM machine.

He put his Bucar in park and left it running while he used the ATM. When he turned around, car was doing circles in reverse in the parking lot, with the driver's side door wide open. The car had to be doing 20 mph, making it very unsafe to try and jump into the open door.

Approximately half of the local fire department, and I am sure, the entire local police department, gathered in the parking lot and tried a number of things to slow the vehicle down enough to allow some brave soul to jump in and turn it off. Nothing worked.

Unfortunately, a local TV news station had its headquarters just down the street and dispatched a news crew to the scene to record the entire thing on video. Every time the car did a circle, it was jumping over a concrete curb and there was more than a little angst that the wheels would straighten out and catapult the driverless vehicle into a main thoroughfare during the morning rush hour. The car had just been filled, so there was no chance that it was going to run out of gas anytime this week.

Finally, an enterprising policeman flagged down a flatbed truck hauling a Caterpillar tractor with front-end blade. Long story short, the car was stopped by broadsiding it with the tractor blade, absolutely totaling the passenger compartment, but stopping the car dead in its tracks, engine still running fine. The poor Agent swore up and down that he had placed the car in park, and naturally we all laughed that one off.

Someone noticed that the VIN of the vehicle contained the numbers '666' and a lot of jokes were made about 'Christine, the possessed Bucar.' Naturally, obtaining a copy of the news station video became the highest priority, and I still have a copy of one of the Bureau's most unusual car stops.

Ordinarily, that would be the end of the story, but not this time. The car was hauled to a garage, one of those old style parking garages with an automobile elevator. The car was stored on the sixth floor where all vehicles being surveyed were stored until they were hauled away.

One morning, one of the garage attendants had to move Christine in order to get the car behind out. YEAP – you guessed it. He put the car in park and left the engine running while he moved the other vehicle. As he pulled the second vehicle onto the elevator, he looked up in his rear view mirror just in time to see Christine traveling in reverse and unoccupied across the garage floor, where it collided with a couple of other junkers.

Only in New York."

AN EMBARRASSING MOMENT

We all had them and sometimes we rather not acknowledge them. Once we utter the phrase or perform the embarrassing act, we can't take it back. We are human beings.

"Perp to the rescue"

"In the ghetto in the early 70's, interviewing a bank robbery subject, threatening him with everything short of the electric chair. As you made a dramatic exit, your keys are in a locked Bucar. May I please borrow a coat hanger? Forget that, watch this.

In two seconds, the car was open without any coat hanger. His final remarks, 'If I get arrested, will you testify to my cooperation with the FBI?' By then, there was a large crowd of kids around me and the car and I said, 'you can count on it.' And I did, after having to explain to a Federal Judge what kind of cooperation he had given. He probably saved me from serious bodily harm, if not worse."

"Love-makers Bucar"

"A certain SA becomes romantically enamored with a certain ravishing damsel. Being the cheapskate that he is, he repairs not to a room but rather to his Busteed, which is handily parked out back. They climb in the front seat and, being that it is winter, he starts the car and turns on the heat. Then, he turns on the heat.

Slipping into the prone position on the front seat of his Buride, a moment of moments arrives, but first . . .

I neglected to mention this lovely lass was deaf.

In the midst of great endeavors, a body part strikes the siren switch, and off it goes. Of course our lovely lady friend cannot hear the damn thing so she thinks the frenzy our storied warrior is engaged in is his 'moment' so she seeks to hold him.

In the midst of other things, he is of course flailing at the dashboard looking for the switch to turn the siren off.

Oh, by the way, we did respond to the siren.

And this, as with so many other stories, will be logged into history. 'Erin Go Bragh'."

"A Special Agent pervert"

"Recently, while attending an in-service training at the FBI Academy in Quantico, I encountered a most embarrassing moment, which has forever labeled me as an FBI sexual pervert.

The training was for sexual child abuse investigations, the malady of Indian Reservation crime investigation, area covered extensively by my FBI office. The FBI had assembled a veritable who's who in this field from major police departments and the FBI.

During one segment of the instruction, a captain from the sheriff's office described a detailed investigation and surveillance of a suspected pedophile. This particular suspect frequented soccer fields, baseball fields, gyms and other places frequented by juveniles. After many days of covert surveillance and no evidence, the suspect was confronted in a public rest room by the officers and asked what he was doing. After much duress, the suspect broke down and confessed that he had never hurt any children and wasn't looking for sex, he became extremely 'turned on' and enjoyed listening to young boys urinate. This shocked me to no end and I more than commented to the class about the suspect's obvious sickness.

Later, at break, I went to the academy rest room and was standing at the urinal when a man walked in and stood beside me at the next urinal. I casually stated to him, "that sounds real nice." When he asked what I was talking about, I said, "listening to you pee in the water."

The man immediately jumped back and stated many expletives to me. I asked, "Aren't you in the class with me?" 'Hell no', he replied, 'nor am I in your 'class', 'you sick pervert'."

For the remained of the week I had to face the ridicule of my class mates and every break the instructor would announce, 'It's time for a break, let's all meet ____________ in the bath room.'

One of my more embarrassing moments."

"Coitus Interuptus"

"Part I: An annual early morning roundup of big time drug distributors, A & D, bad dudes to say the least.

Our six man team surrounded a house and an entry was attempted by ringing the bell and knocking on the door and announcing FBI Open Up and waited a proper amount of seconds. Nothing happened. No response. A two-man battering ram brought down the entrance door and a room by room search began, announcing 'FBI Open Up' at every turn.

My team cautiously opened a door to a possible bedroom, with hundreds of roaches running in all directions. Observed a sheet moving up and down in a rhythm, with obvious action of bodies underneath.

Three of us entered the room, two with shotguns. I jumped on the bed (with my cowboy boots on to prevent a quick hug by the roaches) and pulled the sheet off the bodies. Action still ongoing (sorry for the interruption), and the male cuffed behind his back and arrested. Action terminated. The young lady rolled off the bed and minutes later asked if she could be covered. Searched by a female Special Agent and wrapped in a sheet.

Part II: About 16 hours later when I arrived home, I started telling my dear wife above story. Her first question was: 'Did you take your boots off?' No, not because my boots may have had mud on before I entered our home or taking the boots off before I jumped on the bed to make an arrest. She meant whether I took my boots off outside before entering our home, to dislodge any extra crawling creatures that may have accompanied me home."

"Crawling creatures"

"During the search for the killer of one of our locally based Special

Agents, thousands of citizens responded for our requests on radio and TV, for help. 24/7 investigation by teams made up of local law enforcement officers and federal agents responded to the leads, and lasted for days.

One lead our team covered was in "the hood", at an address identified by a caller as a possible refuge for the killer. After gaining a peaceful entry in the middle of the night, I inquired of the female home-owner if anyone else was in the house. Her answer was negative and she agreed to our request to search the home.

I proceeded to move aside a curtain that was hanging in the door frame normally occupied by a solid door, separating the kitchen from another room adjacent to it. The dim light from the kitchen ceiling illuminated the floor area beyond the kitchen and hundreds of cockroaches were observed moving across the floor and over a completely naked body of a male asleep on the floor, sans sheets and blankets. He was not the subject that we were looking for. The female honestly did not know that her drunk boyfriend entered her house without her knowledge while she was in the bathroom, and he fell asleep on the bare wooden floor."

"A million dollar hole"

"Don't use my name on this one because I don't intend to make light of a very serious situation. The bad part of this incident continues to bother me, but the lighter side is amusing.

Approximately 18 months ago, while serving in this particular RA, I was notified by the division office that a dangerous FBI fugitive, known to be armed, was possibly in my RA area.

After 24 hours of continuous investigation, the fugitive was located at a camp ground on the west side of town. Intricate plans were made involving the FBI and the police department, for the subject's arrest.

To make a long story short, things went wrong and the fugitive, armed with a pistol, confronted and attempted to shoot me. I reacted and shot first, killing him instantly.

After a long and intense crime scene investigation, the Division's Principal Legal Advisor (PLA) responded to the camp ground to explain to the campers that any damage inflicted upon private property by FBI bullets would be paid for by the FBI and, with that, he started handing out the standard government claim form to three couples whose vehicles were struck by bullets.

One man was real serious and wanted the hole fixed in his RV as soon as possible. He was told to take it to nearest body repair shop and have the bill sent to the FBI. Another man, after hearing the circumstances involved, stated that other than the small hole in his RV, which he agreed to repair himself, a bullet passed through this hole and pierced his Play Boy magazine, stopping at the center fold. He requested that the FBI purchase him a new Play Boy magazine and he would forgo any claim. An Agent was immediately dispatched to the local 7-11 convenience store to purchase a Play Boy magazine.

The third damage victim stated to the PLA that he had only two requests. One, don't touch or tamper with the bullet hole in his expensive RV, as he wanted all the bragging rights he is entitled to and if the FBI received telephone calls to verify that, in fact, the hole in his RV was from an FBI shoot out, that the FBI must confirm this. The man went on to say, 'Wow, this hole is worth a million dollars to me! Can you imagine the attention I'm going to get and all the stories that I'll be able to tell?' A reflection on our American society."

AGENT INGENUITY

Is it common sense? Is it in-bred? Is it genes? Whatever it is, it is. Many times it is based on your background, schooling, upbringing. It is highly valued and it gets you places.

"Thinking on his feet"

"Even though I wrote couple of stories, none of them compared to a co-Agent/friend of mine in the RA. With his permission I will summarize the event.

The Agent was traveling from one town to the other with a stop-over in between. As he waited for boarding the plane, an airline gate agent began his announcement: 'We are going to start pre-boarding, would passengers with children, handicapped persons and the FBI Agent please start to board.' After the normal quick thinking by this particular FBI Special Agent, he stood up and started limping all the way to the plane.

Other passengers continued to look around the gate area to try to find the FBI Agent."

"The blind FBI Agent pretender"

"A spur of the moment need for a surveillance outside a city hall came to my partner's attention on an FCI squad. Not a parking spot in the area and no surveillance vehicles available. No Agents wearing other than a suit. What to do? Not a problem for a quick thinking ex-seminarian that originally wanted to be a priest.

As part of his 'shtick', he was almost always prepared for such an occasion. In the trunk of his Bu car he always had an extra well- worn hat, dark sun glasses, a blind man's ID card with a fake name to pin on his shirt or jacket, and an official white blind-person's cane. He quickly changed into his costume and props and voila . . . surveillance proved a success."

"Too long or too small"

"Upon entering the office, in my blue jeans, flannel shirt and gym shoes (I was assigned to a drug squad and this was my regular attire), the squad secretary reminded me that I had a scheduled appointment in court in about half an hour. Being first office agent, I was still on probation. I figured that my supervisor, let alone the SAC, would not understand any excuse I could dream up as to why I would show up in court in this attire (upper management were concerned about Hoover finding out, even though he had been dead for over ten years).

I lived about thirty minutes from the office, so going home to change was out of the question. Trying to call and reschedule was also not an option. I would have to show up as I was and accept the consequences.

Just prior to walking out the door, my partner (he had less time on the job than I did) walked in. He was wearing a nice suit and tie.

Agents are expected to think on their feet, right? I briefly explained to him the situation and told him I would do it for him. The only pivotal question was his shoe size. They were close enough. Let's change clothes.

I'm about 6'1, 185 lbs. He's about 5'9, 180 lbs. For him it wasn't so bad. He could roll up the pants and just sit at his desk until I returned. For me, well I deserved the abuse. The pants were just a little short, to say the least. The sleeves, same story. I had to wear the pants a little low and walk with my arms bent inside the sleeves, but I went to court in a suit.

The Bureau integrity was intact."

"I love sweets"

"I was assigned to a security squad and at least two of us were tasked to do Klan investigations. Others were placed into service as needed.

I was utilized to attend a Klan rally in an old '50 – 60's Plymouth (with the push button transmission). While our attention was on the crowd, a couple of Clansmen snuck up and punctured our rear tire.

My partner, a veteran of this behavior, opened the trunk and gave me a 5 lb bag of sugar and took one for himself. We liberally distributed the sugar where it was most destructive of Klan vehicles, fixed our tire and waited to ultimately see many tow trucks pull up and tow all their cars away.

Bet that's not on paper anywhere."

(Besides, the statute of limitation already ran out and writer's name is not on the paper that the story is on and there is no return name and address on the envelope.)

"A cannon shot?"

(Same type of a case directed against the Klan as above, different Agents involved, different cities, same statute of limitation already running out.)

"A number of us covered a large multi-state Klan rally in a small town covered by our RA. At least five of our Bureau cars were parked in the common parking area, together with Klansmen's cars, but for some reason, our cars must have had a Bureau smell or else we used deodorant and Klansmen did not. Three of our cars were obviously identified by clansmen and had at least one flat tire each by the time the rally was almost ended, with 30 minutes to go.

Our response had to obviously be greater for impression sake. One of the old timer Agents at the rally was always prepared. He had a sack of potatoes in the trunk of his Bucar. These potatoes were used to plug up of at least fifteen exhaust pipes of Klansmen's cars.

It sure sounded like Bastille Day in France … and many cars had to be towed, including ours, and both of our groups were p….d at each other."

"No Bucar for personal use"

"Two of us second office Agents assigned to a new office. A couple of weeks later, we planned a double date with our respective wives, to see the hottest movie of the year, The French Connection , on a Saturday night. The four of us left in one POA (personally owned automobile) to drive the forty five minutes into town to first, show our wives our new office, and then go to a movie.

Parked the POA in the Bu garage and walked to the office. After the office visit, walked back to the garage and . . . the POA just won't start. An ideal double date was to be ruined. What to do?

Plenty of Bucars in the garage. If we had not stopped at the office, we would not break down by the FBI office, but by the movie house.
Took a suitable Bucar, packed in and left for the movie and returned to our respective homes to drop off our wives. Returned early next morning to drop off the Bucar and had my POA hauled to a garage for repair.

The only time (I forgot the other times)that I used the Bucar for personal use."

"Hog blamed in wreck"

"I was a really new SRA in the Division and one night I was in the HQ city reviewing files when I heard my #2 call the night clerk, reporting he had a wreck in his Bu car.

As you can imagine, I quietly panicked as I listened to the radio exchange. The night clerk asked what happened and the reply was as follows: 'I was in route to contact an informant when I observed a wild hog in the road in front of me. I stopped, but the hog charged my car and completely ruined my front end.'

Only from the nimble mind of an FBI Special Agent could this have emanated. It worked, as the hog was blamed for the wreck and no letter of censure was issued."

"Where is my badge?"

"The dreaded inspection team arrived. It was the mid-fifties and they sure cut a wide swath in those days. Jimmy (not a true name), a darned good Agent, was very worried. He could not find his badge after searching his desk, high and low at home, the car, and everywhere else. Such a loss, according to precedents, could be a dereliction, resulting in a disciplinary TRANSFER !!! Jimmy had so many kids, it was said he almost lost his seat in the family station wagon. Oh what a havoc a transfer would wreak upon the family.

He thought it out and devised a plan. Jimmy positioned himself near the inspection staff one morning and waited. Before long, one of the inspectors picked up a newspaper, went out the door, down the hall. Jimmy followed shortly thereafter, out the door, down the hall, and into the booth next to the inspector. He heard the rustling of the newspaper a few times, silence, then a flush. When he heard the inspector washing his hands,

Jimmy pushed the flush lever and, above the whirling, gurgling sounds, yelled, 'Oh my God, MY BADGE!' as he opened the stall door. The inspector came over and asked Jimmy what happened. Jimmy just pointed to the filling commode and repeated his exclamation.

A plumber was soon called to disassemble the fixture and retrieve this piece of assigned Bureau property . . . all to no avail."

"I lost my creds"

"I remember serving on a squad with an Agent whose credentials slid out of his shirt pocket and into the ___________Sound while he was attempting to land a fish on a boat one weekend.

He related his plight to our supervisor on Monday and even confessed that a quantity of beer was involved. The supervisor ordered him to go find his creds, and threw him out of his office.

For three days the hapless Agent covered leads with his little badge, called law enforcement agencies anywhere near the Sound, and visited the supervisor's office, only to be ejected since he hadn't found the creds.

On Wednesday evening, the Agent received a telephone call at home from a citizen who said something with his name on it had washed ashore. Fortunately, the Agent was the only person with that surname in then telephone directory.

On Thursday, the Agent brought the water damaged creds to our supervisor, who ordered him to write a check to the FBI for $ 15 and to go to the photo lab and get a picture taken for his new credentials. The supervisor then enclosed the check and photo with a letter requesting new creds, explaining how the Agent had been on the supervisor's boat when the supervisor's toddler fell over the side into shark-infested waters and 'with total disregard for his own well-being, the Agent dove into the ocean and rescued the little girl'."

The Agent got his new creds and his check back, wrapped in a letter of commendation."

"Agent ingenuity to the fullest"

"About two blocks from our office was a kosher restaurant. Excellent food and loaded with SAs at breakfast and lunch times . . . except during those dreaded inspections when we had to follow the rules to the fullest.

But it didn't stop this particular Agent. During those inquisitions, he would leave the office, put on a pair of horn-rimmed glasses, pull out a copy of the city's top Jewish newspaper from his jacket and enter the restaurant, enjoying his bagel and coffee. The snooping inspectors regarded the Agent as one of the usual diners, not as an FBI Agent.
A true example of Agent ingenuity."

"Mea Culpa, mea culpa, mea maxima culpa…"

"For any venial or mortal sins on the part of any FBI Special Agents, who happened to be practicing Catholics, and may have bent the FBI rules and regulations a bit, they could go and confess their sins. What better confessor than a fellow FBI Special Agent, who was at different times a Commander in the U.S. Navy (and also an Agent) as well as a ???? Priest following his retirement from the Bureau. Add to this a note about also being a CIA Officer and a professional bull fighter."

"Latrine detail…"

"In a U.S. city with a number of foreign embassies, a need existed for a two-man lookout to cover a particular establishment. Unfortunately, the only available space was in a garage without a bathroom facility. Inasmuch as a manned surveillance was necessary, so was the need for a 'toilet'.
What to do? A five gallon covered paint bucket, what else. During the graveyard shift, one of the rolling surveillance crews was detailed to bring a clean bucket and pick up the "slightly filled" bucket and empty it in the wilds of a metropolitan park. Same crew was also responsible for cleaning of this emptied bucket, for use on the next shift.

You could honestly say that this was quite a 'shitty detail'."

"Skid marks…"

"Two FBI Special Agents, Big Mike and Little Chuck (well, not so little)assigned to the 'Black Bag Squad', were on a mission, making an 'installation' of a listening device in the home of a known hoodlum on the

North Coast.

Armed with proper court-issued warrants to make the installation, the two entered the home during the night hours, while the subject of the installation was working a graveyard shift.

One SA was in the basement while the other was upstairs, making sure that the two would not be surprised. The basement Agent heard the toilet flush over and over again and finally hurried upstairs, not knowing what was happening. The upstairs Agent was merely 'erasing the evidence of his deposit in the toilet bowl', noting that he was 'erasing the skid marks'."
(When you gotta go, you gotta go!)

"Decision making"

"On 07/07/1996, when asked about decision making, my ASAC (JP), who moved up in his Bureau career, made the following observation: 'The biggest decision in the FBI is to make it to the bathroom on time.'

"Xerox machine lie detector"

"Pre Bu, as a young police officer in a small East Coast community, we had occasion to arrest a subject who was apprehended in close proximity to a school that one of our patrols had observed being burglarized.

Not witnessing the subject committing the offense nor in possession of stolen property, we had a dilemma on whether to charge him. Let me add that the subject denied his involvement and was not the sharpest tool in the shed. I had an idea. We told him that we were going to give him a polygraph.

We attached two wires to the side of s photocopier (not a common sight in those days) and taped them to his fingers. I put a blank piece of paper on the copier glass and three sheets of paper in the paper tray. Each piece had writing in block letters. We asked him his name and pushed the copy button. We asked him his date of birth and pushed the copy button. And of course we asked him if he had broken into the school.

You can guess the rest. TRUE. TRUE. LIE.

He confessed. Hey, really, I couldn't make this stuff up."

"A 'damsel' in distress…"

"I was assigned to a RA out of a Division on the Great Lakes. I was clearing off my desk when the main phone in the RA rang. Since no one else seemed particularly interested or able to answer it, I took the call.

The woman on the line explained that she was elderly and lived alone and had a problem. I asked her to hold on, while I grabbed paper and pen, and she replied I probably did not have to take notes.

The lady explained that the power in her small house had gone out and she had apparently blown a fuse or fuses. Since her fuse box was placed high on a wall, because of her age and condition, she was unable to reach it. She did not feel comfortable calling a stranger to replace the fuse and didn't know where else to turn.

She stated, 'If you can't trust the FBI, who can you trust?'

Needless to say, even though she lived on the East side of town and I on the West, on my way home from work that day, I made a side trip to replace a fuse."

"A birthday wish . . ."

"I was on a scheduled complaint duty, answering calls from citizens on this particular day. One of the children in a family of a 90 year old black lady called our office and expressed a deep desire of their mother to meet an FBI Special Agent, before she passes on. The caller noted that their mother's birthday was going to be the following week, and if at all possible, a visit would mean so much to mom. I obtained the details and promised a visit.

Never turning down a birthday party, I showed up with a vase of flowers and an Apple II+ generated personal birthday card for the 'young gal'. The lady was very thankful and as gracious as were all the members of her family present. Never mind that I am white. I made her day and the color of our skin has nothing to do with both of our hearts pumping red blood through our body. This was probably one of my best 'leads' during my time in the FBI."

"Claiming luggage…"

"Two fellow Agents had Saturday duty together and were sent to the local airport to arrest a fugitive who was arriving from some far- away place, via a big silver bird.

The arrest was made without incident, and one of the Agents told the other something to the effect that, 'I'll go get the Bucar while you stay with the subject. I'll pick you up at the curb in front of baggage.'

The Agent returned as promised to the curb with a car a few minutes later, to find the subject standing there, handcuffed and utterly alone. He got out of the car and asked the subject, 'Where's the SA FNU LNU?'

The subject responded, 'Oh, he was nice enough to go to the baggage claim to get my luggage.'

I'll bet Tom Clancy wishes he could come up with stuff like this . . . "

OUTTAKE . . .

WHY CARRY A GUN
(Author unknown)

"My old grandpa said to me: 'Son, there comes a time in every man's life when he stops bustin' knuckles and starts bustin' caps and usually it's when he becomes too old to take an ass whoopin.'

I don't carry a gun to kill people. I carry a gun to keep from being killed.

I don't carry a gun to scare people. I carry a gun because this world can be a scary place.

I don't carry a gun because I'm paranoid. I carry a gun because there are real threats in the world.

I don't carry a gun because I'm evil. I carry a gun because I have lived long enough to see evil in the world.

I don't carry a gun because I hate the government. I carry a gun because I understand the limitations of government.

I don't carry a gun because I'm angry. I carry a gun so that I don't have to spend the rest of my life hating myself for failing to be prepared.

I don't carry a gun because I love it. I carry a gun because I love life and the people who make it meaningful to me.

I don't carry a gun because I feel inadequate. I carry a gun because unarmed and facing three armed thugs, I am inadequate.

Police do not protect you from crime, they usually just investigate the crime after it happens and then call someone in to clean up the mess.

Personally, I carry a gun because I'm too young to die and too old to take an ass whoopin.' "

STORIES CONTINUE . . .

"Degrees of death"

"After the mug shots and fingerprinting, the interview began. After the proverbial reading of the rights, I told this mutt that we knew he had killed the victim in the UFAP warrant. I told him we were curious as to why he had shot the victim so many times when a single round would have done the job quite efficiently.

The subject looked totally confused, like a penguin in Death Valley. After he thought for a minute, he looked at me and my partner and calmly said: 'I didn't mean to kill him that bad.'

Apparently he only meant to kill him 'a little bit.' It was on that day that we learned that there are apparently different degrees of death. Guess there is a full spectrum between being a 'little bit dead' and a 'whole lot dead.'

I have never ceased to be amazed at the mind set and thinking (or lack thereof) of these street thugs we dealt with on a daily basis."

CHAPTER 6

BANK ROBBERIES (BR'S) 91 CLASSIFICATION

Of all the different investigations conducted by the FBI, bank robberies take the cake. The cases are worked by the "heavies". After all, everyone knows that it is the FBI that is involved in catching the bank robbers. It is obviously a misconception that bank robberies are the bulk of the FBI's work. Nevertheless, BRs definitely get the headlines in the local rags and they make for good stories. Proud is the Special Agent that comes home after catching a bank robber and telling his kids that he/she were heroes for a day. Following is a sampling of stories about bank robbery investigations.

A GOAT INSTEAD OF A HERO

"I was working on the bank robbery squad in the land of the Choctaw Indians and had stopped at the bank to use the ATM machine. I sat in the car and put on my ankle holster thinking I needed to be armed for that one in a million chance that something might happen while I was in the bank. After several attempts and several minutes, I decided the machine was not working and went into the lobby of the bank to get some money. I noticed that the teller kept looking past me as she waited on me but she didn't say anything. So after turning to see what she was looking at and not seeing anything out of ordinary, I left.

As I got into my vehicle and started toward my office I heard a radio call of a new 91 at the bank I had just come from, so I turned around and started back.

Sure enough, when I arrived, the police were there and said that the bank robber, who had been wearing a suit and tie, had taken one of the managers into her office and then made her go to the vault and put money into his briefcase while he waited for her in her office.

Apparently, I had entered the bank when the manager had returned to her office with the briefcase to give to the robber the money. The teller, not knowing I was an Agent, was watching him walk out of the bank while she waited on me.

Not being told what was going on, I had been unaware of the whole situation. Thinking back, I'm not sure there's anything I could or would have done differently, but it sure was embarrassing when we reviewed the surveillance film and there I was standing at the teller counter.

The kicker to the thing is the silent alarm was tripped and our office was notified of the robbery while I was seated in the car in the front of the ATM. The squad supervisor was notified by the secretary regarding the silent alarm call but he had told her he was too busy working on a report to put it over the radio and waited at least five minutes before notifying dispatch. If (the biggest word in the English language) he had put out the call when it came in I would have been waiting outside when the robber walked out and been a hero. Instead, I became a goat."

TOO CLOSE FOR COMFORT

"While on a surveillance of a spy, I sat in a non-descript sports car on a side street waiting to pick up the surveillance. A broadcast on the FBI radio called for all units in the area to respond to a BR within one block of my location. Radio noted that an armed BR subject was in the bank, ready to exit.

This was going to be my day of glory, as I pulled to the middle of the street, directly in line of site of the front door to the bank, gun drawn, crouching behind the motor block for protection.

A marked local squad car pulled immediately to my behind, with a quickly exiting young police officer with a gun in his hand directing me to drop the gun and do not move. I definitely did not have the look of an FBI Special Agent, with a suit, a tie and an FBI looking car. Instead, I wore a 'Popeye' from the French Connection type hat and short sleeve summer shirt. I quickly placed my weapon on the street and shouted that I was an FBI Special Agent. Additional FBI units arrived and saved my ass…as the officer was sure that I was the bad guy.

It all ended well. The bad guy got caught and I was not carried by six. It was a good day to thank the Lord for another chance in life.

PRISON BETTER THAN OUTSIDE

"We had a typical note job robbery one day on the West coast. The bank still had the old 35mm film system in place but also had recently installed a new video tape system that we were able to review and print out a few small pictures of the robber. So we had a good description of him.

Later in the afternoon, I was sitting at my desk in the office, when the switchboard operator put a call through to me from a guy who claimed that he had robbed the above bank in the morning. The caller identified the motel and the room that he was in. I told him to wait there as we will be there shortly. So off we go and knock on the door and he was still wearing the same clothes he had on that morning. Told him he was under arrest and his reply was as follows: 'I understand, the money is in my pocket.'

In his pocket was half of the money, all in bait bills, amounting to about one thousand dollars. When I asked him where the rest of the money was, the other thousand bucks, he replied that he bought a bottle of vodka and had a young lady from a local escort service show up. I asked him if he gave her a grand and must have been quite a time and he replied: 'No, I passed out as soon as she got here and she just took a bunch of my money and left.'

Then a classic remark for all of us that have ever worked these cases…'think I do better in prison.'

I typed the complaint and found out that he was on supervised release for bank robbery on the East coast. So I had all this info in the complaint, confession, bait bills, prior bank robbery convictions, same clothing and good quality surveillance photos. Took the complaint to a U.S. Magistrate, known to be extremely liberal. I know, big surprise, and having no sense of humor. He read the complaint several times and then looked up at me and stated: 'Just where in here do you think you have probable cause, Agent?' I know I must have had a deer in the headlight look and started to articulately saying, but, but, but, but, he finally took pity on me and stated: 'Just messing with you. This one will never go to trial'…and actually smiled. The Man actually showed a sense of humor."

MALE ROBBER, FEMALE BATHROOM plus THE FAMILY THAT ROBS TOGETHER, STAYS TOGETHER or THREE TIMES IS A CHARMER

"This certain bank was robbed three Fridays in a row. The first, by a male, the second by a female and the third by "A", not the brightest person but par for a BR subject. He ran south from the bank pursued by a police officer and a teller. As this was at lunch time, he ran into the KFC, jumped the counter and hid in the female employee's bathroom.

When the police entered the KFC, the employees told them that the man was in the female bathroom. He was pulled out of the female bathroom and yelled that it was an illegal arrest because the male cops were not allowed in the female bathroom.

But the story gets better. We interviewed his mom and during the interview we happened to show her the BR Unsub surveillance photos we carried around with us. As she thumbed through the photos, she stopped at a photo of a male robbing the same bank. Mom wanted to know what we were doing with a photo of her other son. You guessed it!

The female robber was the second son's fiancée. We executed a search warrant at the apartment and mom was keeping all the BR money in a shoe box in her closet.

I guess, the family that robs together, stays together."

THOUGHTS TO PONDER
(Author unknown)

"I used to eat a lot of natural foods until I learned that most people die of natural causes.

Gardening rule: When weeding, the best way to make sure you are removing a weed and not a valuable plant is to pull on it. If it comes out of the ground easily, it is a valuable plant.

The easiest way to find something lost around the house is to buy a replacement.

Never take life seriously. Nobody gets out alive anyway.

There are two kinds of pedestrians: the quick and the dead.

Life is sexually transmitted.

An unbreakable toy is useful for breaking other toys.

If quitters never win, and winners never quit, then who is the fool who said, 'Quit while you're ahead?'

Health is merely the slowest possible rate at which one can die.

The only difference between a rut and a grave is the depth.

Give a person a fish and you feed them for a day; teach that person to use the Internet and they won't bother you for weeks.

Some people are like Slinkies…not really good for anything, but you still can't help but smile when you see one tumble down the stairs.

Health nuts are going to feel stupid someday, lying in hospitals dying of nothing.

Have you noticed since everyone has a camera on his phone these days, no one talks about seeing UFOs like they used to? Except on moonless nights.

Whenever I feel blue, I start breathing again.

All of us could take a lesson from the weather. It pays no attention to criticism.

Why does a slight tax increase cost you two hundred dollars and a substantial tax cut saves you thirty cents?

In the 60's, people took LSD to make the world weird. Now the world is weird and people take Prozac to make it normal.

Politics is supposed to be the second oldest profession. I have come to realize that it bears a very close resemblance to the first.

How is it one careless match can start a forest fire, but it takes a whole box to start a campfire?

And the # 1 thought for the day: You read about all these terrorists…most of them came here legally, but they hung around on these expired visas, some for as long as 10-15 years.
Now, compare that to Blockbuster: You are two days late with a video and those people are all over you. Let's put Blockbuster in charge of immigration."

The stories continue . . .

DON'T GET EXCITED

"I was working on a bank robbery squad. One of the squad mates located a bank robber one afternoon and the fun began.

While we were gathering the troops, the supervisor said to take the new female SA along, to give her some experience. So we did.

We knocked on the front door of the apartment the robber was in and a short time later the door cracked open and our guy peeked through the crack and asked what we wanted. We shoved the door into him, which propelled him into the middle of the room where he landed on his back screaming.

As we entered we could see he wasn't wearing anything and for lack of better words, was in an excited state. He didn't move as he had shotguns in his face, but kept screaming and stayed excited.

The new female Agent entered and got an eyeful of the situation. Trying to be a little discreet, one of the other Agents told the guy to roll over. He complied but in his excited state, couldn't really roll over very well.

Now he's almost face down, still screaming and for whatever reason, still excited. Probably an even worse picture for our new Agent on her first arrest."

THE DUMB BANK ROBBER

"We just finished a federal BR trial for armed robbery. Since the victim teller was the only one who saw the weapon, for some reason, the jury convicted the robber of unarmed robbery. Due to the error during the trial, our subject was retried for unarmed bank robbery. During the trial, without the jury present, the defendant demanded to speak directly with the Judge. The Judge informed the defendant to speak through his attorney. The defendant insisted, so the Judge let him ask the question. The defendant wanted to know how come he was being tried for unarmed robbery, when he used a gun during the robbery."

WRONG ANSWER

"At the initial Magistrate appearance for a BR, the Magistrate was asking the subject financial questions for bail purposes. The Magistrate asked him if he had any cash and when the subject responded negatively, the Magistrate asked him what he did with the money. He responded: 'I spent it!' "

HAMBURGER MONEY

"I was a rookie, helping another Agent in a search of a bank robber's house. We found majority of the cash in several packages of hamburgers dated prior to the bank robbery. After we thawed all of his meat, regardless of the date, as a rookie I spent an hour in the ceiling with fiberglass insulation, at 90 degrees, recovering another couple grand.

I think I still itch once in a while."

FBI SPECIAL AGENTS ARE ALWAYS ON DUTY

"I am a seasoned Agent, far north, in the territory covered by another FBI office, and I get a call on my cell phone from a 'source'. He tells me that he just robbed a bank, and spent some of the money…and is now at such and such hotel…and have changed my mind…and want to give up to the Agents.

Needless to say, I was upset with him, not because he screwed up the part on the pink sheet that he (as a source for the FBI) filled out previously, that said he would not commit crimes, but because I was fishing in 300 feet of water, on a huge lake, with salmon in the boat, with Agents from another investigative federal agency, on their chartered boat.

Always on duty."

TRANSCRIBING THE MOVIE LINES

"I had a source wired in support of a case. The steno that I used was excited about all the material I had developed for evidence in her rather lengthy transcript…until I told her that the bad guys were listening intently to the movie 'The Godfather' and the only part of their conversations were the grunts and laughs."

NEVER TOO OLD TO ROB A BANK

"On the East Coast, a 95 year old nursing home tenant boarded an interstate bus, after telling fellow friends that he was going to Washington where all the money was. He shuffled into a bank, gave a note to a teller and was given a few hundred dollars. He proceeded to shuffle out of the bank, was passed by two uniformed police officers that were responding to the bank robbery. He was quickly caught and turned over to two FBI Special Agents responding to the robbery. Agents returned the money to the bank manager and put the gentleman back on the bus to return to the welcoming arms of his family waiting at the nursing home. End of story?

Not quite! Two weeks later, he was back at the same bank, the same teller, different note. The teller told him to have a seat and wait for the manager. This time he was taken by the Agents to the U.S. Marshal's lock up where he was kept for a few days. He was later returned on the Marshal's bus and never returned to the bank."

BANK ROBBER IN A WHEELCHAIR

"Why walk into the bank when you can ride. It happened in a Midwest city on Lake Erie. To add fuel to the fire, the wheel chair bound robber even took some hostages and kept FBI Special Agents that surrounded the bank up most of the cold night. The 'hostages' loved the guy and felt bad for his condition."

BR COORDINATOR GOING ON SICK LEAVE

"My first office of assignment was in one of those sleepy southern offices where everything happened slowly. There were quite a few first office agents assigned there, all chomping at the bit to work a bank robbery case. We had plenty of deserter cases to sharpen our skills, but we all wanted to be involved in the real thing…the bank robbery investigation.

Finally, the big day came. Several of us FOAs were in the office dictating when the announcement came over the office PA that a nearby downtown bank had been robbed. We all dropped what we were doing and headed to the switchboard to drop off our #3 cards on the way out to the bank. Imagine our surprise when we had to wait there briefly as the office bank robbery coordinator stood in front of us signing out on sick leave. I guessed that he became sick hearing about the bank robbery that finally happened on his watch, or it was the excitement of it. Never a dull moment."

BANK ROBBER CRAPPS IN HIS PANTS AND DOES NOT GET TO SIT IN FBI CAR

"While working a bank robbery case that happened a week before, I visited the victim bank to show photos to the victim teller. Well, lo and behold, the victim teller was being robbed right in front of me. I stood off to the side and waited for the completion of the robbery, with what can best be described as a sh** eaten grin on my face.

As the robber exited the bank, I walked behind him and announced: FBI…you are under arrest! On the spot, he crapped in his pants. Looking down, he said: 'My shoes have been full of s..t all my life'. He had a gun in his pocket. I recovered his note and brought him back into the bank and called for a local police department car to transport him to our office. There was no way I was going to let him sit in my FBI car. The robber was a slope worker and he had a plane ticket in his pocket to get out of Dodge.

Back at the office, the SAC told me that I hadn't done anything that any hire-a-cop wouldn't have done. No Atta Boy, no letter from the Director, no nothing. Stat was all I got."

WAKE UP AMERICA
(Author unknown)

"Once upon a time, an American automobile company and a Japanese auto company decided to have a competitive boat race on the Detroit River. Both teams practiced hard and long to reach their peak performance. On the big day, they were as ready as they could be.

The Japanese team won by a mile.

Afterwards, the American team became discouraged by the loss and their morale sagged. Corporate management decided that the reason for the crushing defeat had to be found. A Continuous Measurable Improvement Team of 'Executives' was set up to investigate the problem and to recommend appropriate corrective action.

Their conclusion: The problem was that the Japanese team had 8 people rowing and 1 person steering, whereas the American team had 1 person rowing and 8 people steering. The American Corporate Steering Committee immediately hired a consulting firm to do a study on the management structure.

After some time and billions of dollars, the consulting firm concluded that 'too many people were steering and not enough rowing.' To prevent losing to the Japanese again next year, the management structure was changed to '4 Steering Managers, 3 Area Steering Managers, and 1 Staff Steering Manager' and a new performance system for the person rowing the boat to give more incentive to work harder and become a six sigma performer. 'We must give empowerment and enrichment.' That ought to do it.

The next year, the Japanese team won by two miles.

The American Corporation laid off the rower for poor performance, sold all of the paddles, cancelled all capital investments for new equipment, halted development of a new canoe, awarded high performance awards to the consulting firm, and distributed the money saved as bonuses to the senior executives."

The stories continue . . .

NEW SPECIAL AGENT KNOWS BETTER

"Just before my retirement, we had a bank robbery in our RA territory. The RA responded, along with one or two of the new kids on the block, one who will remain nameless. For some unknown reason, one of the new Agents decided to take one of the dye packs as evidence and put it in his briefcase. The banker cautioned him about taking it out of the bank as it would / could go off. As usual, an FBI Special Agent always knows better. The young Agent grabbed his briefcase and walked out the door toward his Bucar.

Several people saw the briefcase explode and die and tear gas filled the air. The young Agent never skipped a beat and kept walking. He placed the briefcase into the car and returned to the RA office. The office, the Bucar and much of the Federal Court House that housed the RA office smelled of tear gas, at which time the Federal Judge got into the act. It never happened again."

BULLET THROUGH THE PRIVATE PART

"Our office had more than its share of BRs. In this particular BR, the perp had a revolver and announced a robbery. To get everyone's attention, he cocked the gun in front of everyone. He then decided to climb over the counter. The young male teller backed up and as the perp climbed the counter, the gun went off, striking the teller.

I was nearby and responded and rode in the ambulance with the teller. When we got to the ER, the on duty DR did a quick exam and came out to tell me that the teller would be OK. He said that the bullet went through the teller's penis and lodged in his thigh. 'NOTHING VITAL WAS HIT'. After I stopped laughing I went back to the bank and shared the doctor's comments."

THE DYE PACK VICTIM WITH VITAL PARTS PROBABLY HIT

"We had a 91-New at a bank in the downtown area. Upon arrival, I was tasked with interviewing the victim teller. She was a 'veteran' of previous robberies as a victim teller. She advised that the subject ordered her to put money from the second drawer on the counter. Of course she included a dye pack. When she saw the subject put the money in the front of his pants, she went to two other teller stations and collected more dye packs which the subject also deposited in his pants. After his escape from the bank, he jumped into a waiting vehicle and departed. A day and evening long search for the subject(s) yielded no results.

The next morning, we get a call from a guy who claimed to have been the person responsible for the robbery. After getting his name and address, several of us went to the house. The subject was waiting for us on his front porch, leaning on crutches in painful agony. I will not go into a description of his wounds; let your imagination take over.

What great experience I had and was thankful to have been able to associate with such fine Agents who taught me so much."

THE REALLY SMART BANK ROBBER

"In this bank robbery, the subject overpowered the security guard and took his gun to commit the robbery. Several days later, in the same area, this robber struck again, but this time he was arrested by the responding policemen as he was running from the bank. He was in possession of the guard's gun. Together with a police inspector, I interviewed the subject. He initially only confessed to the robbery where he was apprehended, but when confronted about the possession of the guard's gun, he confessed to the first robbery.

After confessing to these robberies, he stated: 'You FBI guys think you are so smart you don't even know about the robbery I did cross country in another city.' I told him he was right, so tell us about it. He laid out all the details about the robbery. When we interviewed him in the original city, he was clean shaven and had a shaved head. When we got the surveillance photo in from the second city, the subject had a full beard and a large afro. We would never have put these robberies together based on the surveillance photos.

The best part of this story is when we went to testify in Federal

Court in the second city, the subject again had a full beard and large afro, making him look identical to the surveillance photo. Thank goodness for the really smart ones."

THE SECRET STASH IN THE BUCAR

"Subject robs a bank and makes a good getaway. Within a day or two, however, we get an anonymous tip by telephone. The subject is identified, and furthermore, we're told that the subject is about to fly to another city and buy a big load of drugs with his BR proceeds, that he will bring back to the original city of the bank robbery, for resale.

The source gave us specific flight info. The troops stake out the airport departure, and easy as pie, we get the guy. He is handcuffed behind his back, patted down for weapons, and loaded into the Bucar for trip to our office. All goes well until we realize we have found no money on the subject or in the luggage. This doesn't square with the plan to buy drugs in another city. Subject won't talk and we are baffled. Subject gets convicted for the original bank robbery and is incarcerated.

Some months later, we get an excited phone call from a young kid who is employed at the car wash that we use for the Bucars. The kid knows who is the usual driver of the Bucar and asks for that Agent. 'Come out to the carwash right away.' The Agent goes there. This was the Bucar that we transported the subject in. The kid, cleaning out the inside of the car, found the loot stashed behind the rear seat. Obviously, the subject had stuck the money inside his belt, right at his butt. While we were transporting him, with his cuffed hands behind his back, he managed to grab the dough, remove it from his person, and stick it down behind the seat. The carwash kid found it while cleaning the car. A bit embarrassing for us."

OUTTAKE . . .

NFL FOOTBALL TEAMS
(Author unknown)

1. After AU------------
2. They get broken
3. Military hill builders
4. Streakers
5. They use the Brockway
6. Midnighters at the fridge
7. Top scouts
8. Gringo gauchos
9. Fundamental rules
10. They use credit cards
11. Old time water pipe
12. Louis Armstrong feature
13. Suntanned bodies
14. After the credit cards
15. Lubricators
16. Washington's Fisher goes wild
17. $1.00 per corn
18. 747
19. Use to be a girl
20. Six shooter
21. Six Roman rulers
22. Toy baby with fish fins
23. Cigarette makers
24. Early American leaders
25. Like most apples
26. Animal leader
27. Ocean bird
28. Convicted in summer

The stories continue . . .

SPOILING OPENING DAY BASEBALL GAME

"The SAC and the city's police chief are attending the opening day game. My partner and I are cruising back to the office about 3 pm and stopped at the red light near the bank. We see two guys leave their car at the curb, wearing ski masks and coveralls, carrying shopping bags, entering the bank. I exit the car and my partner pulls to the curb and gets on the radio. I see through the window one guy jumping over the counter. I take cover at the corner of the building. One robber comes out and with a sawed-off shotgun takes my partner hostage and re-enters the bank. Both robbers now exit the bank and run toward their car and toward my position, leaving my partner inside the bank, disarmed.

I yelled at them to stop and they fired several shots, hitting side of building and two cars in the street. I fired once and hit the driver in the face. My partner came out of the bank and grabbed the other guy. A bystander picked up my partner's gun and handed it to him, while the robber tries to grab it, but was struck and subdued by the bystander.

The SAC and the police chief arrived, while a huge team of SAs and local officers handled the scene. The SAC drove my partner and I to the office, stopping at a pub along the way for a couple of quick ones to settle our (mostly his) nerves, before dictating our report.

The driver somehow survived and $37,000 was recovered on the spot. Both robbers had priors. They plead guilty in Federal Court to BR and Assault and got fairly lenient sentences, I think 15 years. My partner and I received $ 300 incentive awards, thus my first set of matched golf clubs.

I left the Bureau later that year, mostly out of sheer boredom from working Selective Service (25 classification) and Conscientious Objector cases in those days. My partner retired years later."

VICTIM WENT TO LUNCH INSTEAD OF CALLING 911

"Two subjects robbed a bank but were spotted by a county deputy in their getaway car. So they drove a few blocks and ditched the car. They next boat-jacked an elderly gentleman and made him take them to the next town. The good news was that we had a witness who observed the boat-jacking and gave us a description of the boat. We called on every agency that had a chopper or a boat and soon we had help from Customs, Coast Guard and numerous others. The witness told us that the Bimini top of the boat was red, but it turned out that it was blue. So, all the choppers and police boats passed on the blue top boat, searching for the red one. The subjects made it to the next port and released the boat owner. Did he call 911 or alert anyone to the subjects who were calling for cab service from a pay phone? No....he went to the nearest bar and ordered lunch and a beer...and 25 minutes later, a taxi picked up our subjects and they disappeared.

Through the ensuing investigation, we did ID the subjects and arrested them at a motel two weeks later."

ROBBERS USING MY STOLEN LICENSE PLATE

"Same bank was robbed again and we did not have much to go on. Then I got a cold call from a young woman who told me everything, including names and addresses and the fact that they were going to rob another bank the next day, but not the identity of the bank. We verified as much information as we could and her info was credible. The rental address of the robbers was just down the street from my house, and on the same canal. County deputies started the surveillance but could not tell if the subjects were there. We decided to send a teletype to all the PDs, warning them about the impending robbery. As I was dictating the report to a steno in the main office, my husband called me and told me that someone had stolen the license plate off my POA. Not believing in coincidences, I noted in the teletype that the robbers might be using my license plate in the planned robbery.

We got the authority to make the arrests and we hit the house that night and had two of the subjects in custody. Guess what was sitting on the counter of their house...Yup, my license plate.

The ringleader cooperated and testified for us. He told us that he knew his days as a bank robber were over, when of all the cars in town, he had to go and steal the license plate from the FBI Special Agent investigating his first robbery.

The bad news was that since my license plate was entered into evidence, I had to go and pay for a new license plate."

PERP BY FIVE

"Here is what I hope to be an informative story about BRs. One day in late afternoon, the call came in that there had been a new 91. Everyone saddled up and responded. After arriving, we discovered we had eight Agents, mostly old-timers, with a lot of experience, to handle the immediate leads.

Problem was, there were no leads. The robber had come in, passed a note, taken the loot and vanished into the afternoon traffic. So after standing around in the bank for an hour, the SSRA who was running the response, announced that we would all leave the bank and reconvene down the road at a nearby diner. When we got there, everyone slips into a corner booth and begins to peruse the menus. As a FOA, I'm a little nervous, but excited to see how we map out our strategy to identify and catch the robber. The waitress took all of our orders and then I figure we're about ready to 'make a plan.'

Instead, everyone just kicks-back and chats about their families, their kids, a fishing trip, vacation plans, and anything else you could think of. Finally, in frustration, I ask them: 'Aren't we going to make a plan? Isn't that why we all came here to the diner?' They all looked at each other, and then one of them says to me very dryly: 'No, we didn't come here to make a plan. The guy's long gone. And we're not going to find him tonight,' and then he resumed his conversation with one of his old cronies.

The veteran sitting next to me sees the confusion on my face and leans over and whispers: 'The SAC has this rule that if you haven't got the guy in custody by 5 o'clock, you have to keep working, and can't sign out until 8 pm. My expression must have been indescribable, and he said: 'I know, I know, just roll with it.' "

BE HUMBLE

"I recall responding to a bank job in my first office. When we arrived the victim teller advised that it was a note job and the perp took the note with him when he left. While the Agents were processing the counter and interviewing witnesses, I thought I'd take a look outside the bank and walk the path that the perp took when he exited the bank. The front of the bank had a row of hedges…one of which caught my eye. Stuck into the center of the hedge was what looked like a rolled up piece of paper. I took it out and examined it. The note read 'This is a stick up, put the money in the bag'.

I ran to my car and found a plastic folder to put it in. I then returned to the bank…walking toward the victim teller with an air of…'who's better than the FBI'.

I showed her the note…and with tongue in cheek asked…does this look familiar? Her response…wait for it…No that's not it. 'The robber's note was on white paper, that one is yellow and the handwriting was different and it only said this is a hold up.'

Life humbles us all."

THE THREE LUNATICS IN A DEBATE

"Back in the early 2000's, we were hunting a serial note job bank robber. After 15 or so jobs he made the mistake of robbing a bank across from the police department. After a foot chase, the cops nabbed him and we got the call…on a late Friday afternoon, of course. My squad partner and I ran over to the PD and took a look at the guy. Covered in tattoos, arms crossed, certainly not amused and certainly not someone who was going to talk to anyone, about anything.

First, a little about my partner at the time, He was a Born-Again Christian, complete with Bible on the desk, parked right next to the MIOG. For fun, we used to debate Evolution versus Creation on our lunch breaks. We would argue for hours about it, non-stop. It would annoy the hell out of everyone around us. I guess there's nothing quite like watching a preacher and a prosecutor debate.

Anyway, we have this guy, I'll call him 'Bob,' placed in an interview room, alone. My partner and I walk in and Bob is sitting back with a sarcastic smile, crosses his arms and legs, and cocks his head, turning it slowly from left to right. Knowing that Bob wasn't going for any 'good cop-bad cop' routine and realizing he wasn't going to give anything to us, I decided to have some fun. I stop in the middle of the room and say to him: 'Evolution or Creation. Which one is the real truth.' Bob unfolds his arms and legs, leans forward and declares: 'Evolution of course. You'd have to be an idiot to believe in Creationism.'

The game was afoot. For the next four hours, it was me and Bob, debating against my partner. Bob would say something supportive of Evolution and my partner would then refute it, at times citing some of the very same biblical citations that Bob himself had tattooed all over his arms and neck. I would then back Bob's position with tidbits of evidence I obtained from taking half a dozen college courses in Geology and Evolutionary Theory. The city detectives would just walk by the one-way mirrors and stare in amazement at these three lunatics in their interview room. We even ordered pizza and sodas and 'broke bread' with Bob.

About three hours into it, my partner had to go use the restroom. As soon as he leaves, Bob leans over and asks me: 'Hey, are we ever going to talk about my bank robberies?' I answered back: 'Not really, I think we are winning the debate. We got him on the ropes, but here's my file of your photos, if you'd like to take a look, autograph the ones you did, and then we can get back to our discussion.' He eagerly went through the four page bulletin form that I always made up for every serial guy, that included every job's details along with the best photo from each one and a Miranda form. He signed each job 'I robbed this bank,' along with his signature and the Miranda form and gave me back the forms just as my partner returned. We then continued the debate for another hour or so. We then thanked Bob and took our leave.

Bob was the Hannibal Lector of bank robberies. He turned out to have some genius level IQ but could not function in society like a normal person. He got seven years in a Federal Prison. After serving his prison sentence he was released in 2011, and he immediately robbed two more banks of more than $500,000. He was quickly caught by my old squad mates.

While housed in the local lockup after his arraignment, he feigned an illness and was brought to a local hospital. While there, he managed to break free of his restraints, attack his guard and attempt to escape. He was shot dead in the process. I kind of missed the guy. I do wish we could have continued our debate."

WITNESS IDENTIFIES HIS HIGH SCHOOL CLASSMATE

"It was a routine one-man note job in the downtown area, not far from the RA. Two of us arrived fairly quickly. And pulled up to an open parking spot at the curb. As we got out of the car, we were met on the sidewalk by a young fellow who asked something like 'why are you guys here?' I suppose we told him we were FBI, and that the bank had just been robbed. He said: 'I wondered what had happened. I just watched a guy tearing down the street right past me. I responded 'well, that certainly might have been the robber'. He then said: 'I know the guy. He was a high school classmate of mine'. I think we had the subject, a confession and the money within two hours. Subject had buried the money in a city park and took us to it."

PANTS ON FIRE

"We had a bank robber who put a dye pack down the front of his pants as another Agent has reported in some other incident. He shred and discolored his Johnsons in the parking lot of the bank. This was years ago, and if I remember correctly, the firing mechanism incorporated a .410 shotgun shell component, sans buckshot, so packed a real wallop."

WHO PLANNED THE ROBBERY?

"We had two brothers-in-law at Christmas time who needed Santa money, got drunk, robbed a bank. Dropped money all the way out to the car where they were arrested fumbling for their keys to the car. When they appeared before the Magistrate, each denied that the other had been involved, that the other one was too dumb to plan a robbery, trying to save the other family member."

LACK OF RESPECT IN "THE HOOD"

"I was fresh out of Quantico in the new city and responded to a 91 in the hood. Being new, I was assigned to do a neighborhood. I knocked on the door of a nearby house and a woman opened the door. I said 'hello my name is so and so and I am an FBI Special Agent', and just as they taught me at the FBI Academy, I held up my creds with my left hand and proudly displayed them. She responded with an 'who gives an F bomb' expletive and slammed the door in my face. I looked at the door for about 20 seconds.

My training Agent said later: 'Welcome to the world of the street in the big city.' I quickly learned the reality of life as an FBI Special Agent."

THE CRISPY CREAM DONUT DELAYS THE VERDICT

We had a career robber, a 50 something Italian guy, rob a brand new teller at one of those trailers they used while building a new bank. The teller, p.o.'ed that he had been robbed his second week on the job, watched the robber run out of the bank, around the side towards the rear of the trailer, and ran out the back door after him. The senior teller, seeing her 21 year old, brand new teller run after the robber, joined him in the pursuit.

A passing cowboy, seeing a guy with a mask, gun and a bag of loot being pursued by a young guy in a suit and a tie, and an older Hispanic woman red in the face, stopped his pick-em-up truck just long enough to knock the dog s*#t out of the guy.

In court, 'Tony' decided to represent himself and his question to the victim teller was 'How was it youse recognized me wit my mask on?' which caused me to lose it and the Judge ordered me to leave his courtroom for guffawing too loud. Took the jury about 20 minutes to return a guilty verdict – would have not taken nearly that long, but they had a box of Crispy Cream Donuts they needed to dispose of in the jury room."

DEA AGENT, FBI AGENT, CIA ??? , CURRENTLY MIA

"An Irishman right off the boat, robbed several banks in town, always with the same demand, that the teller give him all of her money (always robbed females) or he would knock them out of their knickers – none had any idea what a knickers was, but complied nevertheless.

On a Friday night, I got a call from a DEA buddy (I had DEA liaison and was talking to this particular Agent into coming into the FBI as he always wanted to become an FBI Special Agent)who said his snitch had identified the suspect. He was holed up in a flea bag downtown hotel. I called the office's BR Guru and found that he was holding a winning hand in his regular Friday night poker game and didn't have much faith in whatever a DEA Agent said and told me to do whatever I thought was right.

The DEA Agent and I went to the bar in the hotel, talked to the snitch, found out that the suspect had ordered a sandwich to be delivered to his room and I pretended to be delivering it to gain access, find his loot and make the arrest.

(The DEA Agent was my good friend, Bob Levinson, currently MIA in Iran or ??? May God bless him. BRING BOB HOME!"

WRONG BUILDING, RIGHT BANK, OR VICE VERSA

"In a Bucar near downtown one day, the call came in on a BR alarm. Being new and excited that I was close to the bank, I illegally parked in front of the bank building. I rushed into the large lobby, fortunately not with a gun drawn. I looked around and did not see any unusual activity. However, there was an unarmed uniformed guard in the lobby. Asking about the robbery, I was informed there was no bank in this building. The real bank was a block down the street.

With my tail between my legs, I stole out of the building just in time to hear when getting into my car that the robbery alarm had been false.

Although a first office Agent, being of sound mind and thin skin, I never told the other Agents in the office of this."

C'EST LA VIE

"I was a brand new FBI Special Agent in an RA, and was checking records at the PD when a call came in about a bank robbery. The bank was a short distance away and I arrived just before a 'senior' Agent. 'I'll take the victim teller, you take the witnesses', he said.

The first woman I interviewed said she knew who the robber was and gave me his name and address. Other responding Agents were diverted to his residence and arrived in time to observe him drive his car into a tree and stumble out of his car, spilling the loot.

The man pleaded guilty. The 'senior' Agent got the stat. I got nothing."

OUTTAKE . . .

YOU KNOW THAT YOU ARE TOO DRUNK WHEN…
(Author unknown)

1. "You lose arguments with inanimate objects.
2. You have to hold unto the lawn to keep from falling off the earth.
3. Job interfering with your drinking.
4. Your doctor finds traces of blood in your alcohol stream.
5. Career won't progress beyond Senator from State of ______________.
6. The back of your head keeps getting hit by the toilet seat.
7. Sincerely believe alcohol to be an elusive 5th food group.
8. 24 hours in a day, 24 beers in a case – coincidence?? – I think not!
9. Two hands and just one mouth…now, that's a drinking problem.
10. You can focus better with one eye closed.
11. The parking lot seems to have moved while you were in the bar.
12. You fall off the floor.
13. Your twin sons are named Barley and Hops.
14. Hey, 5 beers are just as many calories as a burger, screw dinner.
15. Mosquitoes catch a buzz after attacking you.
16. At AA meetings you begin: "Hi, my name is…uh…"

17. Your idea of cutting back is less salt.
18. You wake up in the bedroom, your underwear is in the bathroom, you fell asleep clothed, - hmm.
19. The whole bar says 'Hi' when you come in.
20. You think the four basic food groups are caffeine, nicotine, alcohol, and (women or men).
21. Every night you're beginning to find your roommate's cat more and more attractive.
22. Roseanne looks good.
23. Don't recognize wife unless seen through bottom of glass.
24. That damned pink elephant followed me home again.
25. Everyone is drunk when you're funny.
26. The shrubbery is drunk from too frequent watering."

THE STORIES CONTINUE . . .

RECLAIMING THE LOOT

"A bank robbery in the inner city, a few days after city firefighters were fired upon when responding to a call in the area. The mood in the area was tense, nevertheless, a neighborhood investigation had to be conducted. A helpful resident advised that about half hour earlier she observed an unknown male jump from a stopped car less than a block away. He ran up the driveway to a garage behind the house and immediately returned to the car and drove away.

The cooperative lady's son came walking up the street as she was being interviewed. He resembled the description of the robber obtained at the scene. He was taken to the bank for possible identification.

As we were trying to placate this helpful lady, she suddenly exclaimed: "There he is now." She pointed up the street, and lo' and behold, the fellow returned to claim his loot and was jumping into a car that sped away. A high speed chase ensued with several Bucars in hot pursuit. The car was finally stopped and the occupants were arrested. Loot was recovered. A good day for the good guys, thanks to a cooperating lady in the hood."

THE UNLUCKY BANK ROBBER MEETS THE "KEYSTONE KOPS"

"To get prepared for the Pan American Games, our division had a regional SWAT training. The bank robbery supervisor took advantage of the extra manpower to help out in catching a guy who had been robbing bank branches on Friday afternoons. The guy used same getaway car twice and then switched to another vehicle. The case Agent spotted the vehicle and we started to follow the car. Since my car did not resemble a typical Bucar, I ended up right behind him when he stopped for the red traffic light and observed the driver checking his rear view mirror. When the light turned green, the driver just sat there. So after a few seconds, I politely beeped the horn and he started up.

A mile or so later, he pulled into an office parking lot and I continued straight ahead. I made a U-turn and saw him removing the back license plate from his car. There was a branch bank on the first floor of this office building. He next drove out of the parking lot and cruised in a nearby subdivision, as the SWAT teams from three other Divisions set up in the parking lot of the office building. Office supervisor ordered us to let him rob the bank and then move in for an arrest.

Subject parked in front of the bank and went in. We decided to converge on him from every direction when he came out, and when he got to his car, two Agents from another Division crashed their cars into each other at the driveway they were supposed to block. I was coming in from that side also, but the robber saw the crash and with two guys each, in four-door sedans with black wall tires, I thought he had made them as cops, so I jumped the curb and headed for the robber. I figured I could crash into him, before I could stop and cover him with a shot-gun across my lap. When I didn't see a weapon, I didn't feel I could crash into him, so I pulled alongside his car, threw open the door and covered him with the 12 gauge loaded with deer slugs. He threw up his hands and I stepped out of the car, but I had forgotten to put the car in park, and it lurched forward.

I dropped into the seat, but the bump caused me to discharge the shotgun and the slug passed by his head and hit the limestone on the side of the building. People in the bank heard the shot and came out to find the 'robber' face down in a puddle of rain water.

He has gone into the entry where they had ATMs, waited a minute or so, and he had come out to get his robbery demand note, which was sitting on the front seat of his car. Oops! He hadn't robbed this bank yet, but he was the guy in the previous robbery surveillance pictures, so he was arrested.

The next day, the newspapers had the story how the FBI

had caught this robber, before he could even rob the bank, and nobody ever said a word about the plan that we had, to let him rob the bank and then take him down. No mention was made of the scar on the limestone wall, made by my slug. Turns out the guy had a gambling problem and was robbing the banks so he could get cash to gamble in Las Vegas."

I'D RATHER BE LUCKY THAN GOOD

"I was a new Agent in 1985 and had the title of 'Bank Robbery Coordinator'. I later realized that every new Agent was given that title in our Division. So much for titles!

We had a series of BR's in the area and it looked as if the same guy was pulling them off. He was wearing us out for a couple of months.

One day, we get a call to respond to a 91 New. I hooked up with the city detective and started the process. While en route, we were told that the state police were in pursuit of a suspect. In the bank, we were told that the state police had a suspect in custody. The detective and I went to the victim teller to ask if she could recognize the subject if she saw him again, thinking of doing a show up.

Between sobs into a tissue, the teller replied: 'Yes, it was my cousin.' I looked at the detective and said: 'I think we got this one solved.' The perp later copped to all the BR's."

ASK THE RIGHT QUESTION

"My BR story involves a serial center-city robber who had robbed 5 or 6 banks in the heart of the city. The cases were all assigned to me, and while we knew that the same guy had committed all of the robberies, we couldn't come up with a name.

A radio call goes out about a new 91 in the center-city, and the description sounds identical to my UNSUB. I rolled up to the bank and asked the Agent handling the scene if I could show the victim teller the surveillance photos from the previous robberies, to see if it was 'my guy'. He said to go ahead, so I sit down with the teller and tell her I'm going to show her some photos of another bank robbery in progress, and I need to know if it is the same guy who just robbed her. So I showed her several photos, all very good quality, and waited for her answer.

She looks at all of them very carefully, and then says, 'No, that's not the guy who just robbed me.'

Disappointed, I thanked her for her effort and started walking slowly toward the front door. As I was about to exit, she called out to me from the back of the bank, 'But I know who that guy is in your photos.' I whirled around and ran back to her and said, 'You know this guy in the photos?' 'Yes, we went to school together,' and she proceeds to give me his name and last address. Turned out to be my UNSUB, and we had him in custody within hours.

When I asked her why she hadn't given me his name when I initially showed her the photos, her response was classic: 'You never asked me if I knew him, only if he was the one who robbed me, and he wasn't. If you wanted his name, you should have asked for it.'

Lesson learned, and I used it frequently when I would instruct on 'Interviewing Techniques' at police schools."

PERPS AND FBI SPECIAL AGENTS USE SAME BANKS

"How about the old story about the bright bank robber who decided to rob the bank near the FBI office on pay day Friday morning, when there were about 50 Agents in the bank cashing their checks.

It had to be a story from the days of yore, when paychecks were handed out in the office and did not get direct deposited in the accounts!"

PERP IN A WHEELCHAIR

"A probation violation subject had been convicted in an armed BR and because he had tried to shoot it out with the arresting officers, he lost the battle and was shot a couple of times and after coming out of the hospital, he was tried and convicted. Because one of the shots he took severed his spinal cord, he was confined to a wheelchair and had a number of other medical issues. He was not sent off to prison, but was put on parole.

Being the kind of guy he was, he soon violated his parole. As the result of being convicted of an armed robbery, he was considered to be A&D. We found the guy with no problem and put him under arrest. Here is where the real problems began.

The frisk for weapons was interesting because of the wheelchair situation and also because of the colostomy bag he was wearing as well as the other medical accoutrements he required. Putting him in the back seat of the Bucar for transport and figuring out where to stow his wheelchair added to the problems. He was completely immobile from the waist down. We were happy to turn the guy over to the US Marshalls."

A LEGAL DISCLAIMER
(Also known in Bu parlance as CYA)

(Author unknown)

"NOTICE: This note, message, letter, teletype, e-mail,

etc. and all its attachments are CONFIDENTIAL and intended solely for the recipients, as identified in the 'TO', 'CC' and 'BCC' lines of this communication. If you are not the intended recipient, and do not know why you should be the receiver, or care to be a receiver, your receipt of this communication and its attachments is the result of an inadvertent disclosure or unauthorized transmittal.

Sender reserves and asserts all rights to confidentiality, including all privileges which may or could apply, in the past, the present or in the future. Pursuant to these and those rights, and privileges, immediately DELETE and DESTROY all copies of the communication and its attachments, in whatever form, and immediately NOTIFY the sender of your receipt of this communication. Under the penalty of death, DO NOT REVIEW, COPY, OR RELY ON, in any way, the contents of this communication and its attachments."

The stories continue . . .

THREE LIMBS NEEDED TO ROB A BANK

"A small town bank is robbed by a W/M who entered the bank with a 32 Cal revolver. To show everybody that he really meant business, he made a big deal of pulling back the hammer on the revolver. After a couple of minutes, he is ready to make his getaway, a cocked revolver in his right hand, a bag of cash in his left. The bank is in an old building, which requires turning a door knob to open the door. The witnesses all remarked how he stood at the door a rather long time considering the situation – both hands were full of required items, the revolver and the cash and no third limb to open the door.

He looked back and forth between the right and left hands several times and then made his decision – stick the revolver in his pants and use the right hand to open the door, while holding the loot in his left hand. You can all guess what happened – BOOM – as the revolver was inserted into his pants."

THE WRONG WAY 91

"This incident happened at a small mobile home bank on a big oval lake, many miles in diameter. A state highway runs close by, on a sort of causeway, miles long.

The guy holds up a bank and gets into his car and heads the wrong way…into waiting arms of several sheriff's deputies waiting for him at the end of the causeway."

THE GOOD OLD TIMES

"Back in the 1970's, one January we had 20 days that the banks were open and 24 bank robberies, all of the armed variety of course. I recall one State Trooper dead, one bank teller dead and a couple of dead hostages, as well as several wounded victims, so it was certainly not all fun and games with these folks."

THE CRAZY BANK ROBBER

"A bank robber was sent to Leavenworth for 20 years and after doing 20 years he came back to the same town and robbed the same bank again - and again in a few days. Having had enough, the banker who was robbed tackled him in the middle of the street and sat on him until the PD arrived.

At trial, the robber invoked the insanity defense, arguing that only a crazy man would rob the same bank three times."

THE BOTTOMLESS BAG

"I was covering another lead when a 91 alert came over the radio, so I responded and was # 3 guy at the bank. The first thing we did, we watched the security camera tapes of the robbery. This was in the day when cameras were just beginning to come into use.

The cameras showed the action one frame at a time, so it took a while for the tape to play after which we interviewed the bank employees. One of the cameras focused on one of the perps who vaulted over the counter (no bullet proof glass protection for tellers back then) and, holding a large plastic garbage bag, instructed the teller, as I learned later, to dump the contents of her freshly filled cash drawer into the bag.

She did so, topping off her 'contribution' to the BR loot by forcefully dropping it into the bag which promptly split open, scattering the cash, currency and coins, across the floor of the teller's work area. The look of surprise on the robber's face was worthy of 'America's Funniest Home Videos'. He kept looking up and down into the bottomless bag until he threw it down in frustration and walked out in frustration.

After watching the silent tape, I interviewed the teller, a sweet young thing who was obviously working on her first grownup job. She said she's been instructed by bank security to cooperate fully with perps if she was ever the unwilling victim of a 91, but the perp's conduct when he threw the bag at her 'pi..ed' her off so badly that she had to do something suitable in response.

According to the young woman, the robber instructed her: 'Put everything in the bag, b..ch and be quick about it." She asked, 'Everything?' His language became even coarser as he repeated, 'Now!' So she followed his orders to the letter and forcefully propelled all of her rolled coins, probably ten to fifteen pounds, into the bag at which time the bottom of the bag exploded, scattering cash and coins all over the floor.

I asked her why she did that. Her reply has stuck with me after all these years. 'I just dumped my boyfriend for talking to me like that and I wasn't going to put up with that kind of sh.t from some foul mouthed thief.'

And to think, they use to pay us for moments like that." (The author of above story was at one time my partner. He died as a relatively young man. RIP)

HOW DUMB CAN YOU BE?

"It has been fun reviewing the misfortunes and adventures of the lesser qualified mopes plying the bank robbery craft. So far, I have been unable to detect any geographical pattern to the ineptitude, but will let you be the judge.

In the NW coast area, circa 1968-69, a group of five or six robbers had hit us for multiple robberies, causing great confusion by their interchange of personnel and disguises. After apprehending one of the group, he agreed to identify everyone in each robbery, but himself. To get around his reticence, I agreed that he could remain anonymous and simply refer to himself as the unknown person, whenever we came to a robbery in which he was a participant. He bit, hook, line and sinker."

THE DEPOSIT SLIP CAPER

"This particular branch of a large bank was robbed at least once a week, whether it needed it or not. One robber was sent in to case the bank prior to arrival of his takeover crew. Becoming nervous, he filled out a deposit slip with fully identifying information about himself and dropped it into the waste basket. Big mistake at trial."

A CONSULTANT

"This particular robber sometimes robber two or three banks a day, continuing until he was caught and sent to the state mental hospital. There it would be determined that at the time of the robberies he was not competent, but was now competent after medication and could be released. The pattern would then repeat itself.

After completion of one such cycle, he showed up at the office to collect property that had been seized from him. The case Agent, a legend in the office, in his inimitable sarcastic voice, said to him, 'Bank robbery doesn't seem to be working out for you, so and so, what are you going to do now'? Drawing himself up with feigned indignation, the guy said without missing a beat, 'I'm going to become a consultant for the bank', leaving the Agent sputtering as he walked out the door."

SAVED BY THE SHOES

"The 70's were the times of double knit suits and platform shoes. One robber fled from the scene, but was run down by my partner. He told the robber that he intended to shoot him, but each time he tried to take aim, his platform shoes caused him to lose his balance and spoil his aim."

THE PRACTICAL JOKE

"While working with the local PD one night in looking for the bank robber, one of the detectives I was working with narrowly missed running over a man standing on the shoulder of the road. The detective was embarrassed, shook his fist and cursed the poor fellow before driving on.

We caught the robber (not the same guy) the next day and after getting a confession, talked him into being part of a practical joke on the detective, by claiming that he had attempted to surrender the night before, but some idiot police officer had nearly run over him, then shook his fist and cursed at him. The detective fell for it and we had great fun at his expense for the next few days as he went around trying to explain himself before everyone heard the true story."

IF NOAH WAS BUILDING AN ARK TODAY
(Author unknown)

"In the year 2014, the Lord came unto Noah, who was now living in the United States, and said: 'Once again. The earth has become wicked and overpopulated and I see the end of the flesh before me. Build another Ark and save two of every living thing along with a few humans.'

He gave Noah the blueprint, saying, 'You have six months to build the Ark before I start the unending rain for 40 days and 40 nights.'

Six months later, the Lord looked down and saw Noah weeping in his yard...but no Ark. 'Noah,' He roared, 'I'm about to start the rain! Where is the Ark ?'

'Forgive me, Lord,' begged Noah. 'But things have changed. I needed a building permit. I've been arguing with the inspector about the need for a sprinkler system. My neighbors claim that I've violated the neighborhood zoning laws by building the Ark in my yard and exceeding the height limitation. We had to go to the Development Appeal Board for a decision. Then the Department of Transportation demanded a bond be posted for the future costs of moving power lines and other overhead obstructions, to clear the passage for the Ark's move to the sea.

I argued that the sea would be coming to us, but they would hear nothing of it.

Getting the wood was another problem. There's a ban on cutting local trees in order to save the spotted owl. I tried to convince the environmentalists that I needed the wood to save the owls, but no go.

When I started gathering the animals, I got sued by an Animal Rights Group. They insisted that I was confining wild animals against their will. As well, they argued the accommodation was too restrictive and it was cruel and inhumane to put so many animals in a confined space.

Then, the EPA ruled that I couldn't build the Ark until they'd conducted an environmental impact study on your

proposed flood. I'm still trying to resolve a complaint with the Human Rights Commission on how many minorities I'm supposed to hire for my building crew.

Also, the trades unions say that I can't use my sons to work on the job. They insist I have to hire only Union workers with Ark building experience.

To make matters worse, the IRS seized all my assets, claiming I'm trying to leave the country illegally with endangered species.

Also, a newly enacted law called Obama Care, something or other, that I have no idea how it operates, has been sending me text messages to get every person and every animal that I am taking along, insured while they are still in the U.S. waters.

So, forgive me, Lord, but it would take at least ten years for me to finish the Ark.'

Suddenly the skies cleared, the sun began to shine, and a rainbow stretched across the sky.

Noah looked up in wonder and asked, 'You mean, you're not going to destroy the world?'

'No,' said the Lord. 'The government beat me to it.' "

The stories continue . . .

CASES THEN AND NOW

"One of the joys of working BR's and other cases in the violent crime arena were the stories that we have been interchanging, not to mention the ones of a more serious nature. These cases gave us our investigative and interrogation skills, informant base and contacts with local law enforcement.

The current Bureau is made up of young people, with remarkable backgrounds. But in my view, their work has shorted them in their skill set with an over emphasis on certain current priorities. It is well, good and important to gather intelligence and foil plots, but it is also nice to know how to conduct interview, file a complaint, testify in court, make an arrest and find the police department. There has to be a happy medium."

(Drinking coffee with fellow Special Agents and having a drink after work gives you a better feel for those you are working with, developing closer relationship with people that may have to save your life someday. Computers in use today are impersonal. Breaking bread together with friends helps in all facets of your career.)

WE ARE THE FBI

"Towards the end of my career, I was assigned to what was back then a 3 Agent RA (1 general criminal, 1 terrorism and 1 FCI). One Friday afternoon, we received a call at the RA about a bank robbery at a local bank. We responded to the scene and began the investigation by interviewing the branch manager.

During the interview, branch manager mentioned she could swear the black male who robbed the branch had also robbed the same branch ten years earlier, when she was a teller at the same branch. She advised that 'I think I saw him sitting out front yesterday and the day before.'

While we continued, I asked one of the local detectives to possibly pull up the ID of the subject who robbed the bank 10 years ago or so. 30 minutes later we had the ID, address and photo. The subject had just been released from state prison + or – 30 days prior. The three of us looked at each other and said: 'What the hell…', so we drove to the address and there he was.

After interviewing him for a while, the other Agent asked if he minded if we looked around.. Subject said 'No…you'll find what you are looking for in a box top of the closet.'

I then mirandized him and sure enough, there was a box of money located in the closet. Subject executed the Miranda form and after providing a full signed statement, asked a simple question. 'How you guys find me so fast?' I simply smiled and said: 'We're the FBI'.

At the end of every interview, I always made it a habit to ask if the subjects wanted to tell me anything else. Subject responded: 'Want me to tell you about the ______________?' I responded…'I was going to get to that now so why don't you tell me.' Long story short, during two evenings prior to the BR, he robbed two stores within two blocks of each other. One night his face was painted white, the next night, his face was black. He advised he used the same weapon to rob all three places. He also told us where to find the weapon in his apartment.

Having a long rap sheet we got creative in prosecuting this subject. We charged him with bank robbery, use of weapon, possession of a weapon by a convicted felon, and here's the kicker: Hobbs Act violations.

The Hobbs Act theory was this. The robberies he committed had an actual effect on interstate commerce when the local CSI unit had to close both convenience stores for hours in order to process the scene after both robberies. We had to obtain each bill of lading, for each delivery, from each warehouse, to prove that most of the products on the shelves came from warehouses out of state. We did. Judge asked if we are sure that we want to pursue this. Yes, and in the trial, we proved all counts.

Subject was sentenced on each count to a total sentence of something like 500 months in the FCI. Won't see him no more!"

A CLEVER SPECIAL AGENT

"As the old TV show said, 'There are a million stories like this in the city.' One day, I was only a few blocks from the victim bank when the alarm came in, so I headed to the bank and was only beaten there by a local cop. He told me about the robbery and that the robber left a note on the counter. He also said that he did not touch the note because of fear he would ruin the fingerprints.

I noticed that the note was written on one of the old IBM computer cards, so I did something really clever. I turned it over. It was a telephone bill with a name and address on it, only two blocks from the bank.

We then did something else very clever. We called the PD records section and found out he had a record for robbery. This is where it gets really clever, we went to the house. The subject was at the kitchen table, still counting the money and asked the inevitable question: 'How did you get me so fast?' I told him that we were the FBI and knew everything.

Thank God they were not the brightest people, but they were fun cases."

NICE LITTLE GUY

"Three weeks out of the FBI Academy, I was the senior agent of two of us sent to a homeless shelter with a mug shot to see if a fellow suspected in a 91-New might be staying there. We were told it was a long shot lead. As my partner tried to interview the bums hanging around the place, I talked to the desk man, who told us that so and so in the mug shot was indeed staying upstairs and he was there now. I got on the phone to the BR coordinator, who told me to put on a discrete surveillance on the man until a more probable cause could be developed. Other Special Agents were en route to the bank to show the mug shot to the victim teller.

As I was getting those instructions, behind me somebody said loudly, 'I hear somebody been asking about me,' and turned to find my partner with his brand new S&W Model 10 revolver trained on the man. The gun was shaking pretty badly as he ordered the man against the wall.

So much for our discrete surveillance. It turns out that my partner had learned from the denizens of the place that the man in the mug shot had robbed the bank that morning, had been drinking heavily and doing drugs all day, was armed with a .357

magnum and had vowed never to be taken alive again. Of course, I knew nothing of this.

The man was a picture of non-compliance. He said something like, 'M…..F…….., I'm going to take that gun and shove it up where the sun doesn't shine', and started to move toward my partner. Vision of headlines about FBI rookies gunning down an unarmed homeless black man in a skid row mission flashed through my mind, and indeed, he did not seem to have a weapon within his reach.

So I grabbed him. Now the perp was short, about 5'6", but went about 250, all of it muscle. I held an arm and gave him a quick frisk, then told my partner to put his gun away (before he shot me), and grab the other arm. It turned out that the man was so screwed up on drugs, that he couldn't really fight, but so strong that we could not do much with him. We just held on to his arms while he swung us around like two sacks of potatoes. I yelled out the office number, and asked the deskman to call for help. I tried out some of my best, brand new Gump-trained (SA Gump was a legendary instructor at the FBI Academy)defensive tactics moves, and nothing had the least effect on the man who was literally feeling no pain. A crowd of about thirty homeless guys gathered and was picking their favorites. I think the betting was going heavily against us. For lack of anything better to do, I just kept giving the man his Miranda Rights, as the man kept swinging us around, but he could not break free.

After what seemed like hours (actually about four minutes), three more agents arrived. That helped slightly. It took one agent choking the man, with two of us holding each arm, to get him handcuffed. But the man had only begun to fight. He was not slowed down much. He was still swinging the five of us around. We kicked his knees out and got him on the ground, but even then he kept on getting up repeatedly, and continued trying to kick and head-butt us.

By then, it seemed like half of our office and half of the local police office, showed up. It took a couple of rough motorcycle cops to soften him up a bit, and finally two veteran Agents transported him, carrying him entirely off the ground by the handcuffs, with him screaming, kicking and spitting all the way to the Marshal's office. I was told the same two Agents had to hold him in reverse wrist-locks, while the Marshals cut all of his clothes off to search him. We never did find the .357 he was supposed to have.

Those that knew him said that once the drugs and alcohol were off, he was the nicest, and meekest of men. He was convicted of the BR, but the AUSA declined on other charges in part because she did not think a jury would believe such a nice little guy could have given a couple of FBI Special Agents such a hard time. I guess nobody considered that he had a local conviction for assault with intent to murder a police officer six months previously."

OLD SAYINGS WITH NEW MEANINGS
(Authors unknown)

- **"Anywhere you hang your @ is home.**
- **The e-mail of the species is deadlier than the mail.**
- **A journey of a thousand sites begins with a single click.**
- **You can't teach a new mouse old clicks.**

- **Great groups from little icons grow.**
- **Speak softly and carry a cellular phone.**
- **C:\ is the root of all directories.**
- **Don't put all your hypes in one home page.**
- **Pentium wise; pen and paper foolish.**
- **The modem is the message.**
- **Too many clicks spoil the browse.**
- **The geek shall inherit the earth.**
- **A chat has nine lives.**
- **Don't byte off more than you can view.**
- **Fax is stranger than fiction.**
- **What boots up must come down.**
- **Windows will never cease.**
- **In Gates we trust…and our tender is legal.**
- **Virtual reality is its own reward.**
- **Modulation in all things.**
- **A user and his leisure time are soon parted.**
- **There's no place like**

(http://www.)home(.com).

- **Know what to expect before you connect.**

- **Oh, what a tangled website we weave when first we practice.**

- **Speed thrills.**

- **Give a man a fish and you feed him for a day; teach him to use the Net and he won't bother you for weeks."**

The stories continue . . .

SOMETIMES YOU GET LUCKY

"Bank robbery is completed and the lone robber allegedly leaves in a taxi. A ring-a-round-ring of heavies and rubber gun SAs responds and a meeting is held in the parking lot, setting out leads. I let the coordinator know that I am going to the downtown area where I'll catch the perpetrator. The somewhat smart-ass Special Agent, considered one of the heavies, who was an attorney and the BR coordinator, made an expletive deleted remark in response to my remark of going to the downtown area. I was a rubber gun agent, of course.

Upon arriving in the downtown area ten minutes later, I headed on foot to the nicest enclosed shopping area, where I inquired of rent-a-cop where a young black male looking to buy an expensive suit would shop. I was pointed to a men's store fifty yards away. There I asked the first salesman whether any young black males shopped within the last thirty minutes and bought a whole new outfit. The response was instant and affirmative. A young Afro-American male, bought a complete suit, shirt, tie, and shoes and paid in cash, wearing the new outfit as he exited the store five minutes ago, and had the old clothes and old tennis shoes packed in a bag, to take with him. Salesman also noted that the male asked regarding where the shoe shine parlor was located. (Definitely a clue to where the young man is now)

By now, two other Agents, who were not needed at the bank, followed me to the shopping center, and entered the store that I was just exiting. The three of us hurried to the shoe shine stand and voila!...the man of the hour was there, getting his shoes shined. A quick arrest followed. His old outfit was still in the bag next to him. The new suit was not needed for where he was heading. A BR stat for the rubber gun Special Agent. Just a lucky day!"

WORST DAY OF MY BUREAU CAREER WITH TOP TEN FUGITIVE BANK ROBBER

"I was assigned to a one man Legat and received a teletype that a top ten fugitive bank robber was reportedly seen in the country where I was a Legat. A TV program reportedly showed the episode that featured the subject and an individual viewer who saw he program had called in and stated that she saw the subject. It took a few back and forth teletypes to narrow the area of search in a mountainous area 6-7 hour drive from my office.

The subject was part of a famous bank robbery gangs from Canada who robbed over 100 banks in the U.S. and who had already escaped from jail twice. The country's national police, patterned after the FBI, indicated that they had located the subject in an area.

Since it was a 6-7 hour drive, I decided to leave early in the morning and if all went well, we could locate and arrest the subject that afternoon. I headed to the area in a Bureau vehicle, which was heavily armored, thus we named it the War Wagon. I was about an hour outside my office area when on a rainy night, on a winding road, I had a flat tire. With help of some friendly local natives, I was back on the road in an hour and arrived at the local office of the host country by 2 pm. By now, they identified the house in a plush gated community where the subject and his new wife were supposed to reside. With a team of 13 host country agents we hit the house at 4 pm.

The only person home was the young wife who indicated that her husband had just left the night before and that he often did this and never told her where he was going. She had absolutely no idea of his past background and that when he was away, she was given a bank card that she used twice a month and took whatever amount of money would come out of the bank machine.

That night, I checked into a local hotel and had a few extra scotch and waters wondering how I could have done this differently since I knew there were going to be a lot of unhappy FBI agents in the U.S. city where the BR occurred and at the FBIHQ. The next two days, we interviewed everybody in the area that subject knew, which were mostly older Ex Pats British or American living in the area. Subject belonged to a bridge group and one time, when they were talking about all the kidnappings, subject opened the heal of his shoe and showed them a small roll of one hundred dollar bills and two master keys for opening handcuffs and doors which he indicated he could use if kidnapped. Nothing much further pertinent was developed, except for obtaining a current photo and aka's of the subject and information developed by the banker who indicated that he had opened an account with several millions in local currency in it and that subject's wife used this to live on the interest of this account when he traveled.

A few weeks later, the case agent where the crime occurred was just ready to leave for my location when the subject was apprehended while robbing a rural bank in the Southern area of the U.S.

A very alert small time police chief had just received a bomb threat at the edge of town and he remembered that the last time a bank was robbed 10 years ago, someone robbed a bank at the other end of town, so he dispatched his men to all the banks in town and that's how the subject was captured. The subject did have master keys and money hidden in the heal of his shoe. During his interview it was determined that after robbing banks in the U.S., he would package up the money and mail it to himself or a friend in the military at the U.S. military post office at the local air base in the country. He also indicated that the reason he took off quickly from the overseas country was because a neighbor's wife told his wife that the police were asking questions about him. While I feel somewhat vindicated, it was still not a good day.

A write-up in the paper noted that the subject was the most likeable bank robber of our time. He was diagnosed with lung cancer and died in the prison hospital at the age of 64."

MY FRIEND… A BANK ROBBER

"We were called to a 91 at bank in the town where I resided. The victim teller advised that the robber, a W/M, displayed a weapon and was given approximately $ 4000 cash. She described him running to a car in the parking lot and he couldn't get into the car, then he ran to a nearby apartment complex.

Upon arrival at the bank, I observed the car that was being examined by the locals. For some reason, the car appeared familiar to me, and upon further examination, it appeared to be a vehicle driven by one of my softball teammates. The registration proved me correct. In fact, my teammate was a Uniformed Secret Service guard at the White House. A call to the White House revealed that he did not report to work that day. An examination of the surveillance film confirmed it was him wearing our softball jersey and hat from the local 'gin mill' who was our sponsor.

To make a long story short, when we finally reached him he confessed to the robbery. The biggest problem was that before we could get our hands on him, he showed up at the White House and used funds from the BR to pay off his gambling debts to his fellow Secret Service colleagues. Efforts were then made to collect these funds from the Secret Service employees.

The following day, this incident appeared on the front page of the Washington Post, with President Reagan chiming in. Sometime later on, I was called to testify at his sentencing. Never had a friend rob a bank before."

BULLET DOES NOT CATCH A BANK ROBBER

"A serial bank robber was hitting a certain area of the city. After his pattern of times and banks was established, we staked out a number of banks one day. Don't recall an exact number, but about 20 as I recall. We worked as twos, with my partner being a metro police detective. We sat in my Bucar in a parking lot across the street and just down the street from a bank assigned to us. Mixed in with other cars, we figured our car would not stand out. It was an older bank located on a corner. We could see the main entrance and the side entrance.

Not wanting to create a situation in the bank should it be robbed, I talked to the bank manager, showing him pictures of the robber. I suggested the manager just get up and walk out of the bank if he saw the robber enter the bank. His leaving the bank would alert us that the robber was there, and we would take action when he left.

Surprise! After a while, the manager walked out the corner entrance, looking around. Why we drove over to him instead of exiting the car and running over, I don't know. But it was a good thing I did, because the manager must have been so excited to follow my instructions that he spooked the robber. When we pulled up to the curb, the manager pointed down the other street from where we had been parked. As fortune would have it, just as he leaned into the car and pointed down the street, the robber turned and looked back. He immediately took off running, with already a half block lead.

No problem, I thought. We've got the car. Speeding down the street, we were almost up to the robber, when he ran into a small neighborhood laundry cleaners. Skidding to a stop, we followed on foot. In the store, the female employee just pointed and said 'he went out the back.' The back, it turned out, bordered one of the famous river concrete channels so many times seen on TV. An 8-foot chain link fence separated us from the river and the robber.

We could see him running on the other side of the fence. The detective decided to fire off a round, which only made the robber run faster. Glad it was the detective and not me – no memos to write.

Now the geographical mistake part. The dumb robber picked the only bank which was located two blocks from the sheriff's office substation. And the dummy picked the time to rob the bank when there was a shift change. With a quick radio call, we had two shifts of eager sheriff's deputies in hot pursuit. Needless to say, another stat was quickly claimed."

"FIELD OFFICE JOB DESCRIPTIONS
(Author unknown)

Special Agent:
Able to leap tall buildings in a single bound.
More powerful than a locomotive.
Faster than a speeding bullet.
Walks on water.
Makes policy with God.

Field Supervisor:
Able to leap short buildings in a single bound.
As powerful as a switch engine.
Just as fast as a speeding bullet.
Walks on water if the sea is calm.
Talks with God.

ASAC:
Leaps short buildings with a running start.
Almost as powerful as a switch engine.
Faster than a speeding BB.
Walks on water if he knows where the stumps are.
Is occasionally addressed by God.

SAC:
Runs into small buildings.
Recognizes locomotives 2 out of 3 times.
Uses a squirt gun.
Knows how to use the water fountain.
Mumbles to himself.

SAC'S SECRETARY:
Lifts buildings to walk under them.
Kicks locomotives off the track.
Catches speeding bullets in her teeth.
Freezes water with a single glance.
When God speaks she says: 'Who is calling, please?' "

Stories continue . . .

FIRE ANTS

" Before I came into the Bureau, I was fortunate to have a mentor and benefactor as I grew up. He was an old country lawyer who was a central city icon. He told me, as we smoked our pipes on his back porch, looking over his cornfields, that as someone who spent time in the hills and forests, as opposed to someone raised in the city, I would be able to 'make it' in the big city where I had just been transferred, just as I could in the country. He suggested that the opposite was not necessarily true. I didn't really appreciate his insight until ten years later. (Hank Jr. later sang this very truism).

The night when with a search warrant our office brought a back-hoe into the woods behind the corn field where the bad guy buried the M-16, we were joined by three of the East Coast finest, including one female, whose names shall be protected. All were cautioned about local dangers of critters and farm life.

The moment of the investigative victory was delicious, but punctuated shortly thereafter by the shrieks of a not-to-be-named East Coast Special Agent, who celebrated the recovery by a rare rendition of the truly southern 'fire-ant strip tease' dance, a dance where modesty never gets in the way of survival (because that is how it feels), until the miniscule rascals (fire ants) – whose reputation for veraciousness far out strip the metal of Tybee Island gnats (those millimeter long bugs with teeth 5 centimeters long) – are brushed off, stomped on and eradicated from one's body and clothing…whipping also comes to mind…

And that is why Agents in Southern __________ carried extra clothes in their Bucars…(how I learned that lesson is a story for another day – and I didn't say anything about snakes!

PS: The Agent, not to be named, was kind and generous enough to send back the jump suit, socks, etc, cleaned and pressed, via BuMail, and some truly bad guys got some of what they richly deserved.

Just an indelible Bureau memory…"

FBI SPECIAL AGENT IN COSTUMES

"In the fall of 1975, my family was involved in 'little theatre' or 'community theater', 'amateur theatre', anyway. This was very popular in the city where I was assigned. I was involved in the play '1776'. Had a small part, as I have no singing voice. We had weeks of rehearsals, the traditional night before opening dress rehearsal and the opening night/cast party was scheduled for next evening.

Yes, my fellow SAs busted my hump for a couple of years while we did these plays. Some actually came to see them.

The afternoon of opening night, I'm on the far east side of town breaking in a new SA. The call comes in about a 91 new on the far west side of town, in the area where I lived and the play was performed. The word hostage is mentioned and it is about 3 pm.

So the two of us proceed to the west side of town. IT IS A HOSTAGE SITUATION. The bank is not far from home of the play's director. His daughter is in the crowd. I spot her and ask her to tell her dad that I will not be there for the opening night as my character, the Rev. J. Witherspoon, a delegate from New Jersey.

As time went on, there were about 150 Agents and cops on the scene. Finally, I got the nerve to tell the SA running the show at the bank of my dilemma re opening night. He said go and do the play and be back in the morning. So, I went to the theater, where the director was rehearsing my lines. His daughter had relayed my situation. After the performance, I called the office and was told to report to the scene in the AM. So, I went to the opening night cast party.

Showed up at the bank early the next am. It was about that time the robber, I believe a former FBI Top Ten fugitive, who had been released from prison, was ready to surrender. Well, don't you know who was part of the team to escort him out of the bank, but yours truly. The TV stations had just started 'live cam' or what we know now as on the scene broadcasting. So, here I am helping to walk him out of the bank, to my neighbors amazement. Had a hangover from the cast party the night before. But, was so young then. Only time I begged off an assignment, the thespian that I am."

(Meanwhile, yours truly was stuck at the bank all night, from the previous afternoon, freezing my buns off, and no cast party and drinks at this play and no leading of the robber out of the bank and live TV so that all of my neighbors would know I was one of the heavies.)

Comment from another Special Agent: "No one in the office would have said a thing or even known you were in community theater except you kept showing up to work in a costume…that Revolutionary War costume from '1776', complete with you trying to shove your musket in your Bu gun holster, was pretty funny, as that BR call came in…and let's not even go over the La Cage Aux Folles episode…we kept thinking you were going to fall off of those 6"heels as you ran out into the parking lot to jump into your Bu steed…and the little red Afro wig from your Annie appearance…priceless…"

CHAPTER 7

THIS - N – THAT

There were/are thousands of FBI Special Agents and it follows that there were/are thousands of stories, with thousands different personalities, characters and talents, yes, even pinheads, reflecting the society around us.

Here are more stories from the FBI Special Agents, with their copyrighted material, some of which has been published in magazines and books, and some of which is seeing their light of day for the first time, with permission granted by the authors.

The backgrounds of the authors in this chapter is as varied as the stories that they wrote. To find additional stories written by them, check their names on the Internet's search engines. ENJOY!

YOUTUBE BARD FERNANDO L. CANDELARIO

Retired ASAC Fernando L. Candelario 1972-2002, loves to compose songs, play guitar and sing. His wonderful renditions about fellow FBI Special Agents, his family, as well as ordinary people that he has met or knows about, can be found on YouTube and are easily searchable. Written below are words to one of his songs, a personal favorite of mine, that causes me to shed tears every time I play it on YouTube.

The Agent ©1991

"They've got a job, a job to do
They risk their lives for people like you.
They're out today, they're out tonight
While you and your loved ones enjoy your lives.

They live for us and they've died for us,
The men and the women, who fight for us.
They love their jobs and do it right,
At home their loved ones are wondering why.

A gun on the hip, handcuffs and badge,
They're taking a risk that others don't have.
A loved one at home is waiting again,
With the hope that their own will come home again.

Now next time you read that an Agent was killed,
Think of all the risks that you take, if you will.
When you get home to your loved one and your dinner is burned,
Think of the Agent who'll never return.

Now their jobs can be made easier then,
If you and your loved ones would help them defend,
All your rights and this system that we're all living in,
Then maybe the Agent will come home again."

FC's short bio: "I worked CT matters for many years and was involved extensively with the EPB-Macheteros investigation in Puerto Rico. I EOD'd as a clerk in 1972 and retired as an ASAC in 2002.

When I entered on duty as a clerk, Filiberto Ojeda Rios, leader of the Macheteros, was a fugitive since 1969. We found him in 1983, during a surveillance. We arrested him in 1985, in a huge roundup in PR. He escaped three years later and was a fugitive for another 15 years.

In 2005, when I was already retired, I was asked if I could identify a photo of an UNSUB who was under surveillance. I positively identified him as Filiberto. A few days later, Filiberto was killed in a shootout with HRT. End of an era. Filiberto was part of my life from 1972 until 2005. I was featured on The FBI Files in an episode called Rebellion in Paradise."

OUTTAKE . . .

THE BOSS
(Author unknown)

"When God first made the body, all the parts wanted to be boss.

The BRAIN said, 'Since I control everything and do all the thinking, I should be boss.'

The FEET said, 'Since I carry my body where he/she wants to go, and get him/her to do what the brain wants, I should be boss.'

The HANDS said, 'Since I must do all the work and carry all the money to keep the rest of you going, I should be boss.'

The EYES said, 'Since I must look and see for all of you and tell you where the danger lurks, I should be boss.'

And so it went, with the HEART, the EARS, the

LUNGS, and then the A&* spoke up, and demanded to be boss. All the other parts laughed at the idea of the A&* (aka 'A') being boss.

The 'A' was so angry that he blocked himself off and refused to function.

Soon the BRAIN became feverish; the EYES crossed and began to ache, the FEET were too weak to walk; the HANDS hung limply at the sides; the HEART and LUNGS struggled to keep going. They all pleaded with the BRAIN to let the 'A' be boss.

And so, it finally happened; all the other parts did all the work, and the 'A' just bossed and passed out a lot of gas.

The Moral: 'You don't have to be a BRAIN to be boss, just an 'A&*%*E.' "

The stories continue . . .

WAYNE A BARNES

FBI Special Agent 1971-2000

A TALENTED STORY TELLER AND WRITER

I am not sure whether Wayne was a talented story writer before he joined the FBI as a Special Agent, or if his talents came alive as a result of his daily output of memos, FD-302s, LHMs, airtels, nitels and teletypes.

One thing was for sure. When his Supervisor was an old-timer with initials DG, many of Wayne's long fictional masterpieces were returned to him bearing nasal mucus on the cover. The SSA plainly loved to pick his nose and deposit the residue on whatever was at hand, in this case, a multitude of Wayne's writings.

Wayne and I were on the same squad, one that was often called the tower of Babel, due to the confusion of voices, languages and sounds, as described in Genesis 11:1-9.

One of the most read FBI stories written by Barnes to date was The FBI Pizza Call.

Still other prose was written for each of his first two sons. In Wayne's words..."The first, Spies in the Woods, appeared in the December 1988 edition of The Investigator, (an FBI publication). After its publication, the folks at the FBI Tour Route saw it and asked permission to publish it. They printed 10,000 copies of it for the children who go through the special tour and get the packages of 'Say No To Drugs', DARE and McGruff handouts."

But, please do stay tuned. When Wayne finishes his long awaited true story spy book, it will definitely be a best seller.

The following stories were written and copyrighted by Wayne. With his permission, the stories are now part of this book.

"THE FBI PIZZA CALL"

Wayne A. Barnes © 08/27/1993

(From the raid at the Southwood Psychiatric Hospital, Chula Vista, Ca.)

"FBI Special Agents conducted a 'search and seizure' at the Southwood Psychiatric Hospital in San Diego which was under investigation for medical insurance fraud.

After hours of pouring over many rooms of medical records, some sixty FBI Agents worked up quite an appetite. The case agent in charge of the investigation called a local pizza parlor with delivery service to order a quick dinner for his colleagues. The following telephone conversation took place:

Agent: Hello. I would like to order nineteen large pizzas and sixty-seven cans of soda.
Pizza man: And where would you like them delivered?

Agent: To the Southwood Psychiatric Hospital.
Pizza man: To the Psychiatric Hospital?

Agent: That's right. I'm an FBI Agent.
Pizza man: You're an FBI Agent?

Agent: That's correct. Just about everybody here is.
Pizza man: And you're at the Psychiatric Hospital?

Agent: That's correct. And make sure you don't go through the front door. We have them locked. You'll have to go around to the back, to the service entrance, to deliver the pizzas.
Pizza man: And you say you're all FBI Agents?

Agent: That's right. How soon can you have them here?
Pizza man: And you're over at Southwood?

Agent: That's right. How soon can you have them here?
Pizza man: And everyone over at Southwood is an FBI Agent?

Agent: That's right. We've been here all day and we're starving.
Pizza man: How are you going to pay for this?

Agent: I have my check book right here.
Pizza man: And you are all FBI Agents?

Agent: That's right everyone here is an FBI Agent. Can you remember to bring the pizzas and sodas to the service entrance in the rear. We have the front doors locked.

Pizza man: I don't think so. (Click !)"

"A COMPLAINT CALL: GAMBLING IN THE COOLER"

Wayne A. Barnes © 04/17/1997

"Last Saturday, I was working the regular 4-midnight shift in the FBI office in San Diego. I took a call at about eleven in the evening from a man with a back-East, Baltimore-sounding accent, who said he wanted to report 'gambling going on.' Further, he thought there was a violation of the health code taking place at the same location.

I questioned whether we would be involved with the health code issue, but I told him I would take his information, especially about the gambling, and listened to his story.

He lives in the Hillcrest section of San Diego and recently left the Navy. He likes to go to one of those sporting grilles where you can watch many games at the same time on several TVs. However, he said he thinks only restaurant employees should be allowed back in the kitchen, and in the large walk-in cooler where the sodas, beer and other food stuffs are kept chilled.

At about nine o'clock, six men walked into the cooler where, the caller was emphatic, he did not think they should be. 'That is only for actual employees.' (He seemed like a real stickler for detail.)

What about the gambling? I insisted.
'Well,' he said, 'six men walked into the cooler, and about ten minutes later, when they came out, two of them were holding a fistful of dollars. Now I don't like it, but the only thing I can think of that they were doing in there is gambling. I just don't want that kind of thing happening in my neighborhood !'

I stifled my comments, wondering how long it would take him to figure it out, and told him I would give his information to the appropriate squad. I just didn't have the heart to tell this straight, former-Navy guy, that where he now lived, Hillcrest, is the gay section of San Diego."

THE FBI JEHOVAH'S WITNESS STORY
Wayne A. Barnes © 04/01/1997

"As part of a routine background investigation for an FBI applicant case, I was to interview several of the applicant's neighbors. He lived in Ramona, CA, a rural suburb of San Diego. The street where he lived was a long cul-de-sac with houses fifty yards apart and large lots, many with horses in the back.

Looking down the road, I saw a white compact car pull into

the first driveway where I planned to stop. Good, I thought, somebody's home. By the time I entered the driveway, two middle-aged ladies were just returning to their car.

'Good morning.' I began. 'Do you live here?'

'No,' one answered, 'We thought you did.'

'No,' I responded, ' I'm in the FBI, and I'm conducting a neighborhood investigation. Was anybody home?'

'No,' the lady said. 'We're Jehovah's Witnesses, and this is our regular route. We don't often find many people home.'

'Your regular route?' I inquired.

'Yes,' she said. 'We come by here every couple of months.'

'Well, good luck,' I said, and turned to walk down the driveway.

'The same to you,' she said and drove off.

I walked to the door and rang the bell. After a moment, I walked around to the back. You can never tell when someone may be outside who can't hear the doorbell ringing. I admired their two horses and petted a friendly calico cat, then returned to the front door. I left my standard 8 1/2" x 11" note, neatly folded, with the FBI seal on the letterhead and just a couple paragraphs indicating who I was, why I had stopped by, and requesting the resident call my office.

I drove to the next house, and the Jehovah's Witnesses were just leaving the driveway. They waved as we passed each other. I went through the same routine, rang the bell, checked around the back and left my note. This went on for the next several houses like clockwork.

Although I found no one to interview, I had left many notes, and was ready to return to my office.

As I passed one of the houses where I had left a note, a lady in rollers came running down the driveway. She was waving a sheet of paper in her hand, my sheet of paper, as it turned out. I pulled over.

'Are you the FBI agent?' she asked, a little out of breath.

I said I was, and she invited me inside. The interview was very cordial, and I finished my questions in about fifteen minutes. I was pleased to have found at least one person home.

'You know,' she said, 'I thought you were with them.'

'What do you mean?' I asked.

'Well, you know, you're wearing a blue suit, white shirt and tie,' she answered.

'I still don't understand,' I said.

'I thought you were with the Jehovah's Witnesses.'

I was a little surprised, but just smiled and shook my head.

'So,' she started anew, 'do you want me to call everybody else?'

'Everybody else?' I asked.

'Oh, everybody's home,' she laughed. 'We all thought you were with the Jehovah's Witnesses, so nobody answered their door. Do you want me to call them and tell them you're here? Then you can interview everybody!'

So, she did…and I did…"

OUTTAKE . . .

A SAD MESSAGE
(Author unknown)

"It is with the saddest heart that I must pass on the following news:

Please join me in remembering a great icon of the entertainment community. The Pillsbury Doughboy died yesterday of a yeast infection and complications from repeated pokes in the belly. He was 71.

Doughboy was buried in a lightly greased coffin. Dozens of celebrities turned out to pay their respects, including Mrs. Butterworth, Hungry Jack, the California Raisins, Betty Crocker, the Hostess Twinkies and Captain Crunch. The gravesite was piled high with flours.

Aunt Jemima delivered the eulogy and lovingly described Doughboy as a man who never knew how much he was kneaded. Doughboy rose quickly in show business, but his later life was filled with turnovers. He was not considered a very 'smart' cookie, wasting much of his dough on half-baked schemes. Despite being a little flaky at times, he still, as a crusty old man, was considered a role model for millions.

Doughboy is survived by his wife, Play Dough; two children, John Dough and Jane Dough, who has one in the oven. He is also survived by his elderly father, Pop Tart. The funeral was held at 3:50 for about 20 minutes."

(FBI used names John Doe and Jane Doe as names for wanted criminals, until their true names were identified.)

The stories continue . . .

DOPEY THINGS CRIMINALS SAID OR DID

© Mickey Mahoney 2004

By Michael J. Mahoney (1971-2004)

"After I retired in 2004, I sat down and wrote the attached from different cases I worked over 33 years as an FBI Special Agent. I wanted to make this into a small booklet for good bathroom reading, by giving it to several writers, but no one was interested. Feel free to use the enclosed and my name in your endeavors."

(Stories by Mickey, titles by the book's author)

Perp with a PHD

PHD – Commenting on how smart law enforcement is.

Dope dealer said: 'Well, I have a PHD. I am a pimp hog dog'.

Know nothing . . .

After a bank robbery in Cleveland, a neighborhood investigation was being conducted. I knocked on one lady's door and she said, before any questions were asked: 'Don't ask me nothin' because I don't know nothin'.

How scared?

A dope dealer's organization was coming apart and his co-defendants were being arrested and he knew his time was coming. He said to one of his associates that 'I'm scared as Joe's turkey'.

The incorrect DOB

A fugitive was arrested and he was trying to con the arresting officers to be released. (The fugitive's date of birth was in February) The fugitive told the officer they had arrested the wrong guy and that they were actually looking for his brother.

The officer asked the fugitive his date of birth and he gave him Feb. 18, 1980. The officer asked him the date of birth of his twin brother, and he responded 'June 20, 1980'.

The darn rope… and OJ

A bank robber parked his get-a-way car outside the side door of the bank. After robbing the teller, he ran out the north door of the bank, only to realize his get-a-way car was parked on the other side of the bank. The robber re-entered the bank and ran through the lobby towards the south door, jumping over the ropes that formed the customer line.

The robber's foot caught the rope and he fell to the floor, knocking himself out.

Later, when being interviewed, he said that when he was robbing the bank, he thought he was Jessie James (the famous bank robber) and when he was running through the bank he wanted to be like the OJ in commercials, running through the airport, jumping over things.

Common response…

Most common response when fugitives were arrested: 'I was just on my way down to turn myself in'.

My tooth brush

A fugitive was chased down and arrested. On his belt he had a little pouch. When asked what was in the pouch, the fugitive responded: 'My tooth brush'. Why do you carry a tooth brush? 'You never know when you have to run and I don't want to have dirty teeth'.

I spent the money

A bank robber was brought into federal court for his initial appearance. An old time Magistrate was questioning the robber about his financial status to determine if he qualified for a federal public defender. The Magistrate asked the robber if he had a job, if he had any assets, if he had money in the bank.

The robber responded with a 'no' to all questions. The Magistrate asked the robber if he had any money on his person or in his possession at the time of his arrest. Again, the robber responded with a 'No'. The Magistrate then asked the robber what he did with the money from the robbery. Before the defense attorney could object, the robber stated: 'I spent it.'

OUTTAKE . . . 

MILITARY WARNINGS THAT VETERANS MAY HAVE FORGOTTEN

(Author unknown)

- "Aim towards the enemy." (Instruction printed on a U.S. Rocket Launcher)
- "When the pin is pulled, Mr.Grenade is not your friend." (U.S. Marine Corps)
- "Cluster bombing from B-52s is very, very accurate. The bombs are guaranteed to always hit the ground."(U.S.A.F. Ammo Troop)
- "If the enemy is in range, so are you. (Infantry Journal)
- "It is generally inadvisable to eject directly over the area you just bombed." (U.S. Air Force Manual)
- "Try to look unimportant; they may be low on ammo." (Infantry Journal)
- "Tracers work both ways." (U.S. Army Ordnance)
- "Five-second fuses only last three seconds." (Infantry Journal)
- "Bravery is being the only one who knows you're afraid."(Col. David Hackworth)
- "If your attack is going too well, you're probably walking into an ambush." (Infantry Journal)
- "No combat ready unit has ever passed inspection." (Joe Gay)
- "Never tell the Platoon Sergeant you have

nothing to do." (Unknown Marine Corps Recruit)

- **"Don't draw fire; it irritates the people around you." (Your buddies)**
- **If you see a bomb technician running, keep up with him." (U.S.A.F. Ammo Troop)**

The stories continue . 

Hand in the cookie jar...

A bank robber had committed several bank robberies and was trying his hand at it again. The problem during his last bank robbery was that he tried to rob a teller who had been robbed twice before and was fed up with it.

The robber approached the teller, in an older branch that had old wooden cash drawers at the teller stations, and demanded money.

The teller did not comply and just stared at the robber. The robber decided since the teller wasn't giving him any money, he would help himself to cash in the top drawer. The robber leaned across the counter and put his hand into the drawer to grab the money. The ticked off teller slammed the wooden drawer closed on the robber's hand, locking it and walked away. The robber's hand was still wedged in the drawer when the police arrived.

Another chance…

A BOLO (be on the look-out) was broadcasted to notify the robbery detail but to not apprehend if a get-a-way vehicle used in a bank robbery was located. The robber was still unidentified.

A rookie patrol officer had located the car but could not remember the details of the BOLO and took the subject into custody.

At this point in the investigation, there was not enough probable cause to arrest the individual. The individual was interviewed and released.

As he was walking out the door, he thought he would have the last say and stated: 'I tell you what, I'll give you another chance to catch me in the act.'

Dog collar broad…

A search warrant was being executed at dope dealer's house. To protect himself against a robbery, he kept a junk yard type dog in the house. Needless to say, the house was flea infested.

What was amazing to officers conducting the search, was the doper's girlfriend, who lived there, was wearing the flea collar and not the dog.

Is pistol a gun?

A doper's house was being searched and before the officers started the search, the doper was asked if he had a pistol. The doper responded that he did not have a pistol, but he did have a gun!

Boots full of money…

A guy was on his way to buy dope in another state and was flying out of the local airport. During the search by the metal detectors, he had to take his cowboy boots off. The inspectors turned over the boots and $ 80K fell out of the boots. The dope dealer said that the money wasn't his and he did not know it was in his boots.

A repeat offender…

A serial robber started returning to the banks he had previously robbed to rob them again. He returned to a bank he had robbed two days earlier and stood in the customer line waiting his turn.

All the tellers noticed him but no one activated the silent alarm.

After the robbery, the tellers were asked why they didn't activate the robbery alarm. The tellers replied: 'He hadn't robbed us yet today.'

Sister, can you spare a dime…

After the individual got the money from the bank, he sat on the sidewalk in front of the bank and counted his good fortune.

The police responded and arrested him for robbery.

The individual turned out to be a homeless person and wasn't robbing the bank. He only asked the teller if she had any spare change and she emptied her cash drawer.

The smart bank manager…

After a violent take-over robbery, the investigators were standing in the bank trying to determine if the surveillance cameras were activated during the robbery.

One investigator, who had over 30 years in working robberies, asked the manager if the 35 mm cameras were activated during the robbery. The manager, who was very pushy and impressed with herself, said to the investigator: 'Where have you been? We only have 9mm cameras.'

One of the bank employees politely informed the manager that a 9mm was ammunition and a 35mm was a camera.

Wrong shoes…

The police were conducting a search of a burglar's home looking for a pair of shoes to match with shoe prints found at the crime scene. The police told the burglar that they found his shoe prints at the scene of the crime.

The burglar responded: 'You can't because I had tennis on.'

He shot the TV…

An undercover drug buy was made at one of the local crack dealers, using marked money. Search warrants were going to be executed the following morning at the dealer's residence.

A minor problem developed during the evening of the buy. The dope dealer was watching a sporting event on TV and got mad at the results of the game and shot his TV.

Neighbors called police and reported shots fired. The police responded and arrested the dealer. The marked money used to make the dope purchase was in the dealer's possession at the time of his arrest and used as evidence to convict him for distribution.

The wrong room…

A warrant had been issued for a bank robber and it was determined that he was residing at a room in local motel. The FBI Agents were lined up on either side of the apartment door and knocked. An individual popped out of the room next door and said: 'Hey, that's my room. What do you want?'

The robber was taken into custody.

Rocks?

An undercover narcotics officer was hanging out near some drug dealers. He dealers did not trust anyone. The dealers felt safe in their sales because all the individuals in the organization hung together since they were juveniles and no one new was allowed to sell.

The gang members even created their own language when talking about weight and sales.

One of the members was not so bright and could not catch

the lingo. The boss was talking in code and the doper could not understand and said: 'Look, all I want to do is sell some cocaine. Give me some rocks.'

Well done…

Warrants were issued for numerous gang members for the interstate distribution of rock cocaine. After being advised of his Miranda rights, one of the arrestees was being interviewed.

A task force member laid out the evidence that implicated the arrestee in the drug organization. The only comment the arrestee made was 'Stick a folk in me. I'm done.'

OUTTAKE . . .

EVERYTHING I EVER NEEDED TO KNOW IN THE FBI I LEARNED AS A HELICOPTER PILOT IN VIETNAM
(Author unknown)

"Once you are in a fight, it is way too late to wonder if this is a good idea."

"Never get into a fight without more ammunition than the other guy."

"Cover your buddy, so he can be around to cover you."

"Decisions made by someone above you in the

chain-of-command will seldom be in your best interest."

"Sometimes, being good and lucky still is not enough."

"If everything is as clear as a bell, and everything is going exactly as planned, you're about to be surprised."

"No matter what you do, the bullet with your name on it will get you. So, too, can the ones addressed 'To Whom It May Concern'. "

"If you are wearing body armor, bullets will probably miss that part."

"If you are allergic to lead, it is best to avoid a war zone."

"Everybody is a hero . . . on the ground . . . in the club . . . after the fourth drink."

"Medals are OK, but having your body and all your friends in one piece at the end of the day is better."

"Being shot hurts."

"Nobody cares what you did yesterday or what you are going to do tomorrow. What is important is what you are doing – NOW – to solve our problem."

"Prayer may not help . . but it can't hurt."

The stories continue . . .

Ice cream maker…

A gang member, arrested as part of an interstate drug distribution organization was arrested at a local ice cream factory where he worked on the assembly line, making ice cream cones. The defendant was taken before the U.S. Magistrate for an initial appearance where the charges were read. The Magistrate informed the defendant that if convicted, he could face up to 20 years in jail and or a $ 1 M fine.

As the defendant was leaving the courtroom, he said to the Agent: 'Man. Do you know how many ice cream cones I have to make to pay off the fine?'

Wrath of a woman…

Investigators learned the identity of the fugitive's girlfriend and where she was living. The Agents went over to the residence and wound up speaking with the grandmother of the girlfriend. The investigators asked if she knew the fugitive and his whereabouts. The grandmother responded that she knew him well and where he was located. The grandmother related that her granddaughter had a toothache and the fugitive refused to take her to the dentist, but he had time to get her pregnant.

The grandmother provided the address of the fugitive and said that now he will have a long time to think about whether he should have taken her to the dentist. Subject was apprehended.

Parrot did it…

Investigators were responding to a call made to the America's Most Wanted television program. The caller claimed that she knew one of the fugitives on the show and provided her name and address so she could be interviewed. The investigators were allowed into her residence by a female occupant.

The female advised that she watched the show every week, but denied making the call. The woman looked over to her talking African parrot and claimed that 'he also watched the show and must have made the call.'

Wrong location…

A not so bright bank robber, after serving 5 years for bank robbery, decided he would go back and rob the same bank. The robber entered the establishment, pulled his gun and yelled that this is a bank robbery.

The employees of the bank froze and finally one of the employees said that this is not a bank. It is a real estate office and the bank moved down the block. The robber insisted this was a bank, because he robbed it before, The employees had to show the robber a telephone book to convince him the bank was up the street.

Dumb s . . t

After leaving the bank, the robber placed the stolen money down the front of his pants. What the robber did not know was that among the loot taken was an exploding dye pack.

Within a block, the dye pack exploded, covering the robber in red dye and burning his private parts.

When the Agents went to interview him, he was sitting off the end of the chair, bent over. The Agent asked the robber his name and he responded: 'Dumb s..t'.

Lunch break…

A bold bank robber hired limos to use as get away vehicles in all his robberies. The robber was out on bail during his trial in federal court. During a lunch break in the trial, he robbed a bank across the street from the federal court house. Agents recognized the surveillance photo and arrested the bank robber at the end of the court day.

Having sex is no alibi…

A criminal was being interviewed about a crime and the criminal told the officers that 'It wasn't me, I wasn't there, I was having sex with my girlfriend, but she may not remember.'

A Christmas gift…

The investigators were searching a house for evidence connecting the individual to a bank robbery.

On a Christmas card found in the house, addressed to the suspect , was written the following: 'The next bank you knock over make sure you get a little for me.'

The virgin – not…

During a dope raid, a female in the house was contacted who had prior arrests for dope. When asked if she was on 'diversion' for drugs, she did not respond.

The officers asked this individual several times and finally she responded, 'I'm no stinkin virgin!'

A true Crack Cocaine…

During a booking search, a small bag of rock cocaine fell from between the suspect's buttocks. The suspect jumped back and exclaimed: 'Who put that there?'

Adjective vs noun…

The police responded to a call at a low rent motel about a

female tenant stealing towels from the room next to hers. The female suspect was contacted and denied the thefts. The officers told the female that she could not take towels out of the adjacent room.

The female responded: 'I don't even know the ADJACENTS !' "

Dirty laundry . . .

Three guys robbed a bank and all three jumped over the teller counter to get to the cash drawer. The surveillance photo caught one of the robbers placing a shopping bag in front of the counter before jumping over.

On his way out, he picked up the bag.

When arrested that night, he was asked about the shopping bag. The robber said that he was on his way to the dry cleaners and his friends asked him if he wanted to rob a bank with them. He said he had his dirty laundry in the bag and did not want to lose it so he brought it with him into the bank.

AN ENEMA BANDIT
(Author unknown)

"Michael H. Cibula, the suspected 'enema bandit', who terrorized coeds at the University of Illinois for ten years, pleaded guilty to six counts of armed robbery in Urbana, Ill.

It was read into the record, that he administered enemas to at least three victims."

The stories continue . . .

Gentleman robber . . .

A robber approached a teller in the bank and was about to rob her. The robber said: 'I was going to rob you but you are too pretty so I'm going to go across the street and rob the other bank'.

The teller watched the robber enter the other bank and called police. The gentleman robber was apprehended.

A victim of a crime?

An individual who aided and abetted in disposing of a murder victim, called into the Workman's Compensation Office, looking for workman's comp because he was a victim of a violent crime.

The individual refused to identify himself and was inquiring if he would qualify. He related that a friend of his had killed an individual and put him in the back of his van. The individual wanted to dispose of the body and encased the body in cement in the back of the van.

The caller claimed that they disposed of the body by throwing it off a bridge into the river. The caller claimed that he got a hernia while lifting the concrete slab. The caller felt he was entitled to compensation, because murder was a violent crime and he became a victim of a violent crime when he got hurt.

He'll need the belt . . .

A bank robber successfully left the area after the robbery. About 40 minutes later, as the witnesses were being interviewed at the bank, the victim teller looked out the window and saw the robber going behind a trash dumpster across the street. The robber was immediately apprehended.

During the interview, the robber was asked why he did the robbery and why he came back after he had gotten away.

The robber stated that he did not have any money to pay for his gym's monthly dues, so he rationalized that if he got caught he could lift weights in jail and if he got away, he had money to pay his dues.

When asked why he came back to the area, he responded that he had left his favorite weight lifting belt behind the dumpster and needed it to go work out.

Double trouble . . .

A very successful bank robber working the West Coast had successfully robbed in excess of 50 banks. After he was caught, he mentioned that he went into a bank in a suburb of San Francisco to rob it. While he was waiting in line to do his thing, he realized that the guy in front of him was robbing the bank. He said he got out of the bank just before the tellers locked the doors.

A perfect dart board . . .

Two bank robbers were working the financial district and had successfully robbed 12 banks. Law enforcement officers were plotting out the time of day, day of week and localities of the victim banks, trying to find a pattern which would help them apprehend the pair.

As luck would have it, and a lot of shoe leather worn out, the two were spotted entering another bank in the financial district. The two were apprehended as they exited the bank.

During the arrest interviews they were asked how they decided to rob a particular bank. They both said independently that each morning when they woke up, and needed money for a fix, they would open the Yellow Pages and throw a dart at it and whichever bank the dart landed on, that was the one they would rob.

What's a grape ?

A guy robbed nothing but one well known type of bank. He tried robbing others but was unsuccessful. The robber always wore an orange three piece suit.

Surveillances were set up at each of the branches in the particular area where the orange suit bandit was robbing. He was spotted entering a bank.

After the robbery, the police chased him down and arrested him. He had a 38 caliber revolver on him but did not pull it out.

The robber said he thought about shooting it out but decided that he 'Didn't want to step on anyone's grape.'

OUTTAKE . . .

TOUGH SHERIFF
(Author unknown)

"Sheriff Joe Arpaio, Maricopa County, Arizona, is doing it right.

He has jail meals down to 40 cents a serving and charges the inmates for them.

He does not allow smoking or porno magazines in the jails.

He started chain gangs so the inmates could do free work on county and city projects.

Took away their weights.

Cut off all but 'G' movies.

He cut off coffee since it has no nutritional value.

When the inmates complain, he told them that jail is not Ritz/Carlton. If you don't like it, don't come back."

The stories continue . . .

Bad commercial . . .

A bank robber was identified and law enforcement waited for him to return to his hotel room. The robber was apprehended and asked if he knew why he was being arrested.

He said: 'Yeah, the banks had identified the name of a particular bank.'

While in route to jail, the robber started smiling as he was being driven past another branch of the same bank. He was asked why he was smiling and he responded 'There's another bank I robbed.'

The robber said he only robbed that particular bank because he didn't like the bank's commercials (that had the Carpenters singing "We've Only Just Begun.")

Later, the bank's security director called, wanting to know what commercial the robber didn't like, because he'd been directed to find out by the CEO of the bank to remove the ad.

Dummy, it's the defense attorney you want. . .

After being arrested, a bank robber wanted to speak with the prosecuting attorney. The Agents contacted the duty attorney and allowed the robber to speak with him in private. After speaking with the attorney, the robber wanted to know how much it was going to cost him to hire the prosecutor to represent him.

Blame it on the elder . . .

A 12 year old boy walked into a bank and gave a demand note to a veteran teller. When he realized that he wasn't going to give him any money, he started to leave.

The teller notified the bank guard who arrested the young robber. The 12 year old claimed that he was forced to rob the bank by a 25 year old.

Further investigation determined that the 25 year old identified by the young robber knew nothing about the robbery and passed a polygraph test. It turned out that the 25 year old had disciplined the youth and to get even, the 12 year old robbed the bank and blamed it on the adult.

Illegal parking caper . . .

A suspect in a series of bank and pawn shop burglaries was under surveillance. During one of the burglaries, rifles and shotguns were stolen.

The suspect was observed carrying out long objects covered in a blanket, from his house and placing them in the trunk of his car. The suspect was followed to a police parking lot where he parked his car illegally. The suspect was inside the PD being interviewed about one of the burglaries.

Since the car was illegally parked it was towed by the PD. During the inventory search, the police found the stolen weapons.

Money will do it every time . . .

During a car burglary investigation, the investigators determined that the reporting party had an outstanding warrant for murder from another jurisdiction.

The investigators contacted the woman and told her to

come into the office for a check to repair the broken window in her car. When the woman arrived at the office, she was arrested for murder. She started yelling to the investigator who called her into the office and said: 'Does this mean I don't get my check?'

Time out . . .

Two defendants were sitting in court for a robbery preliminary hearing. During a break, the bailiff left for a minute and asked the investigative officer to watch them for him.

While sitting by the defendants, the investigating officer overheard the defendants arguing about whose fault it was that they got caught and where they hid the money, etc.

The DA and Judge were informed about the incriminating statements. They both were mad at the investigative officer, the DA and the Judge because they thought it was 'Time out' during the break and thought the Judge had to call court in session before anything counted. They pleaded guilty and each got 15 years for robbery.

Hurry up !

There was a bank robbery in a small town near the FBI Resident Agency, but none of the Agents were aware of the robbery because of poor radio reception in the RA territory.

One of the Special Agents, upon returning to the RA, was informed by the highway patrol that 'your boss was upset' and wanted to know what was going on with the robbery. When we called HQ city, he stated, "Try to get out there before the statute tolls.'

Walking won't do . . .

During an investigation of a Dyer Act case (interstate transportation of a stolen motor vehicle) an Agent interviewed the owner of the used car lot from where the car was stolen.

The dealer stated that the suspect had stated, 'I'm a faith healer but I just can't cure these aickin' feet. I've got to have a car.'

A multiple bed time . . .

An arrestee who was pregnant excused herself to go to the ladies' room while at the prison medical facility. When she emerged, she was carrying a brand new baby, and the shaken doctor, trying to fill out the necessary forms, asked her who the father was. Her response was: 'Do the log know which part of the saw done the final cuttin' ?

More claims, more money . . .

During an investigation, a welfare worker told me the suspect's wife had listed another child, Bebee, who, after four years, finally appeared on the welfare request form.

When she was asked about why Bebee finally appeared after four years, the woman stated that when she was born, 'she was so puny we didn't think she was going to live and we didn't name her until this past year.'

Which target gets hit first ?

FBI Agents saw a fugitive bank robber walking down the street. The Agents proceeded to chase him on foot. One Agent ran up the middle of the street and the other ran up the sidewalk. The bank robber was cornered and surrendered without pulling out his loaded semi-automatic pistol. His comment was, 'I would have shot ya but you outflanked me.'

Mother of Jesus . . . not!

During a bank robbery trial, a prostitute was on the witness stand as a prosecution witness. The defense attorney had represented this witness in a prior local prostitution case.

In trying to discredit her as a government witness, the attorney said to her: 'You told me you thought you were the Virgin Mary.' The prostitute quickly retorted: 'You told me you were Jesus Christ.'

Only a flatulence . . .

A wanted federal fugitive was seen sitting in the passenger seat of a car. The fugitive was a small guy, about 5'5", about 120 lbs and was of Indian descent. This added flavor to the following:

I grabbed him as planned, took him out of the vehicle, braced him on the hood of the vehicle and told him I was going to do a pat down for weapons.

About the same time I started to do this, I smelled a terrible odor that reminded me of a latrine. Since I was about to put my hand in the proximity of his genitals, I asked him if he s… in his pants.

Now imagine someone speaking in an Indian accent replying as such: 'I didn't s… in my pants, I only farted'.

Flunked spelling . . .

A bank robber used a note which read, 'This is a roobery. Put all the money in the bag and if you don't I'll blow your dam head off.'

His misspelling, in addition to other evidence, was enough to convince him to admit guilt.

(Author unknown)

"CERTIFICATE

FOR YOUR VERY OUTSTANDING PERFORMANCE
YOU ARE AWARDED:

'ONE ATTABOY'

ONE THOUSAND 'ATTABOYS' QUALIFIES YOU TO BE LEADER OF MEN, WORK OVERTIME WITH A SMILE, EXPLAIN ASSORTED PROBLEMS TO MANAGEMENT, AND BE LOOKED UPON AS A LOCAL HERO.

NOTE: ONE 'AWSHIT' WIPES THE BOARD CLEAN AND YOU HAVE TO START ALL OVER AGAIN!"

The stories continue . . .

Didn't have no gun . . .

An individual robbed a bank dressed as a woman and made his getaway on a bicycle. Later investigation determined the robber was actually a man. The robber used his money to buy a motorcycle, but didn't learn to ride it well.

A warrant was obtained and as the detectives approached his house, he bolted out of the rear door and fled on his newly acquired motorcycle.

Following a high speed chase, the robber collided with a pickup truck turning in front of him. He must have been going 50 mph, and remarkable, he got up and started limping away. He was arrested.

As he was being interviewed in the hospital, I told him he was being charged with the armed robbery of a bank. He said: 'I didn't do no armed robbery. I robbed the bank but I didn't have no gun.'

The robber was sentenced to 15 years in the federal system.

Admit it !

The bank cameras showed the robber with ski mask and gloves making it impossible to identify him. However, when they showed it on local news, the subject bragged to his friends it was him. Not enough to get an arrest warrant, but we did get a tip and went to see him.

He denied ever saying he was the robber and right before leaving, I took out the surveillance photo and said isn't this you?

He looked at it and said: 'You got me'.

The s....y money!

A rehabilitated bank robber, recently out of jail and on a quest for cash, took it upon himself to relieve another bank from some excess cash.

Running out of the bank, a concerned citizen took it upon himself to give chase, following the fleeing suspect into a nearby train station.

Upon realizing he was being pursued, the desperate criminal, being unarmed, wheeled and told the good citizen 'I will kill you, man'. The citizen, without hesitation, delivered a picture perfect kick to the subject's groin, causing the apparent hardened criminal to immediately #@*t in his pants and drop to the ground, incapacitated in the most primal pain response.

A few seconds later, the police arrived and took the subject into custody, delivering the now reeking subject to the interview room of the nearby station, for an interview.

The newest investigator on the robbery detail was assigned the interview. The rookie arrived at the robbery detail in a new suit and shoes that had been purchased the week before, just for this new assignment. All the detectives were on the verge of laughter, I thought crap, I must look like a rookie with my new outfit. I looked a little out of place wearing this suit with shiny shoes in a room full of hardened detectives with their shoulder rigs. Snickering, one of the detectives stated: 'He's waiting for you in interview room # 1'.

Upon opening the door, it was like being hit in the face , as the stench of excrement was overwhelming. It was then that the laughter erupted full force, rivaling a funny joke at the comedy club.

In brief, the interview didn't last long, as the defiant criminal advised that yes, he did rob the bank, but had thrown the ill-gained money into a trash can during his sprint through the city.

The laughter had died down, as the detectives realized that no smell could thwart the administration of justice by the rookie. I then escorted the smelly subject to the showers, continuing to question the robber as to the location of the money. All the while, the suspect continued to deny any knowledge of which trash can he deposited the money.

The following, still perplexes me to this day, why, as it was blatantly obvious to me and the subject, that he would not be leaving police custody, that he would deny the whereabouts of the money.

I instructed him to take his clothes off and shower and then get into the orange prison jump suit. As I stood in the doorway to the shower, the suspect began a slow striptease. After removing his shirt, he looked at me and said: 'You may want to leave, it's going to be pretty smelly'. I said, just take off your clothes and get showered. Still holding strong to his claims, he slowly started to peel his pants down. Again, 'Hey, seriously, it's going to be pretty bad, you might want to go to the other room.' Just hurry up, you reek and the smell is starting to make me sick.

Slowly, the pants went down, revealing a lumpy pair of s..t soaked white briefs. In desperation, the subject again stated 'really, this is going to be really messy, you might want to wait outside.'

At that moment, being a keen investigator, I noticed the corner of a bill peeking out from under the rugged soiled underwear. I knew the cash was in there.

With a look of dismay, the subject started to peel the briefs off with wads of s..t covered cash spilling to the tiled floor. I looked at one of the veteran detectives, saying the money has been recovered.

It was at that moment, something hit my leg and dropped in to one of my new shoes. Looking down in shock, I saw a trail of &*%#t going down my thigh and ending with the @#!t soaked underwear resting comfortably on my shoe. Shocked, I looked at the veteran detective, who is now on the floor laughing so hard that my growing rage couldn't help but be tempered with a resolute grin that my investigative victory had turned to . . . well . . . !@$t. Perhaps that grin may have given the impression to the criminal that he was about to have an insane rookie commence on a beat down, because he began screaming his apologies, forcing the veteran detective over the edge to tears.

My only revenge was making our scholar wash the %#&*t from every individual bill. I only wondered if this money, someday, would make it back into circulation in our fine city. Why this guy held it out to the last, where he thought he could hide all that !$#&t covered cash, is still a mystery to me. Who really can know what goes on inside a dumb criminal's head.

In the case of the investigative '@$&*t shoe' lesson learned. Never turn your attention away from even the shittiest of suspects.

I did it . . .

A fugitive escaped from prison where he was serving time for murder in a federal case and several bank robberies. When apprehended several years later, he was taken before a U.S. Magistrate, for his initial appearance.

The Magistrate was reading charges and possible penalties and then started discussing bail. The fugitive yelled out 'I don't deserve bail, I'm a dangerous felon.' Bail denied.

Last meal . . .

A fugitive was being sought for the murder of two witnesses in a federal case. When apprehended, he put up a fight but was arrested without injuries.

As he was being transported to jail, they passed a fast food hamburger establishment. Keeping in line with store's commercial, the fugitive said: 'You guys deserve a break today. Can you buy me a few hamburgers?'

What disease?

Old dog fugitive cases were usually given to the new Agents on the squad. The Agent reviewed the case that was given to him and decided to interview some known associate of the fugitive.

The associate would not reveal the whereabouts of the fugitive and was trying to cover for him. The associate said that the FBI should leave the fugitive alone because he was very sick. The associate claimed the fugitive had 'Spinal men in Jesus' and 'Old Timers Disease'.

Blind man's bluff . . .

A blind man attempted to rob a bank. The teller actually gave him money. One big problem – he couldn't find his way out of the bank.

Bank surveillance film shows him surrounded by police inside the bank, a few steps from where he robbed the teller.

Id'd self . . .

The robber walked up to the teller counter and placed his wallet on the counter pretending to do a bank transaction. He even took some ID out of his wallet. The robber told the teller to give him all the money in the cash drawer.

After getting the money, the robber ran out the north door of the bank. Employees as required locked the doors to the bank.

Shortly there-after, the robber returned, banging on the locked doors, demanding to be let in.

The frightened employees were beside themselves. The robber finally left.

Law enforcement later found the robber's wallet and ID on the teller counter where he committed the robbery.

Double robbery . . .

Two robbers went behind the counter and took money from the teller cash drawer. From the surveillance photos, one of the robbers could be seen bending down after taking money from the cash drawer.

The robbers fled and later split the money 50/50, so one of the robbers thought. One of the robbers was apprehended the next day. During the interview he asked if the amount taken in the robbery was correct as reported in the paper.

When he found out that it was, he claimed 'I've been robbed' and gave up the name of his partner.

Investigation determined that the robber who was bending down was actually putting money in his socks so he wouldn't have to share it with his crime partner.

One down, one to go…

A mother of two murder fugitives refused to cooperate with authorities in helping locate her sons, even though they had just committed another murder. The mother knew the police were following her so to antagonize the police, she had a personalized license plate made, with the first names of her two fugitive sons.

Shortly thereafter, one of the fugitives broke into a home and tied up the husband and proceeded to rape the wife. The husband jumped out the window and called the police.

The SWAT team surrounded the house and called in to the fugitive to surrender. The fugitive yelled out 'If you come in, I will kill myself. Two minutes later, the SWAT team broke down the door. One less fugitive.

A week later, the mother was driving away from her home in her car, but she did not notice that someone had spray painted over her deceased son's name on the license plate.

I give you my heart…

A robber was apprehended as he ran away from the bank. He told investigators that the teller forced him to do it.

The teller, who was brought in for an interview, had a very bad attitude. The investigator told her she had great perfume. She responded it was her personal favorite. 'Sweat.'

The teller claimed that the robber had put her up to it. All her life she has had her heart torn out by guys that did not care about her.

The interviewer was so good, he put out his hands and said 'You can trust me. I'll take care of your heart, just reach down and pull out your heart and place it in my hands. The teller reached her hands down and simulated placing her heart in the interviewer's hands.

The teller eventually admitted to setting up the bank robbery.

The next day, the captain saw the investigator and told him that he never wanted to see that again. What are you talking about? The captain said the interview room stunk and that it had to be ventilated so the next time you take someone's heart, you must put it in the freezer over-night.

A confession…

A hard core female bank robber was in custody after her failed get-a-way. Her reputation preceeded her because on her prior arrests, she always told the interviewer to shove it.

One of the new guys on the detail told the old timers that he could get her to talk.

The interviewer tried to establish a report with the robber and started talking about his hard life and how he lost his wife and kid in an accident. The robber felt her life wasn't so bad after all, and wanted to get it off her chest and confessed the robbery.

After the interviewer came out of the interview room, the other detectives, who were in on the interview, told him they were very sorry for the loss of his wife and daughter. The investigator told them he only made the story up about his wife and kid, just to get the sympathy of the robber.

The philosophy major…

An individual was arrested after a series of bombings and confessed to the crimes.

On the way to the jail, the subject got very philosophical and stated to the arresting officers: 'You know everyone is created equal, but some people just have better jobs than others'.

Airplane inspection . . .

An individual on a cross country flight went into the bathroom and after a long period of time other passengers were getting upset because he did not come out.

The flight attendant banged on the door, and when there was no response, she opened the door. To her surprise, all of the passenger's clothes were on the floor, but no passenger. The flight attendant sealed off the bathroom.

The pilot was notified and radioed ahead to the destination field to notify the police about the incident.

Prior to landing, the passenger exits the bathroom fully dressed and returned to his seat. Upon arrival, the passenger was escorted off the plane for an interview.

The passenger had a degree in electrical engineering and claimed he was bored with the flight and thought he would take a tour of the inner workings of the plane. The passenger said he went into the bathroom and took out a ceiling panel and crawled around the plane.

Asked why he took off his clothes, he responded that he did not want to get them dirty.

Light please !

A passenger was on an international flight approximately 14 hours long. The passenger got a little tipsy from drinking and started pinching the flight attendants and jumping over seats.

The passenger was arrested when the plane landed. The subject only spoke a few words of English and had a hard time communicating with the flight attendant.

The passenger told the interviewers, through an interpreter, that he usually read himself to sleep on the long flight, but the overhead reading light was out. The passenger said each time he tried to tell the flight attendant he needed a light, she would bring him a Bud Light which he consumed. The passenger did not remember anything after his third Bud Light.

Incorrect dosage . . . a before TSA story

One passenger on a plane was traveling with his golden retriever and thought it was cruel to put the dog in the belly of the plane as luggage. The passenger calculated how long the flight was and had his friend, who was a veterinarian, give him medication to put the dog out for the duration of the flight. The passenger stuffed the dog into a military size duffle bag and carried him onto the plane and placed the bag into one of the closets at the rear of the plane.

Things were going great and the plane was about to leave the gate, when a bomb threat was called in. The passengers were deplaned without their luggage and the search began.

When a law enforcement officer opened the rear closet, he found the duffle bag moving. The officer thought there was a stow-a-way on the plane and to his amazement, he found the dog.

Apparently, the passenger had not given the dog the correct dosage. Needless to say, the dog and the owner did not make the flight.

He could have sued the bank

A bank robber entered the bank through the main doors of the bank which happened to be a glass (not safety glass) in a wooden frame.

After successfully robbing the teller, he ran to the front door to make his get-a-way. He reached out with his hand to push the door open and crashed right through the glass door and kept going.

The robber did not realize when he entered the bank the doors opened inward. Later that night, the bank robber was arrested at the emergency room getting stitched up.

Handle with caution !

An individual had just thrown a caustic substance in the face of a person with whom he had a disagreement. The individual fled the area, followed by concerned citizens.

The bad guy ran a few blocks away and tried to hide among the people waiting for a bus.

When the police arrived, it was not hard picking him out of the crowd. The individual's hair and skin were peeling off his head. This bright criminal was so intent on getting away that he held the open container, splashing it on himself as he ran away.

Trevor the Cat Burglar

Trevor was a retired guy who loved to sit and listen to criminal trials. He was a regular, known to the judges, prosecutors and defense attorneys. Trevor walked on his tiptoes and shuffled along. You would never know Trevor was there or approaching, because he never made any noise, thus his nickname, 'Trevor the Cat Burglar'.

At the end of the trial, with the judge and jury gone from the courtroom, the attorneys and cops would turn to Trevor for his expert opinion. Trevor would not speak but made hand gestures.

His favorite gesture, if he thought the defendant was guilty, would be to hold up his hands simulating someone hanging from a rope.

Proposal lost in the commode

A non-married couple who were in love, were serving jail time in the county jail, but they were separated by their jail cells.

A strange phenomenon in this old time jail was that the men's and women's bathrooms were back to back and the plumbing pipes were common for both bathrooms.

The inmates figured out that they could communicate through the plumbing pipes if the toilets were flushed at the same time. The conversation could last until the water level rose to a certain point.

The male was expressing to his love through the pipes. He wanted to pop the big question and just as he asked 'Would you . . . ', someone flushed another toilet. His true love did not get to hear the proposal.

The print on the glass

A bank robber had successfully robbed several banks and knew he was wanted by the police. For the next robbery to hide his identity, the robber dressed up like a female, including make-up, lipstick and wearing gloves to hide fingerprints.

After successfully getting money from the teller, the robber ran out the front door. The glass door opened in and the robber slammed his face into the door, leaving red lipstick lip prints on the glass.

The only prints the police were able to lift were the imprint of the lips on the glass door. Investigation determined the identity of the robber.

Under court order, the robber had to give lip exemplars. The lip print on the door was positively matched with the lip exemplar taken from the suspect. Case closed.

Slippers in the snow

On one fugitive raid at a third floor apartment, as all of us were going up the outside stairs (probably for fire escape), the subject passed us going down . . . he jumped off his balcony in his BVD's, landing in a foot of snow, and took off running.

When we got down, the only evidence he had been there, were his slippers in the snow, right where he had landed.

Gave up

You have no doubt heard of instances where the robber tried to rob a bank and was foiled.

In one case, when the robber got to the teller and handed her the note, she actually told him those matters were handled at another window and she could not help him. He changed lines, then left in exasperation, throwing the note on the ground.

Souvenir money

One bank decided to use the new $ 2 bills as bait money. A robber was given these bait bills during the robbery and got away successfully. The robber did not know the $ 2 bills were the bait bills and kept a few in his wallet as souvenirs.

Six months later, when the robber was apprehended, he still had the bait bills in his possession, which linked him to the robbery.

A woman scorned

On the last of a series of several bank robberies, one of the robber's girlfriends drove the getaway car with the robbers in the trunk. When she heard how much money they got, while counting it in the trunk, she pulled over to the side of the road and demanded her one-third cut or she would drive to the sheriff's office.

She wouldn't let them out of the trunk until they passed the money through the seat. A woman scorned. I don't recall if she and the robber ever got close again.

The heavy-weight

One guy who had robbed a bank (he was a getaway driver) was huge. When we arrested him, in order to process him for information on the fingerprint card, we had to transport him to a local meat processor, for him to be weighed. He was over 350 lbs as I recall.

He or she or he/she ?

One night we got an anonymous call that a dancer in a topless dive looked like a fugitive. My partner and I went there and watched all the dancers until sure enough, one came out who had features like the fugitive. She was not well endowed, was about his size and complexion, and had some skin discoloration on her upper left arm where the fugitive had a tattoo.

We got the manager to get the dancer into his office where

we decided we would wait. As they came in, we took hold of the dancer and advised the reason we were there.

First of all, she was furious that we thought she looked like a guy and said she was leaving. The manager knew we would not let her go until we found some way to be sure of her identity, or sure she was not the fugitive.

At that, he told her: 'Tina, take down your G-string and prove to these guys you don't have a Wanger.'

She did, and our thorough examination of the facts determined she was free to go.

Is this a real FBI Special Agent?

A robbery/homicide detective was in his friend's gun store where he engaged in a conversation with an employee. During the conversation, the clerk told the detective he was an old dinosaur and shouldn't be working. The detective spoke with his friend, the owner, who said the new employee claimed to be an FBI Agent who needed an undercover job for a gun sting operation.

The detective was suspicious because he worked with Agents all the time and never knew any of them to be so disrespectful.

The detective called the local FBI Resident Agent who responded and interviewed the employee. The employee tried to convince the Agent that he was really with the FBI, but to no avail. The subject was arrested for impersonation. Investigation determined the subject had convinced his parents that he was an FBI Agent and he made up a non-existent graduation diploma from the FBI Academy. The impersonator was driving a car on which he installed a red light and a police scanner.

It turned out that the car belonged to an elderly couple who had placed a for sale ad in the local paper. The impersonator told the couple that he needed an undercover car but had to take it to the government garage for final approval before purchase. The elderly couple gave the impersonator the keys and he drove off, never to be seen again.

Grounded?

An individual visited a local law enforcement office,

complaining that wherever he went, he was being watched by a satellite. Today, he was able to get out of his house without detection, because he put on a new hat and they did not recognize him.

The individual was informed that his problem was that he was not properly grounded, which allowed the satellite to track him. The individual was given a box of paper clips and he linked them from his belt to the ground, giving him a proper grounding.

The individual felt relieved and left the office because he was grounded.

A bad police chief

An electronic surveillance was being conducted by the FBI, of an illegal gambling operation. The local police chief was picked up as the banker for the operation.

When the site was raided, the chief tried to con the arresting officers, by claiming he was running an undercover operation and the arresting officers just ruined his case.

Quotable one liners . . .

- "You sounded taller on the phone"
- "Spicion is a mother"
- "My bowels are slippin, I got the stomach Jones"
- "Suff goin splode"
- "I throwed up on myself"
- "I'm as clean as a white fish" (Arrestee claiming his innocence)
- "If after twenty minutes, it's more than half an hour, send up a signal"

- "State prisoners being housed in federal prisons are there because those guys got long life sentences"

- "That was the biggest Doberman Sheppard I ever saw"

- "He likes to drink his coffee on the memorandum"

My meeting Mr. Hoover . . .

"Prior to the new FBI Academy being built at Quantico, new Agents had to split training between the Old Post Office (OPO) building in Washington and the range at Quantico. Part of the training in WDC required the new Agents to be to do their physical training in the gym in the basement of the Justice Department building. The gym was next to the Bureau garage for the VIP's, with about a 20 minute window to get from the OPO to the gym.

I and two of my roommates were running down the staircase to the basement. At the basement level, we swung around, holding onto the last railing and came nose to nose with no other than J. Edgar, Clyde Tolson and the driver. The three of us stopped like the Three Stooges, bumping into one another.

Without uttering a word, the three of us sidestepped to the right and kept on running, never looking back. Our Bureau career almost ended before it started."

GEORGE ZELL HEUSTON
FBI Special Agent 1980-2002

George's career in the FBI started as a street Agent and ended as such. He loved being a "hump", acknowledging that it was the best position in the FBI. I wholeheartedly agree.

This talented, but very humble man, spent half of his career working FCI matters and half on the criminal side. His specialties were high tech, computer related crimes and investigations. Add to this his work on the CART team as a forensic examiner and his

affiliation with the elite San Francisco FBI SWAT TEAMS.

In G's own words, "We were Special Agents first and foremost. We swore to protect and defend our country in accordance with the laws and Constitution. SA Jim Reese, from the FBI's Behavioral Science Unit admonished my New Agent's Class to 'Remember, the sun doesn't rise and set on the Bureau. Your family should always come first. If you maintain that perspective, you can make it through a career in this outfit and keep your sanity.'

However, though the sun may not have risen and set on the Bureau, the sun indeed shone on it. The stories here befit the organization, because they are stories of good, well-trained people, doing a necessary vital job. I miss the good people."

George was well prepared for the job in the FBI and beyond. JD, Seattle University; BA, University of Puget Sound; Air Combat Intelligence and Targeting Officer, USAF; Climbing Guide, Mt.Rainier Guide Service; Manager, Hillsboro Police Department; Columnist, Oregon Live.

Look for George Zell Heuston on the WWW when his book, *Avoiding the Sudden Stop*, **Guiding Rainier and other Northwest Mountain Adventures in the 1960s,**
is published in the near future.

A CHRISTMAS RAID
December 23, 1991
By George Z. Heuston

"0630: It is dark in the SWAT Van as eight Team Members fight their cumbersome gear and brace themselves against the corners. The driver takes extra care to drive smoothly, but with the bare interior, bodies cling to the sheet metal. My skin catches the front corner of the battering ram, and I'm assured of at least one bruise to commemorate this action.

It is also hot, and I'm getting queasy in my cacoon of ballistic helmet, ceramic and Kevlar body armor, goggles, balaclava hood, radio, ammunition magazines, black rip-stop uniform, high-top boots, and Nomex flying gloves. The van rocks around a corner and a voice says 'Safety's off.' I thumb the cross-bolt safety on my Remington 870 shotgun and reply 'Off Safe.' Another voice echoes the same words, as a Team Member clicks the fire-select lever on his HK MP5 submachine gun to the 'Full Auto' position. We are ready.

An apartment tract in the Housing Projects of Central Oakland is our destination. The Projects are a teaming and deadly combat zone, where families struggle to raise their children amid daily shootings, gang warfare, and drug deals. It is in another world. Three weeks ago an FBI Agent driving through was shot at from a rooftop. The subject we are after is a '267-homicide-drugs.' He has killed before for a mere five hundred dollars, and is known to carry a cut-down .223 semiautomatic rifle with a 90-round magazine.

'One block to go.' The accelerator on the van surges, and the Team Members not carrying shoulder weapon 9mm Sig Sauer pistols muzzle down, poised to break out the side door. I take my position as 6th man, squeezing in behind Number Five. A hard lurch to a stop, the doors fling open and we are out of the van. This is the first time my Teammates and I see our target 'in person.' It's always different from what the mind perceives from pictures, both those snapped of the scene for tactical planning, and those built from descriptions by Agents collecting intelligence. This building is more squat and narrow than I had envisioned.

0645: First traces of light streak the sky as the Team stages at the outside stairwell, against the south exterior wall. A large picture window is directly above and I elevate the 870 to cover it. Now up the stairs to the second floor, to stage again at the top, next to Apartment D. The team 'stacks' in close to maximize efficiency of movement. The Breechers, two Members with the battering ram, move into position directly in front of the door. The Team Leader nods and the ram slams hard. 'Bam!' The door crashes open, the ram is tossed backwards to clear the path, and the Team streams in. 'FBI

Freeze! FBI Get Down!' I'm into the living room behind Number Five. A man is on the couch, but Hs not moved as the MP5 and several Sigs pan across him to clear the room. Number Two Man takes him, and Number Five and I cross the living room. According to our rehearsal, Number Five picks up the ballistic shield from Number One, who had used it as cover on the entry, and advances with my 870 over his left shoulder, to the hallway and the first bedroom – our objective. We kick the door and yell 'FBI, Get Down!'

The room is dark, and the light switch doesn't work. I squeeze the light built into the slide forestock of the shotgun. The beam reveals a shambles, mirroring the rest of the apartment. Cockroaches take cover under heaps of clothing and discarded food wrappers. On the bed is a small boy, perhaps five years old. His face reflects a combination of bewilderment and familiarity. He sits half upright and remains quiet. I drop the muzzle, feeling slightly remorseful that I had covered such a small child, but am thankful for the touch-index training – the finger is not on the trigger until a threat is identified. 'Is there anyone else in the room?' No answer. There is a commotion in the hallway as Team Members shout orders to an adult male in one of the back bedrooms. The little boy just stares back. Quickly Number Five and I clear the rest of the room and call out 'Clear, one child in the bed' to the Team Leader. 'It's okay young man. What's your name?' The little voice, with a slight lisp, says 'My name is Matt.' 'Matt, that's a pretty name. Several people in my family are named Matt.' There is a glimmer in the child's eyes. The Angel of Innocence has not yet completely left him, though he remains detached and impassive with two heavily armed Agents in his room. My kids would have come unglued at such a violent awakening, but the hardening of this child's soul has already begun. 'You're doing fine, son. Just stay under your covers and keep warm.'

The Team Leader calls us out to clear a back bedroom and hallway closet. The large and vocal adult male has been cuffed and contained in the living room with the other adults. 'Clear, Five and Six coming out,' shouts my partner to the Team Leader, and to Number Four, who's covering the hallway with the MP5.

0655: Apartment D has been cleared, the older occupants handcuffed and searched for weapons. The primary suspect and the .223 are not there. The only weapon seized is a .38 revolver. Our Team Leader keys his radio: 'SWAT Team One to TAC CP (Tactical Command Post). The apartment is secure. Bring in the Search Team.' TAC CP replies 'Ten Four,' and in three minutes a group composed of FBI and DEA Agents and Oakland Police Detectives, arrives to scour the area.

The large adult male is passed to the Oakland PD Officers for transport and booking – ex-felon in possession of a firearm. One of the SWAT Team informs a four-year-old girl in one of the bedrooms that her mother may have to go down to the police station and asks if she wants to go. The child replies 'Can I go with you?'

Another hour spent providing perimeter security for the search team, and our job is completed.

The ride back to the staging area is mixed with relief and reflection. The image of the little boy, caught in the bead of my sights, haunts me. A glance at my partner reveals he is also in a pensive mood, perhaps pondering the same scene. I wonder about that child and all the thousands of other children similarly trapped in these dens of squalor and terror.

Maybe the Angel of Innocence can remain long enough with these little ones, these orphans in a deadly war, to lift them out of the fire. One can only hope . . . and pray."

"Note: This raid culminated a two-year drug task force investigation into Oakland gangs. Twenty different locations in the Bay Area were struck simultaneously in the pre-dawn hours of 23 December, in an attempt to still some violence and drive-by shootings that have earmarked the Subject's activities, and to strive to bring one peaceful Christmas to the Projects."

SAN FRANCISCO SWAT OPERATION 1990 By George Z. Heuston

" 'The subject in this drug investigation has AIDS,' the case Agent cautioned. 'He's a mid-level dealer. He lives in the Sunset District of San Francisco, and has mentioned that if he's ever caught he's not going to jail. He'll shoot it out. He doesn't care, because he's got AIDS.'

We geared up and got into the SWAT van. Ron Baker handed out surgical gloves. 'Put these on under your leather gloves. With this guy we'll need extra protection.'

The operation went smoothly. The subject's car was boxed in on an Oakland side street. I was carrying an MP-5 sub machine gun. The subject was wearing a black leather jacket with a red '8 Ball' in the middle of his back. It made a perfect aiming point. The subject gave up passively, was cuffed, searched, and placed in a Bu car for transport to jail. The subject's car yielded 3 kilos of cocaine.

'OK, we got the nod, let's get out of here,' Baker said, walking back to the SWAT van.

'I have to go to the bathroom,' I said. 'I'll go across the street to the battery shop.'

'Make it quick,' Baker replied. 'We want to get breakfast.'

I crossed the street and was allowed to use the restroom. I had taken off my outer leather gloves, but not my surgical gloves. When I zipped up my fly I got the middle finger of the glove caught.

'Heuston, let's go!' the cry came from the Team in the van.

In my haste I yanked on the glove. The middle finger pulled off and was hanging out of my fly. I ran for the van.

Of course my predicament got a big laugh from my Team and more than a few comments.

'I noticed that a lady on the street stopped you on the way out of the shop,' Baker observed. 'What did she say?'

'She just looked at my fly.' I told her 'Move on lady, there's nothing to see here.'

'Boy, you can say that again,' she said, as she casually walked away."

OUTTAKE . . .

NOBODY IS PERFECT
(Author unknown)

"Each one of us is a mixture of good qualities and some perhaps not-so-good qualities. In considering our fellow man, we should remember his good qualities and realize that his faults only prove that he is, after all, a human being. We should refrain from making harsh judgement of a person just because he happens to be a dirty, rotten, no-good son-of-a-b*#@&."

The stories continue . . .

Romeo, oh Romeo…

A first office Agent during Mr. Hoover's era is interviewing a pretty young lady. Business and pleasure get mixed up, and the feeling is mutual.

The Agent asked for a date and the lady agreed.

The young lass can't remember Romeo's name, so she asked her dad, a local police chief, to inquire at the FBI. A call is placed by her dad to his friend, the SAC, who promised to help.

SAC contacts all the single Agents in the office, but none have a date planned with the described lady.

What to do? The SAC, with police chief's concurrence, tasks two old-timers to conduct a discreet surveillance to identify the Romeo. ID is made. You guessed it, the Agent is married. The ending is unknown.

Wire hanger auto fix…

With the statute of limitations long past, I'll admit to being the owner of a front bumper, grill, headlamps and hood to one of Mr.Hoover's vehicles and without his knowledge. The one part that could never be found was the hood release lever. If a certain former Inspector is reading this, he will know the reason for the wire coat hanger that protruded through the grill.

Semper Fi!

CHAPTER 8

DIRECT QUOTES OF HOGWASH, MISQUOTES, DOUBLESPEAK & GENERAL WORDINESS

No, I am not exaggerating. Every quote that you are reading in this chapter is either of words spoken or personally seen by me on various communications to or from one office to another, or an FBI division to the FBI Headquarters or vice versa. For all the years of my FBI career, 3 x 5 cards were always available to commit these gems to memory. Every time I looked at these cards, there was a smile on my face. Hopefully, if you are a retired Agent, reading these quotes, you will remember some of the characters that are being quoted and will further explain these to your children and grandchildren. If you are a casual reader, you too may wish to start writing down quotes that you read or hear, and write a chapter or a book someday. Thanks for the memories, my dear fellow FBI Special Agents.

"He wants to be a manipulator, rather than a doer. His arrogance is an arrogance of command. He is a deviser and schemer, a pontificator, a person who enjoys being both the center of attention as well as 'eminence gris'. "

"His lips are always searching for a new ass to kiss." (SA GA re a fellow SA.)

"You are an extension of a horn, you don't do any actual blowing if you are at FBIHQ." (SSA TM newly assigned from FBIHQ re fellow SSAs at FBIHQ.)

"Above classified confidential to protect the source which Chicago has not yet been able to contact."

"Peachy-keen verbiage to use in a report." (SA CH)

"The source responded with a nebulous rejoinder." (CH TT)

"Soupy and Fred are pickling themselves." (SA JB)

"Throws out a smooth, subtle double entendre remark."

PPPP INVENTION(

"A quiet, rainy Friday afternoon in the big city. SSA PP and the squad are drinking coffee and discussing the Oklahoma City bombing case. Crazy ideas are being thrown around on who done it. At one point, SSA fixes his sight on the newly painted ceiling and paint spots on the fire prevention sprinklers. The SSA, a member of Mensa, an exclusive organization of highly intelligent people, wonders aloud how the sprinkler heads could be protected when the ceiling would be painted again, to prevent paint spots.

One lowly street hump, not exactly a Mensa product, but definitely a common sense guy, takes his own empty styrofoam cup, stands on the desk and places the cup over the sprinkler head on the ceiling, in a perfect fit. Problem solved....except!

Every invention needs a name for the product. Among laughter, a conclusion is reached to name the invention after the SSA, namely: **PPPP, which stands for Peter's Perfect Paint Protector. (Don't even think of getting this name copyrighted. It had already been done. . . by the hump.)"**

The stories continue . . .

"Many of his non-governmental American interlocutors evidently predict such passivity."

"Marko knows as much about terrorism as a bird flying over terrorism

manual." (SA GA)

"Your cases are cloning themselves." (SSA TM to SA JP...how right TM was.)

"We are flimsy shufflers...the emphasis on the shuffling." (SA TB to his son who needed to give a speech at schools re dad's job. TB claimed he was the only one in the world with his sir-name. Following his death, two other individuals have been identified with the same name, and TB's son got to meet at least one of them.)

"Buzzards missed Hinckley and arrived here." (SSA TM) (Hinckley, Ohio is known to welcome buzzards every Spring.)

"A multi-purpose expert in the collection, transportation and elimination of steel wastes and debris." (Description of a job as a garbageman, given to a defector working at a steel plant.)

"Made in Flushing, New York" (An Imprint on a cup found in an FBI office bathroom.)

"...or people of his ilk, is an exercise in futility...we need disingenuous, sophisticated approach to ascertain in advance the terrorist game plan." (CV TT)

"Prioritization" (priority matter)

"Repond" (respond and report) (FBIHQ TT)

"We need Catalytic Agents for recruitment operations, misdeeds, derelictions and indiscretions of the Russian diplomatic colony."(SAC's memo)

"Existing statutes and regulations pertinent to unauthorized disclosures of confidential information suffer from vagueness and underbreadth." (FBIHQ TT)

"SA did not operate his vehicle in a wreckless manner." (IN LHM)

"BU work is abhorrent to a free society." (Washington Post newspaper)

"These Agents fought for decency while others blasted it or piously mouthed its shibboleths in the halls of Congress."

"Thus any report which downgrades the Bureau stirs glandular satisfaction in some circles."

"One was a traffic scofflaw."

"Infiltrate and destroy." (SA BL)

"Traditionally, the BU car coordinator has had a car assigned that he could pick." (SA JH)

"Trans- national terrorists will not respect our border only our resolves." (SA JH)

"You have more money than a cat has hair on its ass." (SA PJ)

"If I had your money, I'd burn mine."(SA RW)

"He who dies with most software – wins." (SSA PG)

ARKANSAS DAYVORCE

(Author unknown)

“A farmer walked into an attorney’s office wanting to file for a divorce.

The attorney asked, ‘May I help you” The farmer said ‘Yea, I want to get one of those dayvorces.’

The attorney said, ‘Well do you have any grounds?’ The farmer said, ‘Yea, I got bout 140 acres.’

The attorney said, ‘No, you don’t understand, I mean do you have a case?’ The farmer said, ‘No I don’t have a case, but I do have a John Deere.’

The attorney said, ‘No, you don’t understand. I mean do you have a grudge?’ The farmer said, ‘Yea, I got a grudge, that’s where I park my John Deere.’

The attorney said, ‘No Sir, I mean do you have a suit?’ The farmer said, ‘Yes Sir, I got a suit. I wear it to church on Sundays.’

The attorney said, ‘Well Sir, does your wife beat you up or anything?’ The farmer said, ‘No Sir, we both get up about 4:30.’

The attorney then said, ‘Well, is she unfaithful or anything?’

The farmer said, ‘Yes, she’s a little gal, but our last child was a #@&*!$ and that’s why I want this dayvorce!”

The stories continue . . .

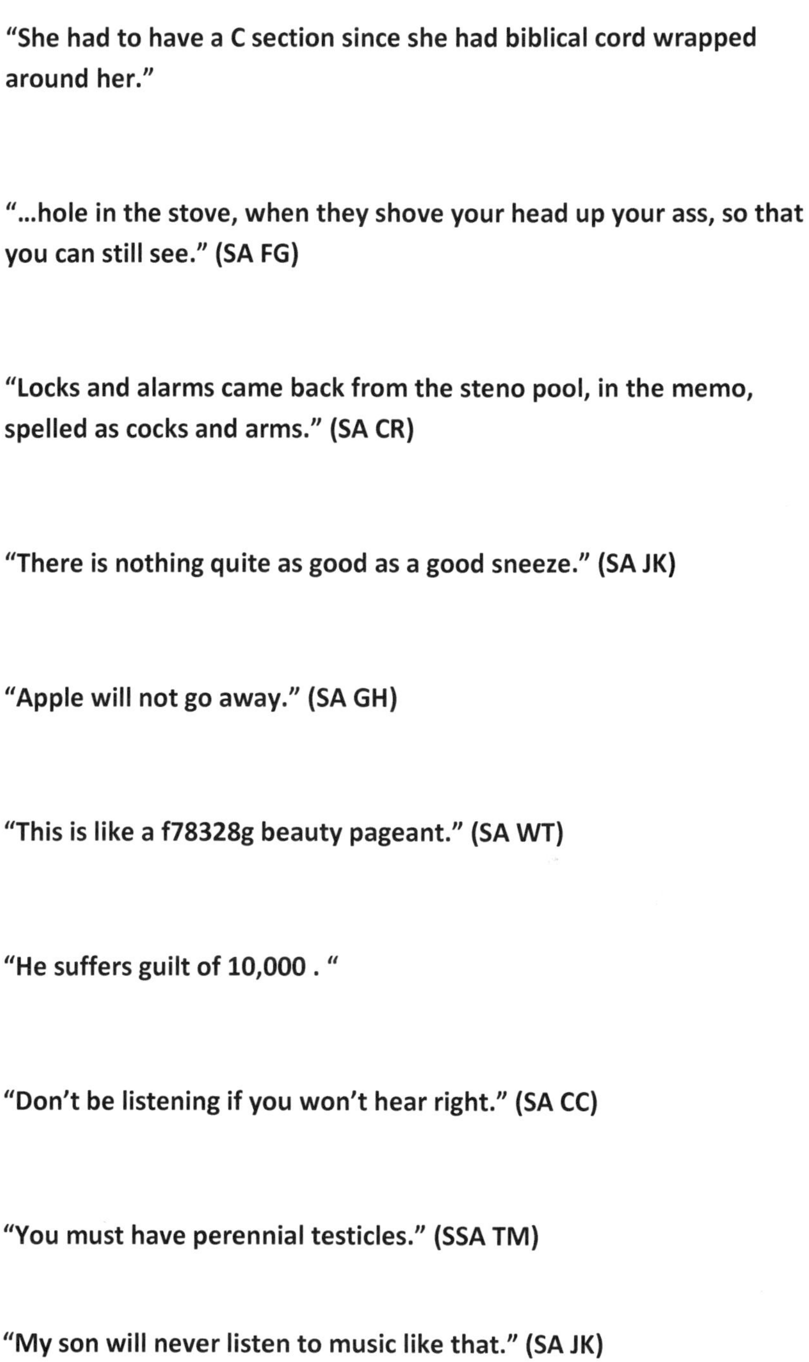

"She had to have a C section since she had biblical cord wrapped around her."

"...hole in the stove, when they shove your head up your ass, so that you can still see." (SA FG)

"Locks and alarms came back from the steno pool, in the memo, spelled as cocks and arms." (SA CR)

"There is nothing quite as good as a good sneeze." (SA JK)

"Apple will not go away." (SA GH)

"This is like a f78328g beauty pageant." (SA WT)

"He suffers guilt of 10,000 . "

"Don't be listening if you won't hear right." (SA CC)

"You must have perennial testicles." (SSA TM)

"My son will never listen to music like that." (SA JK)

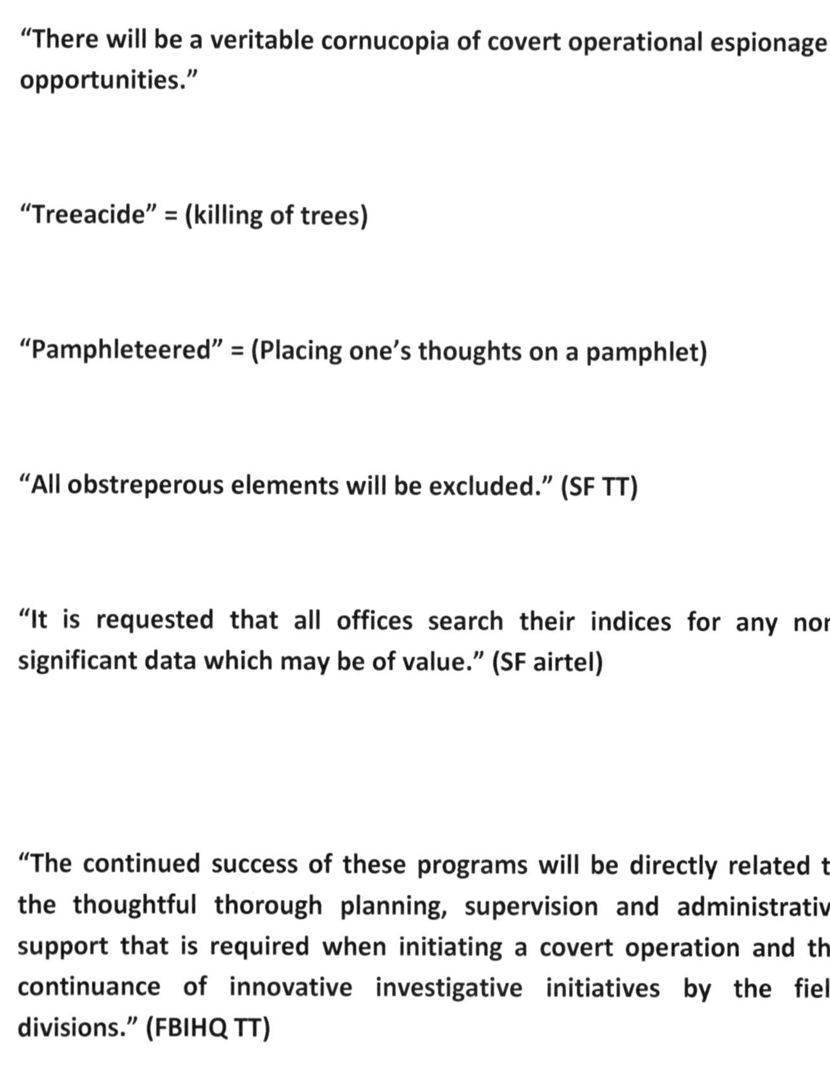

"There will be a veritable cornucopia of covert operational espionage opportunities."

"Treeacide" = (killing of trees)

"Pamphleteered" = (Placing one's thoughts on a pamphlet)

"All obstreperous elements will be excluded." (SF TT)

"It is requested that all offices search their indices for any non-significant data which may be of value." (SF airtel)

"The continued success of these programs will be directly related to the thoughtful thorough planning, supervision and administrative support that is required when initiating a covert operation and the continuance of innovative investigative initiatives by the field divisions." (FBIHQ TT)

"If he was on fire I would not even pea on him to put it out."

"The gerontocracy of the cybernetic managerial cadre at FBIHQ

responsible for integration of WFO elements into the counterintelligence and counterinterferencial force has again been demonstrated." (WFO TT)

"SA J.B. is fat, dumb and happy."

"The era of the explosion of knowledge...the information age...is upon us. Eighty percent of all the scientists who ever lived are alive today, rapidly distributing technology advances to our society. Were it not for a misunderstood Italian named Galileo, we would not have binoculars and telescopes in the lookouts. The eraser-tipped pencil greatly facilitates making log entries. But it is now time for another great leap forward into the present." (NY airtel)

OUTTAKE . . .

GREETINGS

(Author unknown)

"For my Democratic Friends:

Please accept with no obligation, implied or implicit, our best wishes for an environmentally conscious, socially responsible, low-stress, non-addictive, gender-neutral celebration of the winter solstice holiday, practiced within the most enjoyable traditions of the religious persuasion and/or traditions of others, or their choice not to practice religious or secular traditions at all.

We also wish you a fiscally successful, personally fulfilling and medically uncomplicated recognition of the onset of the generally accepted calendar year 2014, but not without due respect for the calendars of choice of other cultures whose contributions to society have helped make America great. Not to imply that America is necessarily greater than any other country nor the only America in the Western Hemisphere. And without regard to the race, creed, color, age, physical ability, religious faith or sexual preference of the wishee.

By accepting these greetings you are accepting these terms. This greeting is subject to clarification or withdrawal. It is fully transferable with no alteration to the original greeting. It implies no promise by the wisher to actually implement any of the wishes for herself or himself or others and is void where prohibited by law and is revocable at the sole discretion of the wisher. This wish is warranted to perform as expected within the usual application of good tidings for a period of one year or until the issuance of a subsequent holiday greeting, whichever comes first, and warranty is limited to replacement of this wish or issuance of a new wish at the sole discretion of the wisher."

For my Republican friends...

Here's wishing you all a Merry Christmas and a Happy New Year!"

The stories continue . . .

"We mandate commitments to reactive matters."

"From all quadrants, reports indicate that we are losing the battle." (WFO memo)

"Phone is fun and it is informative because the speaker's personality is injected into the air lanes."

"He has galvanic personality."

"From all quadrants, reports indicate that the Russian diplomats abuse American willingness to get along."(NY TT)

"He has latent leadership qualities." (Written in my MAP evaluation report, letting me know very politely that there is no chance in hell in getting a promotion to a supervisory position.)

"I hope you are cognizant of the fact that you are expected to modify and ameliorate the methodologies with which you demonstrate productivity in order to conform to the desired objectives of the program." (Words...more words)

"If brains were dynamite you would not be able to fart." (SA GA)

"One who is all knowledgeable in supervisory techniques." (Supervisorial) (SSA TM)

"Clean underwear on the same dirty ass." = (Definition of someone that had just been promoted to the Headquarters) + (SA JC upon hearing the announcement that a new Director of the FBI has been named)

"Creative intelligence" (Common sense)

"The information descended upon the recipient Senators in a cacophony of macaronic dissention." (SA JH)

"I am on Meridian time." (SA GH)

"Pilot read the note and said: 'Oh shit, this plane is being hijacked." (FBIHQ TT with the understatement of the day)

CHAPTER 9. . .

SOURCES, ASSETS AND RECRUITMENTS

Finding and developing sources and assets is as important to FBI's solving of cases, as are the meals of meat and potatoes for a typical farming family. You just got to have them.

There are only so many FBI Special Agents to cover different interests and varied investigations, only so many boots on the ground. By means of sources and assets, FBI can exponentially increase amount of information obtained on a particular case or on individuals and organizations.

Likewise, by use of recruitment, FBI can get inside the heart of the organization, a diplomatic or terrorist establishment, and get to the family jewels, to determine what type of an operation is necessary to bring forth the desired information.

Recruitments are worth their weight in gold and are prized by any organization, whether it's intelligence or a competitive private business.

THE FATHER FIGURE

"One of my jobs in the FCI field was to 'babysit' new recruitments and defectors that decided to jump the fence from the various diplomatic establishments. Many were recruited in place and worked for us and at our direction in providing information of interest in our investigations. Some were recruited while serving in other countries and when it was time to defect they were brought to the U.S. to be resettled here.

Some of these assets were given a new identity and started a new life in the U.S., while others lived openly in big cities, with no new identities or new covers. Some had a fairly good understanding of the American way of life, as well as a working knowledge of the English language, while others were like babes in the woods. This was a new country and a new life-style for them. They had no friends, except for the FBI Special Agents that they met. Most came with the clothes on their backs and no extra clothes in the suitcase.

Shopping that we take for granted was a huge task for them, after all, it is hard to even decide which shirt to pick out from the 100's of different colors and styles in typical American stores. This was now a problem for them. In their previous country, all decisions were made for them…there was only one style and one color for a shirt available on the store shelf.

One particular recruitment was resettled in the city where I was assigned. I was tasked to find suitable housing for the family, furnishings for the apartment, school for the kids as well as a doctor and a dentist and a gainful employment for the head of household. I was their babysitter. After months of involvement with the family, the principal subject made the following observation: 'You are a father and a mother to me. Thank you for that.' I can only thank the fellow Americans, who when approached for assistance in these cases, did so willingly, without a thank you from Uncle Sam, and without publicity. They too were sources who were either previously developed or developed at a moment's notice, trusting the FBI Special Agent that requested their assistance.

An old timer Agent that worked cases in the former Eastern Bloc countries told me the story of a funeral that he had to stage for a diplomat's family member. He had to use other Agents as pallbearers and a reverend who was an FBI source, to conduct the service in subject's language. It took good old GI ingenuity to pull it off."

OUTTAKE . . .

EARLY RETIREMENT PROGRAM

(A memorandum to all employees from the Director, FBI in February, 1971... tongue in cheek)

(Author unknown)

"As a result of automation as well as a declining workload, steps must be taken to reduce our work force. A reduction of staff plan has been developed which appears to be equitable under the circumstances.

Under the plan, older employees will be placed on early retirement permitting the retention of those employees who represent the future of the Bureau.

A program to phase out older personnel by the end of the current fiscal year by means of early retirement will be placed into effect immediately. This program shall be known as RAPE (Retire Aged Personnel Early).

Employees who are Raped will be given opportunity to seek other jobs within the Bureau, provided that while they are being Raped, they request a review of their employment status before actual retirement takes place. This phase of the program is called SCREW (Survey of Capabilities of Retired Early Workers).

All employees who have been Raped and Screwed may then apply for a final review. This will be called SHAFT (Study by Higher Authority Following Termination).

Program policy dictates that employees may be Raped once and Screwed twice, but may get the Shaft as many times as the Bureau deems appropriate."

The stories continue . . .

BULGARIAN SHIP-JUMPER

"Headlines in the morning newspaper over a few days caught my attention. A Bulgarian ship-jumper apparently left a Bulgarian ship and asked for political asylum in the U.S., claiming prosecution by the Communist government in Bulgaria.

INS was contacted and a lengthy interview by the INS followed, utilizing a Bulgarian translator. The young man claimed he did not speak the English language and Bulgarian émigré community started a campaign to help the young man, by providing monetary and social support.

As far as I was concerned, his story, as featured in the newspaper, did not pass the smell test. I called the familiar INS Agent that handled the case and asked him to allow the FBI to interview the man after INS's investigation was complete, to determine if he had any information that would be of interest to the FBI, regarding Bulgarian intelligence activities. Promising a two minute interview brought a hearty laughter on the part of the INS Agent, who was familiar with my style of 'please give me two minutes of your time' interviews.

A couple of days later, an interview was scheduled in our office. I arranged to have our own familiar translator present for this interview, without presence of INS Agents.

The young man was brought to the FBI office. Introductions were exchanged with help from the translator and I was assured that the man had zero knowledge of the English language. My two minute interview began. I asked through the translator for subject's name and date of birth and was given a translated answer. I duly wrote down the name and date of birth on the legal pad. I next asked if the subject understood or spoke English and received a translated NO in the English language, writing same down on the pad.

Putting down the pen and directly addressing the subject, I asked: 'Would you like a Coke?' The answer from him was almost instantaneous . . . YES PLEASE!

I got up and left the room ostensibly to get a Coke. While outside the room, I called the INS Agent to return and arrest his subject. The FBI interview was completed. The man was a fake."

UACB
(Unless advised to the Contrary by the Bureau)

" An intelligence officer (a spy) of an Eastern European country, left the U.S. before there was a chance to pitch him for recruitment, as the FBIHQ and the U.S. State Department could not get into a higher gear and make a decision before it was too late. The last teletype from the FBIHQ was a one liner, 'Wait for the other shoe to drop'.

A few years later, this same individual returned to a U.S. posting. The Special Agent that had the case reopened sent an equally short teletype to the FBIHQ, namely: 'UACB, the other shoe is ready to be dropped'."

The GRU Officer who peed in his pants
(For a full story, read the chapter on "Jai Aflai" in *Spy vs Spy* by Ron Kessler)

"The Russian military intelligence officer (GRU) drove around the metropolitan area for over eight hours, dry-cleaning himself, attempting to identify a surveillance. He could not identify one, so he decided that he will go ahead and clear a drop site.

Under cover of darkness, he stealthily approached the wooded area and the location of the buried top secret documents, placed there by an American. As he crouched down to pick up the package, all hell broke loose and flashlights exploded all around, as FBI Special Agents, secreted in covered foxholes all around the area, jumped out of the ground, yelling 'FBI DO NOT MOVE'. The Russian was startled., claiming to be looking for a fishing hole (no rivers or lakes or ponds anywhere nearby). He promptly peed in his pants.

As an aside, the following story also developed at the same site, approximately one hour earlier:

A jogger who resided in the area, by sheer coincidence, an Air Force officer, needed to "take a dump" and did so within an arm's reach of two of the Agents hidden in a foxhole surrounding the drop site. He continued his run, oblivious to the trap that was to ensnare a Russian military attache, a GRU Officer . . . a spy, later that night."

OUTTAKE . . .

110 YEARS AGO
(Author unknown)

- "The average life expectancy in the U.S. was 47 years.
- Only 14 % of the homes in the U.S. had a bathtub.
- There were only 8,000 cars in the U.S. and only 144 miles of paved roads.
- The maximum speed limit in most cities was 10 mph.
- The average U.S. worker made between $200 and $400 per year.
- More than 95% of all births in the U.S. took place at home.
- Sugar cost four cents a pound.
- Most women only washed their hair once a month and used borax or egg yolks for shampoo.
- The population of Las Vegas, Nevada, was 30.
- Crossword puzzles, canned beer and iced tea hadn't been invented."

The stories continue . . .

THE IO WHO WANTED TO MAKE AN INVESTMENT

"An officer in the foreign intelligence service had come to our attention. He had some extra money to invest and was looking for a deal.

It just so happened that two out of town businessmen, representing farmers from a nearby state, appeared on the scene, with a lucrative proposal. They offered a high return on investments and the deal was ready to be signed. The intel officer agreed to return on the following day to the same hotel room and bring the money, often asking to be excused for his minimal knowledge of the English language.

The officer returned on the following day, bringing a bottle of his country's favorite alcoholic drink, to seal the deal. Small talk ensued, glasses clinked and alcohol consumed, but the officer apparently smelled a rat and headed for the door. All appeared to be lost.

At the very last moment, in desperation, one of the businessmen asked the IO not to leave, in the officer's native language. The officer turned around and hugged the two businessmen.

Now an additional bottle of the best American whiskey was ordered and delivered. The man cried and drank to his heart's content and the deal was sealed.

The FBI Special Agents developed a new friend."

CAR DEALER ONE CAN COUNT ON

"I suppose that every city has businessmen that have assisted the FBI when the FBI came calling. In my experience, none has been greater than one I am now describing, without actually naming him or her.

This particular businessman is a big-time car dealer. If the FBI called and asked for a 'loaner car', it was ready when you went to pick it up. If the FBI needed an undercover car, one was available at a moment's notice. If a defector that you were baby-sitting needed wheels and had no credit record established yet, wheels were easily obtained. Monthly payments could be arranged later.

An hour after 911 occurred, this wonderful human being and an outstanding U.S. citizen, called a lowly FBI street hump that he personally knew and told him that he has not been able to contact the SAC, and he wanted to pass a message to him, as follows: 'If the FBI needs a large fleet of cars or trucks to carry on its mission, please just say so and the vehicles will be provided, at no cost, for the duration of the crisis and until the case (911) is solved."

On numerous occasions, this same individual also provided, at no cost, a pilot and a plane, if he learned that a sick child had to be transported out of town for special treatment. No publicity for his business was requested., or given, in return.

This man was given a special blessing, by the Almighty, and it was his way of thanking Him."

WASPS

"As a clerk in the late 1960's, I saw an exchange of routing slips between the SAC and the SRA in a border town in SW U.S.

SAC, per Bureau instructions, had to prepare a nitel to the SOG, regarding any potential civil unrest by racial minorities in the division. He sent a routing slip to each SRA asking for their assessment.

In one two-man RA, response was as follows: 'Boss, as WASPS, the two of us assigned in this RA are the only racial minority in town. We don't plan any unrest.' "

170 INFORMANTS

"Up to mid-1970's, Bureau required each FBI Special Agent to develop classification 170 Informants, aka, Ghetto Informants. Most of the divisions mandated two Ghetto Informants per Agent, with monthly contacts. Their negative info on potential riots was actually considered a positive information for stat purposes.

As a FOA, I developed one of my two required Ghetto Informants, in a very ingenious way. During the first week in my first office, I was directed to acclimate myself to the area by taking out a bureau car and driving around the city. At one point, I parked the car and started walking. As soon as I turned away from the car, I heard the sound of a vehicle being hit. It was my bureau car for that day that was hit. Quickly returning to the car, I observed an elderly Black gentleman surveying the almost non-existent damage to the bureau vehicle. I identified myself as an FBI Agent and the driver of the vehicle. to this man who expressed a deep remorse. I proceeded to obtain his driver's license and copied down the identifying data. Based on this info, I was able to open him up as an informant. Subsequent contacts with him were always negative."

A POEM FROM 'THE YEAR OF THE SPY'
(By "Debbie")

"T'was the night before Christmas, when all through the USA, not a creature was stirring, not even an SA.

The package was hidden by Walker near the pole with care, in hopes that Tckchinko soon would be there.

The cash and gold were safely buried by Ed, while visions of disappearing acts danced in Howard's head.

With Pelton's flopped caper and Pollard's ill-fated scheme, also Larry Wu Tai Chin's bombed out dream.

When out of the such a group with such muster, everyone in the community wants to know who are the Spy-busters.

Away to New Mexico they flew like a flash, also covered Annapolis with such a splash.

At Dupont Circle and 14th Street, they artfully covered the subject's meet.

Near Landmark Center on Yokum Parkway. Some of the troops made Larry Chin pay.

With their disguise and manner-at-ease, we knew in a moment it must be the G's!!

More rapid than grease lightening they came, they whistled and shouted and called subjects by name.

Now Edward, now James, now Michael and Johnny, on Jonathan, on Ann, on Larry and Ronnie.

To the prison, the slammer, and behind the wall, now dash away, dash and a Merry Christmas to all !"

A BELATED GUILTY STORY

"One particular Agent was on the surveillance team in the 70's in the city known as car capitol of the U.S.. They had an RV with all the goodies this particular day, in case a big snow storm came in. Sometime that day, they stopped for a few drinks and parked the RV in a big lot.

When they came out a few hours later, the RV was gone. All hell to pay, but the RV was recovered sans a lot of equipment.

Years later, this same Agent was assigned to another division. His job was to protect a witness who was in the witness protection program. One day, the subject of the initial city noted above, came up. The 'witness protection' individual stated that once upon a time he stole an FBI RV from a parking lot in that city.

The FBI Special Agent lost it, telling the man how much trouble the incident caused him."

THIS BOOK'S AUTHOR, UPON RECEIVING RETIREMENT CREDENTIALS (Author unknown)

"Whose bletcherous, malar-ific face is this, sad ancient physiognomy, pretending to be Al? What twisted those features to rhyparography?

Where hides the young hero, who bethought himself a modern Achilles donning U.S. Army's 1LT bars, and a

golden badge? Surely never in the sixties?

The image on the plaque is the one I recall; some schism of photography made awful morphallaxis of our minor Adonis; it had to be evil sorcery.

Those ears, that hanging underlip, eyes of crepe. How many Rieslings will be needed to expunge the pain of this unkind clout to the testes?

And . . . I can't help but wonder:
Would my picture be pert-ier , my hair curlier . . . hm hm fuller, my teeth pearlier?

If they had only just sent the damn things to me ten years earlier?

Al Zupan 1970-2002"

(Ah, well. Never mind. Only a belated gripe; X-G's have that license)

The stories continue . . .

AN EASTERN EUROPEAN ASSET

"While meeting with a targeted female Macedonian diplomat, in a woman to woman informal discussion, I asked her in the Serbian language if Yugoslav intelligence officers of Croatian nationality would make good recruitments. Her answer was very outright: 'Pas menja dlaku a ne chut' (A dog changes its hair but not its brain)."

MEETING A FAMOUS PERSON

"One day I interviewed a lady who called the office and requested an in-person contact with an Agent. She volunteered information regarding a subject of one of our investigations in the FCI field. Her information was of value and I asked if she would be willing to provide additional information, should it become available to her. She agreed.

Next day, while out covering other leads, my supervisor contacted me requesting a quick return to the office. He advised me that the SAC received a call from the FBIHQ, requesting that the Supervisor and I come to the FBIHQ at a designated time that day, due to a problem with a contact of mine.

When we arrived at the FBIHQ, we were introduced to Mr. Ross Perot, a proud Texan and the 1992 and 1996 Independent presidential candidate, who was deeply involved in the Vietnam War POW/MIA issues at one time.

Mr. Perot looked down first and noticed the brown leather cowboy boots that I was wearing that day. He looked up at my face, reached out with an outstretched hand and said: 'Are you from Texas, boy?' The ice was broken, the rest was strictly business.

This was an only time in my career that I actually met a famous person. Too bad that I did not purchase any of the shares of Mr.Perot's EDS Corporation or ask to talk to him privately about my potential future employment opportunities with the EDS after my retirement from the FBI."

A PROFESSIONAL HOOKER

"The young lady volunteered to help in a criminal case and identified a fugitive who was on the lam. I opened her as a criminal informant and had regular contacts with her, simply business related to criminals.

During one of these contacts, she let it be known that if a 'paying customer' knocks on the door, she will politely ask that I hide in a nearby closet, while she carries on the business of the oldest profession in the world.

It happened a few minutes later and yours truly hid in the closet for fifteen minutes while there was bed action a few feet away.

(What a torture to put a man through, all for the sake of the FBI business …and to even get paid to do the job.)

A year later, before transferring to another division, I introduced her to another contacting Special Agent and thanked her for her cooperation. She noted, in the presence of the other Agent, that she always hoped to get me in bed, but did not succeed. She lamented the only failure that she ever had.

I often stated that I have a deep respect for the 'ladies of the evening, selling their wares', because they honestly provide the service that you pay for, nothing more and nothing less, and they will even let you charge it on a credit card."

"DON'T STAY AWAY FROM CHURCH BECAUSE"
(Author unknown)

- **You are poor. There is no charge.**
- **You are rich. We can help you resolve that problem.**
- **It rains. You go to work in the rain.**
- **It is hot. So is the golf course.**
- **It is cold. It's warm inside.**
- **No one invited you. You go to movies without being asked.**
- **Churches have emotional religions. A ballgame is emotional, too.**
- **You have little children. Churches welcome children.**
- **You don't like the preacher. He's human, like you.**
- **There are hypocrites there. You associate with them daily.**
- **You have company. Bring them with you or ask them to wait for you. They'll admire**

you for it.

- **You need a weekend vacation. God never takes a vacation. From loving and caring for you. What if he did?**
- **Your clothes are inexpensive. Church isn't a fashion show.**
- **The church standards are high. Look at the Bible's standards.**
- **The church always wants money. So does the grocer.**
- **You have plenty of time ahead to get saved. Are you sure?**

The stories continue . . .

FAMILY ASSISTANCE

"A simple assignment on an important FCI case. Bring your kids along tonight in a Bureau car, a non-descript station wagon, and park yourself in a shopping center adjacent to a dead-end townhouse development at a designated time frame, plus or minus an hour, with a good view of a vehicle that was being used by an American double agent as a dead drop to be cleared by a foreign spy. Pretend that you are a happy family man babysitting kids in a family car, while your wife is shopping.

Two dozen other non-descript FBI cars, with two Agent teams in each, are strategically located inside a two mile radius circle of the target vehicle, ready to descend at moment's notice, after the dead drop is cleared.

A vehicle belonging to a foreign country military intelligence officer is observed passing your station wagon. This was not the expected individual but the actual officer in charge of the military office . . . and having a rank of a General. No other team observed him in the area. You are in the closest surveillance car and advises the other units when the drop is cleared. The General takes off as a bat in hell, heading for the nearest entrance to the seven lane freeway. You follow at an even higher speed, shouting to your kids who are safely buckled in the back seat to unbuckle and hit the floor between the seats. The proverbial s#&t was to hit the fan and the smell will be bad. If his vehicle reaches the freeway, only a direct collision with his vehicle will prevent him from reaching his diplomatic establishment.

With less than 50 yards to go, and half a vehicle length ahead of his, I squeezed General's vehicle against the right side of the road, against a high berm, so as to block him from driving away or exiting the car, without actually causing the two vehicles to crash. Shouting to the kids to stay down, so as not to have them observe what may happen next to their dad, I jumped out, hi-stepping to subject's vehicle, as flashing lights and sirens from the rest of the crew descended at high speed into the area and engulfed both of our vehicles. Arrest of the spy followed.(I have a picture to prove it.) Everyone was safe. The General was declared PNG, Persona non grata, and expelled from the U.S.

Many years later, my wonderful young daughter told me that despite my warnings, she 'peeked' to observe what was happening with all the lights and sirens. Women, at whatever age, have a way."

PROMISE OF HELL

"Information was received re possibility of a contact by an individual with a known foreign country intelligence officer, of interest to us. Two of us interviewed him, using good cop – bad cop technique. I was usually the bad cop.

Individual denied having contact. I told him point blank that he was not truthful and he will burn in hell for telling a lie to FBI Special Agents. I then walked out, by design, while my partner tried being the nice guy and win the man over.

A few days later, read a story in the local newspaper regarding some individual committing a suicide. It was the man noted above. Unless God forgave him, he is burning rightfully in hell."

A SNAKE NEST

"A male called, claiming to have knowledge of a GRU (Soviet Military Intelligence) officer visiting a certain bar on a regular basis. Caller believed this to be a trolling operation conducted by the GRU. An appointment was made with the caller to meet him in his apartment, for an interview.

I knocked on the door and the man opened the door, with a boa wrapped around his neck and countless other snakes observed in the cages and directly on the floor, slithering behind him.

Sorry, wrong door. No questions asked. Obtained a business card from him and left."

FINAL FCI TEST AT FBI ACADEMY
(Author unknown)

"Four spies in trench coats sat in four facing seats as they traveled the Peking Express. With two by the window and two by the aisle, the arrangement was strange (as you guessed):

The English spy sat on Mr. B's left.
Mr.A had a coat colored tan.
The spy dressed in olive was on German spy's right.
Mr.C was the only cigar-smoking man.
Mr.D was across from the American spy.
The Russian, in khaki, had a scarf round his throat.

The English spy stared out the window on his left.
So who was the spy in the rust-colored coat?"

The stories continue . . .

SWEATING NITROGLYCERIN

"A confidential informant called early one Saturday AM. He was calling from a pay phone and asked to meet at McDonalds. He said it was urgent I show up.

I made it there in 20 minutes and /McDonalds was dead on a Saturday morning with only four customers inside. As I sucked on a greasy Egg McMuffin, I told the source that this better be damn good.

The source claimed that he was able to 'solicit' an explosive device away from a radical group; he wouldn't testify about it, and he had 2-3 days to return it or they'll know he was up to something with it. He told them he had to move the device for safety reasons, so he came from another state, through the tunnel, to meet with me.

He said the device was of plastic composition; 2 blasting caps, and appeared very old. He wanted to know how we can spare his identity, keep him active, and 'do something with this thing', to further our investigation.

Simple, I thought; we'll substitute an identical looking 'inert' device and the source can return it, and we can track it. Sounded good, so I told him to arrange to show us and appropriate bomb squad personnel where he had hidden the device; we had to move on this thing immediately, and I had a lot of calls to make.

And that's when it all happened. . . that 'oh, crap' moment of our careers. It was only then when he said he saved us the trouble and the explosive device was in a paper bag under the exact table we were sitting at in McDonalds! But it only got worse from there . . . when I bent down to examine it, the paper bag was wet. I asked him if the device was 'sweating'. He said he thought so; that it was sweating nitroglycerin!

I lifted the bag, figuring it weighed about 2 – 3 pounds.

And so, I sat frozen for what seemed to be hours, realizing this bozo (who was really a bright guy), just drove with the device through a tunnel; it was sitting now in a place with us and others, and there was a possibility that this thing could go off at any moment because it was 'sweating'.

I told the source to get into his car and get lost. I then ID'd myself to the manager and we evacuated the place, calling for the bomb squad at the same time. Uniform and bomb squad members arrived and the downtown area was lit up like a Christmas tree. 'Hell' had nothing to do that morning, and the PD brass had me cornered, grilling me like they had just captured Jack the Ripper; ready to put the cuffs on. Police radios were chattering that an FBI Agent was in McDonalds with a live explosive device. A member of the bomb squad that knew me came over and said, 'Don't tell me a damn thing . . . just what do you want to do with this thing?' He had a look on his face like a friend of his was about to end up on the front pages of the newspaper and none of it was going to be good.

Monday morning at the office was a day or reckoning; someone somewhere was going to have a piece of yours truly for allowing (which I did not) a source to bring a live explosive. And so I spent the next 2 weeks explaining the whole thing to the high up honchos in the PD and the Bureau.

I ended up unscathed by it all. We duplicated the inert device and gave it back to the CI. Believe it or not, none of this story ever appeared in the media at the time, or even later.

But during the ensuing weeks, my bar tab was double what it normally was.

One night after this incident, a fellow Agent who was my partner in crime, pulled up a stool at the bar, ordered his scotch and water and muttered to me something I heard for the first time, 'Big cases, big problems; little cases, little problems. No cases . . . no problems'."

OUTTAKE . . .

COUNTERESPIONAGE
(By Eric Ambler, *The Light of Day)*

"I think if I were asked to single out one specific group of men, one category, as being the most suspicious, unbelieving, unreasonable, petty, inhuman, sadistic, unbelieving, double-crossing set of bastards in any language, I would say without any hesitation: 'The people who run counterespionage departments.' "

(Above sign was hanging on the wall above my desk as a constant reminder.)

The stories continue . . .

170 CASE WITHOUT A BODY

"My favorite 170 case involved a car pool mate. He was working on the old commie squad, hence never got near the ghetto. None the less, he was required to have a ghetto informant. So a little creative writing developed a black female who lived in the ghetto and could tell him 'nothing happened'. His rationalization was, who the better to say nothing happened than a fictitious source.

This worked great until the criminal check he sent in came back from the Bureau, that his source's name, DOB and description matched someone wanted in another state. He got a lead to contact the source and determine if she was the fugitive.

So what to do? He responded that 'attempts to contact the source again were negative and she had apparently moved with no forwarding address'.

No one ever found out what happened and he went on to become an ASAC."

DO YOU SPEAK RUSSIAN?

"A foreign diplomat, of interest to the U.S. intelligence community, was scheduled to be polygraphed overseas as the last step before being accepted as a bona fide recruitment in place.

A polygraph examiner from another U.S. intelligence agency was flown in to conduct an exam. The examiner was told by the FBI Special Agent responsible for the case not to discuss subject's nationality and not to use the word 'Russian' with this particular subject, so as not to agitate the subject. The examiner agreed.

When the subject entered the room, pleasantries were exchanged and the examiner's first words were, 'Do you speak Russian language?'

The diplomat stormed out of the room using choice X#^&*+ words in several languages that he spoke, including Russian.

The polygrapher was sent packing back to his own Agency. The case was set back a few weeks because the examiner could not follow the rules of engagement that were set."

A RECRUITMENT APPROACH

"A certain SA wanted to familiarize a recruitment target to feel at ease as every day the same SA leaned on Bucar bumper in vicinity of subject's parked vehicle. The subject was quite aware that he was being surveilled. This was going on for over two weeks, and subject acknowledged SA's existence.

In the past, the target had been approached by a sister agency overseas, and turned them down for cooperation. Likewise, subject had been approached by other FBI Agents, with similar results. In no uncertain terms, subject stated that he was not interested. He continued with his dastardly work, recruiting Americans. It was time to put a stop to his endeavors.

When it was learned that a relative of his, who was a highly placed individual in their country's intelligence service, had died, a condolence card was placed on target's car windshield, expressing sorrow and condolences.

Subject picked up the card, opened it, ostensibly acknowledged SA's presence within his view, and was visibly shaken as he shed a tear.

Within 24 hours, target was packed on a flight to his homeland, only to be replaced by another spy, who was more receptive to our approach.

There are definitely many ways to skin a cat."

WILL YOU HAVE A JOB?

"A foreign diplomat, of interest to the U.S. intelligence community, was being debriefed in a high-rise hotel room, for possible grooming as a recruitment-in-place, while being posted in the U.S.

To create white noise, and muffle our conversation, a TV channel was set to a continuous news station. The FBI Special Agent told the potential recruitment that he would be monetarily rewarded for his cooperation with the FBI. At the same time, a news bulletin on the TV announced a headline story of the FBI possibly laying off FBI Agents, since funding had not as yet been approved for them.

The diplomat, who spoke and understood English fluently, asked the Agent how he can guarantee reward when the SA was not guaranteed of getting his next paycheck. The only thing the Agent could do was to start laughing and stating that apparently, neither of our countries could guarantee our jobs and existence. We both raised our glasses to that and had a drink, for friendship's sake."

AMERICAN HEROES
(Written by "Debbie")

"There are some American heroes who caught a Russian spy,
Their patriotic effort gave them a natural high.
To the American public they have remained unknown,
And one would imagine them as a 'Superman' clone!

These Americans are brave, courageous, and true,

They magnify freedom in our red, white, and blue.
That must have been a fabulous team, the FBI and the OSI,
To have convinced The Russians there were many secrets
they could buy.

Trading secrets for money on nights that were more than cool,
Must have convinced comrade Vladimir that he had
an American fool!

When the 'commie' fell for the sting, it was even better than pay,
And to cuff the Russian diplomat, made the Agents' day!
So let's raise a glass of vodka and have a memorable toast,
To the unsung American heroes who should be praised the
most!"

OUTTAKE . . .

AN OBITUARY FOR COMMON SENSE
(Author unknown)

"Today we mourn the passing of a beloved old friend, Common Sense, who had been with us for many years. No one knows for sure how old he was, since his birth records were long ago lost in bureaucratic red tape.

He will be remembered as having cultivated such valuable lessons as:

- **Knowing when to come in out of the rain;**
- **Why the early bird gets the worm;**
- **Life isn't always fair;**
- **And maybe it was my fault.**

Common sense lived by a simple, sound financial policies (don't spend more than you can earn) and reliable strategies (adults, not children, are in charge).

His health began to deteriorate rapidly when well-intentioned but overbearing regulations were set in place.

Reports of a 6-year-old boy charged with sexual harassment for kissing a classmate; teens suspended from school for using mouthwash after lunch; and a teacher fired for reprimanding an unruly student, only worsened his condition.

Common Sense lost ground when parents attacked teachers for doing the job that they themselves had failed to do in disciplining their unruly children. It declined even further when schools were required to get parental consent to administer sun lotion or an aspirin to a student; but could not inform parents when a student became pregnant and wanted to have an abortion.

Common Sense lost the will to live as the churches became businesses; and criminals received better treatment than their victims. Common Sense took a beating when you couldn't defend yourself from a burglar in your own home and he burglar could sue you for assault.

Common Sense finally gave up the will to live, after a woman failed to realize that a steaming cup of coffee was hot. She spilled a little in her lap, and was promptly awarded a huge settlement.

Common Sense was preceded in death, by his parents, Truth and Trust, by his wife, Discretion, by his daughter, Responsibility, and his son, Reason.

He is survived by his 4 stepbrothers; I Know My Rights, I Want It Now, Someone Else Is To Blame, and I'm A Victim.

Not many attended his funeral because so few realized he was gone, if you still remember him. If not, join the majority and do nothing."

The stories continue . . .

BLAST FROM THE PAST

"New Agent classes at the OPO (Old Post Office); White shirts, dark suits, and 'shoes with a thousand eyes'; Pens with only black ink; Mr. Hoover used blue ink; Getting weighed by the ASAC every quarter; A set amount of pencils allowed in your desk; Live dictation to real life stenos; When requesting stenos, single Agents would normally get single stenos, while married men got older married women stenos; A percentage of time that you could be in the office (TIO); Voluntary overtime (VOT); # 3 Card to note work done on daily basis; # 1 Register for signing in and out; AC taken out of Bucars since Mr. Hoover believed that 'it would look bad for Agents to be riding around with AC on, while most taxpayers in those days did not have the AC'. Those were the days!"

WORTH OF AN FBI SPECIAL AGENT

"It had sometimes been said, if one could buy someone for what they are worth, and then sell them for what they think they are worth, one could make an enormous profit !

The pay raises were not that great, but the checks still kept coming in. And most of us never knew that we were poor.

As it turned out, the job was worth a lot more than what they paid us. I am still fearful the FBIHQ will find out how much fun I had and how much I enjoyed the job (minor travails not withstanding) and they will demand a refund on all what they paid me."

FBI SPECIAL AGENT GIVES MORE THAN 100%

"What makes 100%? What does it mean to give more than 100% ? Ever wonder about those people who say they are giving more than 100 % ? We have all been to these meetings where someone wants you to give over 100 % ? What does it really mean ?

Here's a little mathematical formula that might help you answer these questions:

If: A B C D E F G H I J K L M N O P Q R S T U V W X Y Z
Are represented as:
1 2 3 4 5 6 7 8 9 10 11 12 13 14 15 16 17 18 19 20 21 22 23 24 25 26
Then:
H-A-R-D-W-O-R-K
Is
8+1+18+4+23+15+18+11 = 98%
And
11+14+15+23+12+5+4+7+5 = 96%
But
A-T-T-I-T-U-D-E
Is
1+20+20+9+20+21+4+5 = 100%
And
B-U-L-L-S-H-I-T
Is
2+21+12+12+19+8+9+20= 103 %
And, look how far ass kissing will take you:
A-S-S-K-I-S-S-I-N-G
1+19+19+11+9+19+19+9+14+7 =118 %
So, one can conclude with mathematical certainty that while hard work and knowledge will get you close, and Attitude will get you there, it's the Bullshit and Ass kissing that will put you over the top."

PEOPLE WHO ARE RIGHT
(Author unknown)

"Never attempt to reason with people who know they are right all the time."

The stories continue . . .

THE 1ST NON-WHITE SHIRT WORN BY AN FBI AGENT

"When L. Patrick Gray became an Acting FBI Director on May 3, 1972, he visited the Washington Field Office (WFO) of the FBI on the morning of the same day. A question was asked by one of the street humps: 'Do we still have to wear white shirts as FBI Special Agents?'

Mr. Gray's quick answer was: 'Negative. I don't care what color shirts you wear !' Over the lunch period, the same hump went shopping and bought a colored shirt (can't remember the color) and wore it in the office that afternoon. The SA rose to the position of an Assistant Director. His initials were JG."

FBI HAT

"On August 6, 1951, 44 of us reported for training to become FBI Special Agents. Just before lunch break, a Bureau official asked the class how many of us had a hat. As I recall, only one put up his hand. We were told that when we reported back from lunch, we would all have one, (a fedora style dress hat)."

CHAPTER 10

FRUGAL FBI SPECIAL AGENTS?

HISTORICALLY, FBI SPECIAL AGENTS WERE FRUGAL . . . OR WERE THEY JUST PLAINLY CHEAP . . . OR WERE THEY ABUSING THE "BUREAU CONTACT" ARRANGEMENT? YOU DECIDE!

THE COOKIE CONTACT

"There was an SAC in an East Coast office who had an SA drive him each month to a cookie factory so he could buy a bag of broken cookies at a greatly reduced price. SAC justified this as being part of source development."

BELOW WHOLESALE PRICES ON BUSHES?

"A newly arrived SAC and a newly arrived SA were having new houses built in a suburban housing development. SAC found out that the SRA covering the area known for the abundance of greenhouses had a contact for bushes. Arrangement was made for the SAC to visit the greenhouse where he could buy eighteen dollar bushes at wholesale price minus Bureau contact price.

SAC had a problem with bringing the bushes home since he did not have a truck or a van. A call to the newly arrived SA (who was on annual leave that week)determined that the SA had a personal truck and also needed bushes for his newly built house . . . but was not ready to spend the thousand dollars for the needed bushes.

SAC advised the SA that there will be a great deal. He suggested and persuaded the SA to come to the office on Saturday morning with his personal truck and the SAC would drive SA's truck to pick up the bushes, while the SA would use the FBI van (a big NO NO using a government vehicle for personal use) and meet with the SAC at the green house.

A trip was made, bushes loaded up to the vehicle's capacity and brought back to the two construction sites. The price for bushes was fifty cents each, with the SA ingratiating himself with his neighbors, as he was able to bring back way more bushes than he needed and gave some to his neighbors.

Another Bureau contact dried up."

CHEAP SAC?

"The SAC in my office, identified as being very frugal, was known to be interested in magical tricks and used the tricks in an office setting to charm his flock . . . until something went wrong.

While this self-taught magician showed a trick involving matches (on Bureau time, of all things), his suit pocket caught on fire, to dismay of his audience.

Perhaps this boss should have spent some money and attend a magician's course on playing with fire."

OUTTAKE . . .

WHY AM I HERE?
(Author unknown)

"God put me on earth to accomplish a certain number of things. Right now I am so far behind, I will never die."

The stories continue . . .

A 3 CENT STAMP ARGUMENT RUINS A CARPOOL

"Once upon a time . . . three SAs bought an old Ford specifically to use for car-pooling into the office each day. Every time they purchased gasoline, they split the cost. They paid $ 6.00 per month to an old lady that had a home near the FBI office, to be able to park in her back yard, and they split the cost.

The argument ensued over who should pay for a 3 cent stamp to mail the payment.

Another car-pool bites the dust."

THE CHEAPEST AGENT

"An older SA, who was rumored to be a millionaire (in the 1960s), parked every day on the street far away from the FBI office, near a football stadium, because parking was free there and he always arrived very early in the morning to be sure he got the spot.

One day, a big storm moved in and the SA, walking from the parking spot, was drenched upon arriving at the office. With no one around on his floor, he removed his clothes and hung them over the baseboard heaters to dry. He also removed his hearing aids that were wet and began to do paperwork. He was surprised by a 'primal scream' from the oldest female support employee that was also an early bird.

Same individual, while attending office shindigs, regularly helped himself to extra cold cuts that he placed in plastic-lined coat pockets. He was also followed to his home by two fellow SAs and braced to return a bottle of booze that he 'borrowed' at a gathering following a funeral service for a fellow Special Agent. A book could be written about his cheapness, but one would probably be sued by him, since he is still around kicking."

(Another fellow FBI Special Agent reported that following above Agent's retirement an awful smell was detected in the area where the coats were usually parked for the day. Two days later, the awful smell was finally traced to a box of fish that were well fermented, secreted in the same room. So much for trained investigators. Was the box checked for fingerprints?)

YOU GET WHAT YOU PAY FOR

"In my second FBI office, in a large East Coast city, the office had a suit contact. One day I was working with another Agent wearing one of the suits he purchased from the contact. We were going to the parking lot at the end of the day and got caught in a thunder storm. By the time we came to the parking lot, his wool suit had shrunk so much that you could see the tops of his white socks. We were laughing so hard we had tears running down our cheeks.

What a great contact that was."

FOUR IDENTICAL SUITS, SHIRTS AND TIES

"In my first office, I learned that most of the FBI offices historically had suit contacts. Since SAs were required to follow the dress code . . . suit, tie, white shirt, dark shoes (and in the Hoover days also a hat) . . . I also needed to buy another suit.

A fellow old-timer introduced me to the contact and I purchased a suit at a fair price. What a surprise it was when a week later I wore the new garb and identical duds were worn by three other SAs on the squad of 16 that I was on."

PAY FOR ONE, GET ONE FREE

"The only reason we could buy quality suits at one time was because companies that we bought suits from, considered it cheap advertising to have FBI Special Agents wear their suits and look good in them."

OUTTAKE . . .

NOTICE AT FBIHQ !
(Author unknown)

"This Department requires no physical fitness program: Everyone gets enough exercise jumping to conclusions, flying off the handle, running down the boss, knifing friends in the back, dodging responsibility and pushing their luck."

The stories continue . . .

SENIOR DISCOUNT

"One of the senior SAs would even ask for a senior discount in addition to the Bureau contact discount."

HENRY'S ROAD KILL

"During SOG surveillance, out in the country, a rabbit crossing the road was hit and killed by one of the Bucars. This particular Special Agent, whose first name began with letter H, known for his frugality, home-made sandwiches and a tiny fishing boat, pulled off the road, spread newspaper on the trunk's floor and picked up the rabbit.

He was asked by another Agent re this and he claimed that he will make road-kill stew when he gets home."

THE GREEN MONSTER

"In the late 60's I took out an early 50's green surveillance van that alternated as the trash truck to take classified trash to a steel company for burning in their furnace. I was to use this truck for surveillance that day.

A couple of pea-sized holes were drilled in the side of the van to peep through and I assumed the rear windows were one-way. After all, I was in the FBI, wasn't I? I should have checked but didn't and got made when someone in the neighborhood came up to the truck and looked in the back window. I did not think he could see me as I sat motionless staring at him as he pounded on the door. When he started yelling at me, I realized I was in the naked city and had some embarrassing explaining to do. The guy was not the subject and I don't think he was connected to the subject in any way.

Sometime later, I had the same truck out trying to do a surveillance with a couple of Agents in the back. I was driving by a the surveillance site, looking for a parking spot to set up, when I heard all this pounding and shouting in the back of the van. Couldn't tell why so I pulled away to find a safe spot. I stopped the truck and opened the back door and all this black smoke came pouring out with two coughing, sputtering FBI Agents. Seems as though an electrical fire had started in some kind of built-in ventilator or heater in the back. The truck could not be opened from the inside when locked from the outside.

Only the best (and cheapest) equipment money could buy."

A BRICK AGENT IN TRUE SENSE OF THE WORD

"In Hoover's time, SAs were issued brown leather briefcases that SAs carried when outside the office. One enterprising SA was known to make it a daily ritual to pick up two free bricks every day, from demolition sites or from trash bins at construction sites. It did not matter to him what color , design or quality the bricks were. He placed these bricks into his briefcase and took them home at the end of the work day. He was doing this for three or four years, so as to build a brick-walled garage in myriad of colors."

BUS TOKEN CAPER

"Years ago at WFO, when the office was located at the Old Post Office Building, at 11th and Pa Ave, N.W., within walking distance of the USDS, the Capitol Hill and the White House, many leads were covered on foot. Due to traffic and parking problems, it was easier and more expedient to walk or take a bus in the pre-Metro days.

Instead of using cash and claiming the expense on a voucher, one could sign for bus tokens, round metal disks the size of a dime.

Years later, tokens were eliminated and any tokens that were unused could be turned in at the Metro office for cash. Many old timers collected boxes of tokens that they were hoarding or obtained them from other SAs that were transferred or merely left behind the tokens in their desks. On the first day of the advertised turn in, many an SA took the left over tokens and traded them for cash, in some instances, for a lot of cash.

If this was today, tokens would be sold on E-bay"

MIXING BU BUSINESS AND RICE-A-RONI AT THE NAACP CONVENTION

"For a few months at WFO, I had a black (yes, it was officially and politically correct term in those days) partner. A great guy who worked hard because he wanted to climb the ladder of success in the FBI.

One day, he received a call from a long lost college friend, who was in town at the NAACP Convention, as a rep for a food chain. The two of them had not seen each other in years. This friend recently learned that my partner joined the FBI and was now an FBI Special Agent, and he expressed an interest in possibly doing the same.

It just so happened that my partner and I worked applicant cases and looked forward to getting another stat for a minority applicant.

It was the last day of the convention and this friend was at the convention representing Rice-A-Roni products. Pleasantries were exchanged and an applicant brochure was given to him. All his questions about the Bureau were hopefully answered.

The potential applicant noted that he had 50 cases of Rice-A-Roni promotional products that he had to discard, as it was too costly to ship it back to the company. Neither my partner nor I believed that food that was well within expiration date should be thrown away. 50 cases of the promotional boxes were loaded into the Bureau car and taken to the nearest 'shipping port/distribution center' . . . my house.

Our families enjoyed the gift from the NAACP Convention for months to come. I do admit that it was years after this gift was consumed, before we bought Rice-A-Roni from the store, since we were probably sick of it, but it was free.

Every time we eat this product now, we remember that the NAACP was good to us. How can one argue with that."

CHEAP LUNCH OR CHEAP SPECIAL AGENT

"When I arrived in my second office in the Midwest, I was assigned to the Fugitive Squad. On the squad we had a few old-timers to balance out the rest of us young chargers.

One of these old-timers was 'Ed', who had reputation for being notoriously 'frugal'.

Next to the Division Office was a famous German restaurant, complete with surly waiters. When you were seated at a table, they immediately brought a glass of water and a plate of rye bread and butter for each patron.

The 'Kinzer Lunch' was simply a piece of apple pie with cheddar cheese. 'Ed' put the cheese on the rye bread for a sandwich, drank the water, and had the pie for dessert."

FOUR FBI SPECIAL AGENTS IN THE BAR

"Four FBI Special Agents are walking down the street. They turn the corner and see a sign that says 'Old Timer's Bar', 'All Drinks 10 cents'.

They look at each other, and then go in. The old bartender says in a voice that carries across the room: 'Come on in and let me pour one for you; what will it be, gentlemen?'

There seems to be a fully stocked bar, so the men all ask for a martini.

In short order, the bartender serves up 4 iced martinis and says: 'That'll be 10 cents each, please.' They can't believe their good luck. They pay the 40 cents, finish their martinis, and order another round. Again, four excellent martinis are produced with the bartender again asking for 40 more cents.

They pay the 40 cents, but their curiosity is more than they can stand. They've each had two martinis and so far they've spent less than a dollar. Finally one man couldn't stand it any longer and asked the bartender 'How can you afford to serve martinis as good as these for a dime apiece?'

The bartender says: 'I'm a retired cop from New York, and I always wanted to own a bar. Last year I hit the lottery for 25 million and decided to open this place. Every drink costs a dime. Wine, liquor, beer, all the same.'

'Wow. That's quite a story', says one of the men. The four of them sipped at their martinis and couldn't help but notice three other older guys at the end of the bar who didn't have a drink in front of them, and hadn't ordered anything the whole time they were there.

One man gestured at the three at the end of the bar without drinks and asks the bartender, 'What's with them?' 'They're retired FBI Special Agents, they're waiting for the Happy Hour'."

(New generation of FBI Special Agents, same frugality!)

OUTTAKE . . .

THE G-MAN'S WIFE
(James J. Metcalfe ©1951)

"The G-Man's wife must be resigned
To hours spent alone
And to a kind of daily life
She cannot call her own.

Her husband may be gone for days
Or even weeks on end
And when in town, he may not have
A lot of time to spend.
She has to be prepared to pack
And move from place to place

And in each new surrounding strive
To find some living space.

Sometimes his task is dangerous
And she must wait and pray
That God will guide and keep him safe
Throughout the night and day.

But in every sacrifice
And as they kiss good-bye
She is immensely proud that he
Is in the FBI."

Thanks Kathleen M.
for being my wonderful wife since 08/16/1969.

Thanks to our son and daughter, who actively participated in the arrest of the highest ranking Soviet military intelligence (GRU) officer. They suggested that I write a book of FBI stories, so that their kids, and grandkids of other fellow FBI Special Agents will know what grandpa or grandma did for a living.

A big hug and a kiss to the following possible
future FBI Special Agents:
Shay, Dane, Theo and Connor,
who call me their GRANDPA and 'ATA' and will fully
understand when they read this book in a few years, that I
proudly served with "the Greatest Generation"
and "Baby Boomer Generation"
as an FBI Special Agent.

The stories continue . . .

APPLE OF MY HEART

"There was an Agent in a Midwest office who was known for being very frugal. He was really a nice guy. He told me that he realized that he was very frugal, but said that it was the way he was brought up.

The following part of the story about this frugal Agent was told to me by a steno.

This 'frugal' Agent asked her out and they went to a free movie. After the show, he asked her if she would like something to eat. When she replied that she would, he told her that there was an apple in the glove compartment."

(I would bet that this frugal Agent had parents that were immigrants from Europe. My own mother told me years after my dad died, that my dad was so frugal, or just plain broke, that he brought a loaf of bread from home on their honeymoon.)

CHEAP SUIT – BUT NOT EMPTY SUIT

"There was an Agent in a SW FBI office, famous for his frugality. He came to work one morning in a pale blue new suit and was showing it to us in the break room. He said he got it on sale at the Jaques Penney (J.C. Penny) store down the street. It was extra cheap because it was a window display model. He then showed us the back of the suit which was a much darker color than the front. He explained that the front had faded from being exposed to the sun in the window.

He further explained that no one could see his front and back at the same time, so it would not be noticed.

Had to love the man."

PLAIN FRUGAL

"My parents were very poor and they shopped for their clothes at a St.Vincent de Paul Thrift Store, a fifteen minute walk from our one bedroom apartment, where we did not even have a refrigerator or a TV. It followed that at the age of eleven, I finally received a nice coat, few sizes too large, that I tried on at the store (St.V of course), and bought.

Almost 30 years later, when I was already an FBI Special Agent, a write-up about St.Vincent de Paul appeared in the local newspaper. St.V was trying to locate the 25 oldest customers of their thrift store and asked that each write a short story about their first encounter at the store and the year that it occurred. Offers of coupons, on monthly basis, for a whole year, were to be given to the 25.

I was one of the 25 winners and the coupons started coming, from 25% to 80% off. SUCH A DEAL ! One month, at probably 80% off, I actually purchased almost 500 hospital mattresses, professionally cleaned, from St.V's and sold them at a good profit..

This encounter with mattresses actually started a sickness that has not ended to date. Reselling of repurposed items, that is now in vogue, is now in my blood.

What did the FBI get from my experience in finding items of value for resale? Dumpster jumping training, of course, which is not taught at the FBI Academy or at the in-services!"

A la NEW YORK SPLIT

"I have had many an expensive hamburger myself in a 'New York Split'. The downside of the split was the price you paid for arriving late, and the upside was the privilege of being a part of such events. Early, late or in-between, I never regretted attending a single one of them."

A TEACHABLE MOMENT

"The New York Split stories have brought back many fond memories for this New Yorker.

Yes, there was an occasional raised voice or two about the system, but in my view, it worked very well. I do have a story about the split, and it involves a certain NY ___________Party, that was held at a restaurant that is still in business.

We had three squads in attendance, including support staff. The place was famous for German dishes, over the top décor and generous steins of beer. Most of us over-indulged in all of the above during the celebration. The tab was running.

One of our group showed up late, sat down and ordered a hamburger and a glass of water, as our merriment continued.

One of the fellow SAs deadpanned to the late-comer that 'it will be the most expensive hamburger you will ever eat.' A teachable moment."

A LABEL ON EVERY FBI MACHINE
(Author unknown)

"This machine is subject to breakdown during periods of critical need.

A special circuit in the machine, called a 'critical detector'. senses the operator's emotional state in terms of how desperate he or she is to use the machine.

The 'critical detector' then creates a malfunction proportional to the desperation of the operator.

Threatening the machine with violence only aggravates the situation. Likewise, attempts to use another machine may cause it to also malfunction. They belong to the same union.

Keep cool and say nice things to the machine. Nothing else seems to work."

The stories continue . . .

NO SPLITS

"I don't believe in splits or splitting the cost of the party. I do not drink anything that has alcohol in it and it burns me that at one of the parties I had to pay out of pocket for a simple Coke, while alcoholic beverages were included in the price."

SPECIAL AGENT AT A GARAGE SALE

"I recently invited a fellow retired FBI Special Agent to accompany me to garage sales. I am sorry I did. At one of our stops, he inquired if the quarter collector's booklet, wrapped in the original cellophane, priced on the sticker at 99 cents, contained actual quarters."

(Need to meet this man. He is actually cheap, while I am frugal.)

OUTTAKE . . .

A CHEAP AGENT AND A CAT
(Author unknown. Sick but funny.)

"A single Special Agent in one of the SW Divisions lived very frugally and had a cat as a companion. In order to keep the

water bill low, he improvised and trained the cat to take a bath, as follows:

- **Put both lids of the toilet up and add the required amount of pet shampoo to the water in the bowl.**
- **Pick up the cat and soothe him while you carry him towards the bathroom.**
- **In one smooth movement, put the cat in the toilet bowl and close both lids. You may have to stand on the lid.**
- **The cat will self-agitate and make ample suds. Never mind the noises that come from the toilet, the cat is actually enjoying this.**
- **Flush the toilet three or four times. This provides a 'power-wash' and rinse.**
- **Have someone open the door to the outside. Be sure that there are no people between the toilet and the outside door.**
- **Stand behind the toilet as far as you can, and quickly lift both lids.**
- **The cat will rocket out of the toilet and run outside where he will dry himself off.**
- **Both the commode and the cat will be sparkling clean."**

The stories continue . . .

HILARIOUS TALE OF A CHEAP AGENT

"The same Agent that bought the suit at JC Penny (on his lunch period I'm sure), was in the dressing area when, as he dropped his trousers, his Bu-issued Model 10 S&W slipped from his Sloan holster and slid out into the main sales floor, causing the expected pandemonium…"

CONTACTS

"If you are interested in discounts, I have two deal sites that I check in on a daily basis. People post all the deals they find on those internet sites. The deals include all types of travel, entertainment, electronic items, restaurants and just about anything else. I would venture that the FBI Agents were ahead of the times for finding deals, sans the computers.

In the old days we had deals with Bostonian Shoes, Palm Beach Suits, Hart Shaft Marx out of Chicago and appliances at Sears."

EMBARRASSING DISCOUNTS

"I've even heard rumors of senior discounts. How demeaning. What's the world coming to.

What's embarrassing is when they give the discount without my mentioning it."

(Bumper, I knew where you were buying the suits. After you left town, the owners mentioned you often and said that every time you bought a suit at a discounted price, you would insist on two pairs of pants and a tie.)

IS IT FBI OR BFI ?

"A Midwest Division, bordering on one of the big lakes, had a well-known suit contact straight at the factory. An account for the FBI Agents was made in the name of a business known as BFI (Browning-Ferris Industries, a waste collection and disposal business), so as to protect the real buyers, the Agents.

One day, as an SA was being fitted and measured for a suit, the company employee noted that he was surprised that so many garbage company employees get fitted for suits. SA had hard time telling the tailor the truth."

CHAPTER 11

OLD ODDS AND ENDS

THIS CHAPTER WILL HAVE SOME OF THE OLDEST AND LONGEST STORIES IN MY COLLECTION, OBTAINED FROM OLD-TIMERS IN THE EARLY 1970s AND WRITTEN BY THEM IN THE 1950s AND 1960s. BUT, THIS CHAPTER WILL ALSO HAVE SOME OF THE NEWEST STORIES, RECEIVED AFTER THE REST OF THE MANUSCRIPT WAS ALREADY WRITTEN.

YOU WILL NOTICE THE NEW YORK ATTITUDE, BASICALLY, WHO GIVES A HOOT. THE SPECIAL AGENTS ASSIGNED TO NEW YORK WERE PAID THE SAME AMOUNT OF MONEY PER YEAR AS FELLOW SPECIAL AGENTS IN PODUNK, MONTANA. IT WAS HARD FOR THEM TO RAISE A FAMILY IN THOSE DAYS. THE ATTITUDE WAS, "WHAT CAN YOU DO TO ME? TRANSFER ME!"

IF THEY SCREWED UP AND COMMITTED VENIAL AND MORTAL SINS, THEY WERE TRANSFERRED OUT OF NEW YORK AND THANKED GOD FOR IT. UNFORTUNATELY, IF A SECOND AND THIRD SPECIAL AGENT IN NEW YORK COMMITTED THE SAME MORTAL SIN, AND EXPECTED TO BE TRANSFERRED, THAT WAS NOT THE CASE. THEY WERE FIRED, INSTEAD. IN THOSE DAYS, THERE WERE BUREAU RULES AND NEW YORK RULES . . . BUT, NEW YORK ATTITUDE REALLY HAS NOT CHANGED MUCH.

WHAT ARE FBI SAs MADE OF ?

"An SA is a composite of what all men and women are, a mingling of saint and sinner.

An SA is at once the most needed and the most unwanted.

An SA is strangely a nameless creature who is 'sir' or 'mam" to his or her face, and a &@^+ behind their back.

An SA must be such a diplomat that he can settle differences between individuals so that each of them thinks they have won.

But, if an SA is neat, he's conceited; if he is careless, he's a bum; if he's pleasant, he's a flirt; if he's not', he's grouch.

An SA must make in an instant those decisions which would require months for a lawyer.

If he hurries, he's careless; If he's deliberate, he's lazy. He must be first on the scene of the bank robbery, but he'll be criticized if he speeds.

He must be a doctor at times and a nurse on another. He must know every gun, draw on the run and hit where it doesn't hurt.

He must be able to whip two men twice his/her size and half his age, without damaging his suit and without being brutal.

If you hit him, he's a coward; if he hits you, he's a bully. He must know where all the sin is, but must not partake.

If he catches the criminal or a spy, he is lucky; if he doesn't, he's a dunce. If he gets promoted, he has political pull; if he doesn't, he is stupid.

The SA must be a minister, a social worker, a diplomat, a tough guy, and a gentleman. He must know everything, and not tell.. And, of course, he has to feed a family on a Special Agent's salary."

OUTTAKE. . . 

AMISH BUGGY PULLED BY A CAMEL
(Author unknown)

In Pennsylvania, the FBI issued a warning in Lancaster County. They suspected a terrorist may be hiding among the Amish community when a photo of a camel, pulling an Amish buggy, was found in possession of an Amish Bishop.

(FBIHQ was probably not aware that one of my closest friends, born in Lebanon, carried a business card in high school, identifying himself as a "Lebanese Camel Jockey" and his niece, who calls me "uncle", is presently an FBI employee.)

The stories continue . . .

ACCORDING TO HOOVER
(Author unknown)

(Substitute FBI Special Agent for every time the word man is used, please. There were no female FBI Special Agents when this version of the Baltimore Catechism was written.)

- Who made you ? The Director made me.
- Did the Director make all things? Yes, the Director made all things.
- Why did the Director make you? The Director made me to show forth His goodness and to make me happy with Him in the Bureau forever.
- What must you do to be happy with the Director in the Bureau? I must know Him, love Him and obey the Manual of Rules and Regulations.
- Where is the Director? The Director is everywhere.
- Does the Director know all things? Yes, the Director knows all things.
- Can the Director do all things? Yes, the Director can do all things.
- Did the Director have a beginning? No, He had no beginning. He always was and always will be.
- Will the Director always be? Yes, the Director will always be.
- Is there only one Director? Yes, there is only one Director.
- How many persons are there in the Director? There are three persons in the Director: John, Clyde and Helen Gandy.

- How do we know that there are three persons in the one Director? Because we have the Director's word for it.

- Did one of the persons of the Director become man? Never.

- How did the Director satisfy for the sins of all men? By organizing and directing the FBI and devoting His life thereto.

- How does the Director help all men to gain Heaven? Through incentive awards.

- What is sin? Sin is disobedience to the Director's laws as set out in the Manual of Rules and Regulations.

- Who committed the first sin? The first Special Agent.

- Is this sin passed on to us? Yes, this sin is passed on to us.

- What is this sin called in us? This sin is called New York Attitude.

- Was anyone ever free from New York Attitude? Yes, Assistant Director J.F. Malone was free from New York Attitude.

- Is New York Attitude the only kind of sin? No, there is another kind of sin called Actual Sin.

- What is Actual Sin? Any violation of the MRR or the MI.

- How many kinds of Actual Sin are there? There are two

kinds: Mortal and Venial Sin.

- What does Mortal Sin do? Mortal Sin (1) embarrasses the Bureau; (2) makes us enemies of the Director and robs us of His graces; (3) can get us fired.

- What is Venial Sin? Venial Sin is a lesser sin.

- What does Venial Sin do? Venial Sin displeases the Director and gets us Letters of Censure, probation and transfer.

- What does the NYO do to help gain grace in the Bureau? The NYO gets us Incentive Awards and Letters of Commendation.

- What is a Letter of Commendation? A Letter of Commendation is an outward sign, instituted by the Director to give grace.

- What does grace do to the Agent? Grace makes the soul pleasing to the Director.

- Have you received a Letter of Commendation? Yes, I have.

- What did the Letter of Commendation do for you? It washed away the New York Attitude from my soul and made it pleasing to the Director.

- What is penance? Penance is he process of telling our sins to the Inspection Staff and receiving the forgiveness of the Director.

- What must you do to accomplish this process? You must: (1) Remember your sins; (2) Be sorry for your sins; (3) Make up your mind to obey the MRR and all SAC Letters; (4)Tell your sins to the Inspectors; (5) Do the penance the Inspector gives us.

- How do you make your confession? In this way: (1) I go to the Inspector and kneel; (2) I say: 'Bless me, Mr.Gale, for I have sinned'; (3)I recite my sins; (4) I listen to what Mr.Gale tells me; (5) I say an Act of Contrition loud enough for the whole Bureau to hear me.

- What do you do after leaving the confessional? After leaving the confessional, I (1) Worry (2) Call my friends in high places at the Bureau (3) Wait for the axe to fall.

- What must I do when the Director forgives my sins? I must thank the Director and write Him a nice letter every time He gets an award from B'nai B'rith.

THE HUMAN SIDE OF THE F.B.I.
(George E. Saunders 1941 -1977)

"During the early 1960's, David Murphy, an Agent assigned to the Washington Field Office of the F.B.I., became critically ill with cancer and was a patient at the Bethesda Naval Hospital for more than fifteen months, before passing away in 1963.

At the time, I was assigned to cover Montgomery County in Maryland, the county in which the Bethesda Naval Hospital is located. As one of Dave's closest friends, I asked to be the Agent who would visit him and maintain contact with his family to make sure that the needs of his wife and four children were taken care of. It was my privilege to serve in this capacity.

During the lengthy period of his hospitalization, fellow Agents visited Dave on a regular basis and many hours were spent by Agents and clerical personnel of the F.B.I. looking after the needs of his family. I relate this story to remind us as former Agents how genuinely concerned Mr.Hoover was about F.B.I. personnel who were ill or experiencing family medical problems.

I recall on one occasion during Dave's hospital stay, Mr.Hoover and Mr.Tolson informed the SAC of the Washington Field Office that they wanted to visit him at the hospital. I was in the hospital on that particular day and received word of their pending visit, but stayed in the background and did not identify myself to the Director. They spent a considerable amount of time visiting with Dave and his wife, Evelyn, which was a big boost to Dave's morale and greatly appreciated by his family.

Later that day, the SAC informed me he had received a call from the Director inquiring about how the Agent's personal and family matters were being handled. The SAC informed the Director that there was an Agent in the hospital at the time of his visit and that the family as well as Dave were being contacted on a daily basis.

We who were part of the F.B.I. over the years were always aware of the concern and compassion shown for our fellow workers in their time of need as demonstrated not only by this particular case but also by countless others that could be related.

Following in his father's footsteps, his son, who was a teenager when his father passed away, now serves with distinction in the Washington, D.C. area of the F.B.I."

OUTTAKE . . .

"PERFORMANCE TEST FOR PROSPECTIVE FBI SPECIAL AGENTS (1977 VERSION)
(Author unknown)

Instructions: Read each question carefully, Answer all

questions. Time limit – four hours.

1. MANAGEMENT SCIENCE: Define management. Define science. How do they relate? Why? Create a generalized algorithm to optimize all managerial decisions. Assuming an 1130 CPU (Now an IPAD would do it) supporting 50 terminals, use each terminal to activate your algorithm, design the communication interface and all necessary programs.

2. POLITICAL SCIENCE: There is a red telephone on the desk beside you. Start World War III. Report at length on its socio-political effects, if any.

3. ECONOMICS: Develop a realistic plan for refinancing the national debt. Trace the possible results of your plan in the following areas: inflation, cubism, unemployment, and the Donatist controversy. Outline a method for preventing these results. Criticize your plan from all possible points of view. Point out the deficiencies in your plan as demonstrated in your answer to the last question.

4. SOCIOLOGY: Estimate the sociological problems that might accompany the end of the world. Construct an experiment to test your theory.

5. Take a position for or against truth. Prove the validity of your position.

6. PSYCHOLOGY: Based on your knowledge of their works, evaluate the emotional stability, degree of adjustment and repressed frustrations of each of the following: Alexander of Aprodisias, Remeses II, Gregory of Nicea, and Hammurabi. Support your evaluations with quotations from each man's work making

appropriate references. It is not necessary to translate.

7. **ENGINEERING: The disassembled parts of a high powered rifle have been placed in your desk. You will find an instructions manual printed in Swahili. In ten minutes a hungry Bengal tiger will be admitted to the room. Take whatever actions you feel is right. Be prepared to justify your decision.**

8. **BIOLOGY: Create life. Estimate the differences in subsequent human culture if this form of life had developed 500 million years earlier, with special attention to its probable effects on the English parliamentary system. Prove your thesis.**

9. **LANGUAGES: Two thousand five hundred rioting aborigines are storming this office. Calm them. You may use any ancient language, except Latin or Greek.**

10. **MEDICINE: You have been provided with a razor blade, a piece of gauze, and a bottle of Scotch. Remove the appendix. Do not suture until your work has been inspected.**

11. **MUSIC: Write a piano concerto. Orchestrate and perform it with flute and drum.**

12. **PHILOSOPHY: Sketch the development of human thought. Estimate its significance. Compare with the development of any other kind of thought.**

13. **GENERAL KNOWLEDGE: Describe in detail. Be objective and specific."**

(In all probability, above test was prepared for those aspiring to become a President of the U.S. in the 21st century, and not an FBI Special Agent.)

CHAPTER 12

ON BEING A RETIRED SPECIAL AGENT & FUNERALS

They are a different breed. The retired Agents tell you they are happy that it is over, but that is really not the case. They definitely miss the job they had.

Some planned for years on what they will do, but the unexpected happens. Some die in place, others lose their spouses, still others divorce and remarry and now have a trophy wife in reverse order, at the tail end of their lives. Some stay in the same town where they served in their last FBI office and they know the territory. Others retire in the usual retirement villages in Florida and in climates that they thought they would enjoy. Some are happy, others are not. Most still love to argue over old cases, via e-mail on the WWW's x-G list and at social functions.

The executive types finally realize that they are now simply street humps like the rest of us were for the duration of our careers. For some, that is definitely hard for them to take.

The former street humps are just as happy now as they were then. For them, the grass is not greener on the other side of the fence.

With most of the stories in this book not attributed to authors by

name, any of the current or retired Special Agents will be able to claim the story as their own, and it will result in more mayhem and squabbles when meeting in person over a beer or on the golf course or on the XG's net.

Yours truly has not changed in my retirement. I still get up at 0500 hours, seven days a week. Despite being officially retired, I am still gainfully employed. I do not play golf. Thank God, my wonderful spouse supports my habits and I support hers.

On July 11, 2013, our life changed drastically.

An 84 year old female driver hit my wife and I in a legal crosswalk, with a blinking WALK sign, right after our entire family completed a pizza dinner at a local restaurant. My wife had to be brought back to life after a 20 foot flight in the air and both of us ended in separate ambulances to the ER. Months and now over a year later, our life is still different. Many of our plans had to change. The precious seconds between the hit and the recovery at the accident scene had me going through my whole life.

What will happen now?

We are alive, and my plan to write a book with stories from the fellow FBI Special Agents, is on a fast roll. God willing, the book will be completed.

If God did not intervene that day in 2013, three generations of my family would be "living" in underground seven foot long condos. Six adults and three and a half kids would have been dead.

WHY I LIKE RETIREMENT

"Get up at 6:00 AM; check comes. Get up at 10:30 AM; check STILL comes.

Perfectly acceptable to begin conversation with 'Well, the way we used to do it…' –then not do anything at all.

Even if you get Alzheimer's, if no one tells you about it the next day, you're fine.

By 60, you know which organs are okay to donate.

Without your bifocals, your wife could be Drew Barrymore. (Be careful to yell out the right name just before, though.)

Those arrests in 25, 42 and 88 cases become heroic shootout in which everyone but you was killed.

Socks last a long time if you only wear them to go downstairs to the refrigerator.

A documentary about WWII pin-up girls gets you more excited than

'Debbie Does Dallas'.

New law: beer is covered under Medicare.

And most importantly: honor, like good wine, ages well."

POST RETIREMENT JOYS

"A fellow Agent posted a list he received from his brother, of some post-retirement joys, and suggested there might be some other serendipities we retirees have learned about now that we have had a little time to cogitate on the matter. And I believe there are a few, albeit there are obvious trade-offs to secure their usufructs. Still, aren't you glad you about these little pleasantries?"

ON BEING A RETIRED AGENT

"Q: What do retired Agents find hardest about their new status?
A: Paying for photocopies and pens.

Q: What most amazes new retired Agents?
A: They're so busy now, they don't know how they ever had time to work.

Q: Why don't retired Agents protest the stereotype that says they're either hyperactive or always napping?
A: They're either too busy to care what other people say, or they're asleep, or they just plainly don't give a %&*+.

Q: What's the retired Agent's favorite bumper sticker?
A: 'Go ahead and pass me. What do I care.'

Q: Just how much free time does a retired Agent have?
A: Enough actually to stay on the line until his/her call to the HMO, government agency, or computer help line is answered by a human being.

Q: What do retired Agents call a long lunch?
A: Normal.

Q: When is a retired Agent's bedtime?
A: Three hours after falling asleep on the sofa watching TV.

Q: Why do retired Agents hate holidays?
A: There are too many workers with the day off cluttering up stores and movie theaters.

Q: What's the best way to describe an Agent's retirement?
A: The coffee break that never ends.

(And, lastly … why do you know this applies to retired Agents?)

Q: Why don't retired Agents mind being called a 'senior citizen ?'
A: The term comes with a 10% discount."

RETIREMENT CELEBRATIONS IN SMALL CITIES

"Executive Assistant Director's Party = $ 30
Section Chief's Party = $ 20
Street Agent's Retirement = BYO in brown paper bag, Fritos available at vending machine….
The more things change, the more they remain the same."

RETIREMENT CELEBRATIONS IN NY, SF, LA, WDC

"Hundred bucks gets you into the room and one drink. The rest is up to you and your eating and drinking habits. Same-o, same-o."

AGENT'S LIFE

"An Agent's life is not measured by the number of breaths we take, but by the moments that take our breath away."

UPON ONE AGENT'S DEATH

"Now, suffer this old man, me to reminisce a moment. He was a great Agent. I've heard it said that he could handle anything but an irate old woman. I suspect that there was a story behind that.

You know that the toughest cases are always assigned to the best Agents. He would explain it this way: 'You always whip the mule that pulls.'

You have also noted that in approaching potential witnesses, reluctant witnesses, that a little empathy and understanding is more rewarding than officiousness. He said, 'I always approach hat in hand.'

Another, 'When looking for advice, go to the head of the stream where the water is fresher and better to drink.'

And advice to a young Agent, 'Don't do anything that is not to your advantage.'

Wonder what he meant by, 'The older the ram, the stiffer the horn' ?

He was great at training new Agents. Here is a testimonial from a former Deputy Assistant Director. 'It has been a long time, but this first office Agent in 1976 never forgot all the valuable lessons learned from him during the short two years I spent working cases with him.'

Another Agent once sat in awe as he saw him interview an embezzlement subject. He (the Agent) feigned dumbness. He was good at that and in the course of the next hour gently led the subject into a complete confession. After leaving, the observing Agent expressed amazement. His response, 'Just push the wagon hard enough to get it rolling.'

He was deeply religious and at the funeral a mutual friend remarked, 'I guess it was decided that some country humor was needed in heaven.' "

HOW WE USE OUR WORDS
(Authors unknown)

"The words you speak today should be soft and tender . . . for tomorrow you may have to eat them."

"I lived my FBI in the best of times, with the greatest of men, and the best of cases."

"If you think you are too small to be effective, you have never been in bed with a mosquito."

"I am now 60. One half of my life was spent in the FBI. I don't regret one day of it."

The stories continue . . .

REFLECTIONS BY A RETIRED SPECIAL AGENT

"What has happened that our parental training does not make us reflexively call all men Sir and all women Ma'am, regardless of race, age, color, crime, creed, and treat them as such, as we are not the judge or jury, but merely a conduit to the justice system.

I will never forget a 45 year old Black man (not African-American) from the ghetto, (not his fault) who I arrested for murder (UFAP). I received a call at 2 AM from his mom, whose trust I had apparently gained, at home, and told me to please come get her son before he was killed by law enforcement (early 1970's and listed as A&D). I did not tell my SAC, but went and picked up the man in the ghetto peacefully and took him to the local Federally approved jail. When I called him 'Mr. Smith' he told me he had NEVER been called 'Mr.' in his life. Frankly, that astonished me, but reinforced a value of my parents. True, all arrests cannot be made this way, and I recognized that. Sure, there were plenty of Subjects that would pass the test of pure EVIL, but we are not at the GATES judging them. I can't say I was a particularly religious man, just spiritual. But beyond that, if all Agents spent their training time simply utilizing the Golden Rule with ALL the folks they met from week one, would they need this training?

I am of course referring to today's FBI training. It puzzles me. PC is bad for the future. Perhaps this is an anomaly in the Bu, but I doubt it. I didn't have to be handcuffed, although we were so trained how to do it. Didn't have to go to a museum to respect all other human beings. Was gassed, but there was a hose.

These new measures make me question society as a whole.

My rule of thumb was to treat all Subjects with respect until they proved they did not deserve same. Then it became my rules."

ANOTHER REFLECTION…

"In circumstances where Subjects were wanted on murder charges, and they had at least one parent, I normally made a short visit with the parent and explained the facts of life to them. I told them that a typical police officer or an FBI Special Agent would see the picture of their dear son, with words WANTED on the picture and think of the worst case scenario. This would be followed by a possible shooting and a loss of life, their son's or daughter's or the life of the officer. Parent agreed to assist and promised to talk to their 'child' and call me when the child was ready to turn themselves in. If a promise was made, it followed with an easy arrest at a public place. It never failed for me, especially with Black Subjects."

MUSIC TO MY EARS

"My observation is that developing sources is somewhat like music. Some musicians are gifted and others struggle. Ability improves with training and practice.

That said, JD was greatly gifted, as a musician. I remember one case when JD was assigned to interview a country preacher who we had reason to believe was an accessory to a triple murder case. The preacher, protesting loudly, contended that he, a man of the Bible, could never be involved in such a heinous crime.

Sitting on the front porch of the preacher's cabin, JD noted a guitar leaning against the log wall. Picking it up, JD began to strum. The preacher was impressed and soon they were singing that old mountain hymn, 'Unclouded Day.' At preacher's suggestion, they then knelt in prayer. The preacher tearfully admitted having held the 'blood money.'

Yes, JD was a musician, but more importantly to the FBI, he was very gifted at developing informants, information if you will.

Recently I talked to JD on the phone. I had remarked on what an outstanding Agent he was. In his customary self-depreciating way he protested, 'In all my life I never solved a single case, lessen somebody tole me who dunit.' What a statement ! What a great guy!"

THE AMERICAN WHO WANTED TO TALK TO THE KGB

"Sometimes it's pure luck and not institutional knowledge that catches a fish. Such was the case with a lonely American male that believed he had information of value to the foreign intelligence service and he allegedly had minimal knowledge of the language spoken by that service.

The American was 'intercepted at the pass' before he could reach the building housing the diplomatic establishment of the particular country. Unfortunately, the Agent that normally handled this type of a contact, because of his knowledge of the particular language, was out of town. In this case, an alternate SA was used that spoke a language closely resembling the language used by that particular establishment.

On this particular day, there was no time to change clothing worn by the Agent or the cowboy boots warn by the Agent. Time was of essence. The American male quickly picked on the shoes worn by the supposed foreign intelligence officer and when the male tried talking the language of the particular country, the Agent had to remind the American that since we are in the U.S., we must speak the English language, so as not to expose ourselves as being intelligence officers of a foreign intelligence service. The American swallowed all this BS and a successful contact was established.

The rest is history."

TRASH COVER

"The young man worked for a copying service that handled information classified up to Top Secret.

One day he decided that a foreign intelligence service may be willing to pay for copies of paper containing classified information. On this particular day, he made 'extra copies', and was particular in discarding copies that were not quite perfect. He made sure that he tore the sheets into small pieces and discarded them in the trash can.

A few hours after information came to our attention, two FBI Special Agents visited the young man's employer. One of the Agents requested the contents of the trash can in young man's immediate vicinity, and received permission from the company.

Over the next 48 hours, working non-stop, day and night, the Agent collecting the trash pieced together three documents, including one with Top Secret designation, enough to bring the young man to trial and conviction."

WORDS OF WISDOM FROM A 94 YEAR OLD RETIRED FBI SPECIAL AGENT

(JOHN A. ERWIN FBI SA 1951-1974 . . . just an ordinary guy who has led an extraordinary life)

"94 years ago today, December 7, a Sunday, a doctor gave me a slap on the behind. I gulped in some air to bawl in protest, and thus began my time here. This puts me in the Greatest Generation category, and I accept the accolade that goes with it. We done good! Sadly, the most recent statistic indicates we are shuffling off at the rate of one every 90 seconds.

I well remember the last half of the Roaring Twenties with such things as 'Speakeasies' where, due to the 18th Amendment prohibiting booze, my dad could drink the hard stuff and come home happy. Gals in those days, with heavy rouge, thick lipstick and fashionable short hair were called 'flappers'. My mom belonged.

The Great Depression hit us hard and many times I stood in line to get a government handout: a pair of

shoes, a 5 pound bag of flour or a pound of oleo. Love and laughter got us through that period.

The next birthday of note was the 21st - - maturity and legality at last!! With friends I hiked to a local bar with the attitude 'Today I am a Man'. Number 22 was a bummer . . . and the POTUS dubbed it 'a day which will live in infamy'. The 25th was spent aboard a troop ship on the Pacific, en-route to the U.S., home, and changing from khaki to civvies. One's 40th day is kinda game-changer, hence worthy of a party. When I walked into our house about 30 friends and relatives screamed 'Surprise !' and the one-on-one toasts began. I didn't make it to the 'Good Night' part of the evening nor do I recall much of the occasion!

With all those years behind me, I call my life a reasonable success, considering what I've done and where I've been. And y'know what, I owe it to bad guys. A week after Pearl Harbor I upped with about 11,000,000 others to wipe bad guys Hitler, Mussolini and Tojo off the planet. Among many benefits there came the GI Bill, college, and a degree. In July 1951 my background was sufficient for entry into the FBI. A personal goal was to help get bad guys off the streets and it happened. Yeah . . . reasonable success.

One of the many things for which I thank My Maker every night (aloud) is my mind, which continues to serve me so well. There are but a few things I cannot reprise, not entirely, but enough to converse or write about. Hell, if the Bureau were to contact me and ask me to return, I'd say 'Sure, just show me the laws and elements added to our jurisdiction since, 1974, and I'll be ready in two days'!

Now I offer my personal secret to longevity: Faith in the Almighty, Love, Laughter, Music, Dancing, Fun, Multivitamins, AND, Never A Dull Moment.

Thoreau, the great essayist, wrote: 'Most men lead lives of quiet desperation and go to the grave with the song in them'. Not I ! I've been singing for over 92 years, and many songs remain to be sung.

Looking back, I have but two regrets. Were I to go through it all again, I WOULD HAVE LEARNED TO JUGGLE AND I WOULD HAVE LEARNED TO TAP DANCE."

(I personally talked to Mr.Erwin . . . Sorry, "John" on February 20, 2014, and he admonished me for calling him "Mr.Erwin", noting that both of us are equal, as both of us are retired FBI Special Agents. What a man! When I grow up, I want to be just like "Mr.John A. Erwin".)

Author's note: So much for the "Bureau's 57 and out policy". While U.S. Congressmen and Senators can die and stay in place, until discovered petrified and carried out and buried, an FBI Special Agent has to retirc at age 57. Go figure.

THE LAST OUTTAKE . . . 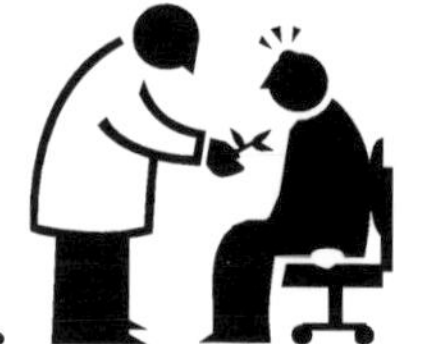

(Author unknown)

"The song of the birds I cannot hear, the flowers I cannot smell.

I cannot remember the ones that I loved, and the things that I knew so well.

I cannot see the wondrous sights, my eyes no longer can see,
The setting sun, the stars at night, the beauty of a tree.

I cannot cry, I have no tears, and yet my heart is filled with fears.

I cannot speak as I did before, my voice has faded away.

I'm in a world all of my own, I cannot even pray.

I know no difference between day and night, time means nothing to me.

I cannot tell the wrongs from right, oh God what has happened to me.

I long to feel the tender touch, of someone to light the way.
Someone to lead me out of my world, and turn the night into day.

I need a strong and gentle hand, someone who understands,
Someone who would guide me, out of these strange and distant lands."

HEAVENLY E-MAIL

When I read about a death of an FBI Special Agent, or a local police officer, in the line of duty, or of death of innocent children in school shootings, or a death of a close friend, yours truly sends a "Heavenly E-mail" to those left behind. Following is the letter sent to the grieving families and community, from the dearly departed victims, following the Sandy Hook Elementary School shooting.

"HEAVENLY E-MAIL Date: January 1, 2013

FM: The Twenty Youngest Angels

TO: Our Dear Earthly Family

This message of love is being sent to you via the HEM (Heavenly E-mail), since the much-slower HSM (Heavenly Snail-Mail) would not reach your earthly location in due time for the 30-day anniversary of our burial. (We bet that you are surprised how fast this message got to you. You know, in heaven we have instant one-way only communication with earth, via Heavenly E-mail, but Skype, texting, Facebook and tweets for some reason are not available to us as yet. The twenty of us will work to hopefully change that in the near future since we are aware that you are much more comfortable to using this type of communication.)

We wanted to take this opportunity to have a chat with you and thank you for loving us as we love you. Our presence at this location was offered to us by The Almighty. Apparently, there was a need here for ever-smiling, lovable young angels, that could get along with everybody, including legions of old angels that have been around for a long time and were hard to convince about usage of computers and

the internet. So The Almighty picked us to make what you adults call "the supreme sacrifice". For us, it was merely a super opportunity to explore the heavenly full-time theme park. At the relatively young earthly age, we were offered an opportunity of a lifetime to join a newly developed 'choir' of very young angels, to act as messengers of God to the earthly beings that we left behind. Apparently, the older angels were not very successful in leading the earthly human adults on a path of love, care for each other, and peace. We truly considered ourselves to have been just average youngsters that loved our moms and dads, our siblings and our grandparents. As a matter of fact, we had complete trust in everyone that we met.

You were our beloved family and we thank The Almighty for having you as our parents, sisters and brothers, grandparents and aunts and uncles, neighbors and friends. All of you have shed a tear and you miss us. Because of your faith, however, you have to understand that our stay with you on earth was always meant to be a temporary one, sort of a visit, before reuniting with Our Creator, for eternal life, where we are all well taken care of by God, with help from the 'old chaperones' that came with us.

We deeply treasured our close family relationships and we wish a peaceful time on earth and much love to all of you, our family and friends. Please remember the Almighty God and praise Him in your respective human ways, by praying for us, as we pray for you.

All our unconditional love,

The Twenty Little Angels from Sandy Hook Elementary School.

(Comments/criticism to: JOHNMERCINA@YAHOO.COM)

John Mercina is a "nom de plume" of a retired FBI Special Agent, a former city cop and a U.S. Army officer during the Vietnam War, writing a column gratis in two newspapers since April Fool's Day, 1991, hoping to change the world for the better, one person at a time.

ONCE I THOUGHT I WAS WRONG BUT I WAS MISTAKEN !

(Author unknown)

If you served as an FBI Special Agent, or are presently on duty, write your personal stories and notes on the blank pages and in empty spaces in this book. Your children and grandchildren will have a loving memory of you when you have departed, reading your stories.

At the same time, if you wish, send copies of your stories to the author for inclusion in the next book. (Yes, the postage will be refunded to you.)

ABOUT THE AUTHOR

Al Zupan was born in Slovenia, which was one of the republics of the Socialist Federal Republic of Yugoslavia, but is now an independent country and a member of NATO. He arrived in the U.S. on Thanksgiving Day, 1956.

After being taught by Notre Dame Nuns in grade school, Marianist Brothers in high school, and Jesuits at John Carroll University, Al joined the Cleveland Police Department as a patrolman.

Following his service commitment as a U.S. Army officer during the Vietnam War, Al served as an FBI Special Agent for thirty two years, retiring in 2002.

Al has written a freelance column in two separate newspapers since April Fool's Day, 1991, utilizing a nom de plume, to protect his identity.

Al enjoys that he is alive, surrounded by his loving wife, married children and grandchildren.

Made in the USA
Charleston, SC
05 January 2015